The Second Life Herald

The Second Life Herald

The Virtual Tabloid that Witnessed the Dawn of the Metaverse

Peter Ludlow and Mark Wallace

Cambridge, Massachusetts
London, England

For information about special quantity discounts, please email special_sales@mitpress.mit.edu

This book was set in Stone Serif and Stone Sans on 3B2 by Asco Typesetters, Hong Kong. Printed and bound in the United States of America.

Library of Congress Cataloging-in-Publication Data

Ludlow, Peter, 1957–
The Second Life Herald : the virtual tabloid that witnessed the dawn of the metaverse / Peter Ludlow and Mark Wallace.
p. cm.
Includes bibliographical references and index.
ISBN 978-0-262-12294-8 (hardcover : alk. paper) 1. Second Life (Computer game) [proposed] 2. Avatars (Computer graphics) 3. Tabloid newspapers—Fiction—Computer programs. 4. Shared virtual environments. 5. Internet. I. Wallace, M. (Mark), 1955– II. Title.
GV1469.25.S425L83 2007
794.8—dc22 2007002794

10 9 8 7 6 5 4 3 2 1

To the memory of Candace Bolter

—Peter Ludlow

To my mother, who inspired so many
—Mark Wallace

What are his nets and gins and traps; and how does he surround him
With cold floods of abstraction, and with forests of solitude,
To build him castles and high spires, where kings and priests may dwell
—William Blake, *Visions of the Daughters of Albion*

"Don't get broke off for free."
—Evangeline, The Sims Online

Contents

Acknowledgments

We are grateful for the time, ideas, and support that were given to us in the writing of this book by any number of game developers, academics, legal scholars, and editors, but most of all by the gamers who occupy the same worlds we do, without whom this book and the worlds described in it would not exist. If we've left you out of the list below, it's not because we don't appreciate your contribution. We would like to thank the *Herald* staff and freelance writers, and particularly Pixeleen Mistral, Fiend Ludwig, Heartun Breaker, Prokofy Neva, Matthias Zander, Neal Stewart, and Budka Groshomme, for their service; Richard Bartle, Andy Phelps, Rich Thurman, Don Hopkins, Randy Farmer, Deep Max, and Don Woods for their insights; Ted Castronova and Dan Hunter for early and continuing support; Denise Lopez at Blizzard Entertainment and Kjartan Emilsson at CCP Games; Philip Rosedale, Cory Ondrejka, Robin Harper, and Catherine Smith at Linden Lab; Jeff Brown and The Borg (as well as Electronic Arts' public relations department for forcing us to use our The Sims Online screenshots under fair use principles).

This story begins in The Sims Online, and there are plenty of people to thank for teaching us about the world of "social" massively multiplayer online games, including (but not limited to) Kale, Respected Banker, Daywalker, Snoopy Magoofee, Mr-President, JC Soprano, Mistress Juliana, Maria LeVeaux, Toy, Stella Dives, Pimcess Julie, Cocoanut, AJ Down, Granny Celestie, Mimi C., Cassandra Jackson, Dyerbrook, Sir, Twitty Robespierre, Mia Wallace, and, of course, Evangeline.

In Second Life we've benefited from contact with at least as many avatars, including One Song, Cyanide Leviathan, Lance LeFay, Gina Fatale, YadNi Monde, Prong Thetan, Grim Hathor, Anshe Chung, Diamond Hope,

Francis Chung, Marilyn Murphy, Father Callahan, Miravoir Psaltery, Mimi Coral, Clark Ambassador, Eva Tal, and Wandering Yaffle.

More thanks go to Bruce Wallace for bringing home that dumb terminal in 1978, Jeremy Wallace for staying up late online, and Marilyn Wallace for love and inspiration, especially in her last days; and Jennifer Carlson, Amy McKenzie, Micah Sherman, Jerry Paffendorf, StateCorp, and the TerrorNova guild. Thanks to Robert Ludlow, Pat Ludlow, and Sarah Milbrandt for showing that values are important, no matter how they are encoded, and extra special thanks go to CTRL Key Pinkerton for playing with her dad in lots of online worlds.

Finally, we would like to tip our hats to the growing group of games writers known as the New Games Journalists—albeit they are known by that moniker somewhat inaccurately and only under protest. What unifies them is the knowledge that computer games are more than the sum of their software, and that Johan Huizinga's "magic circle," the conceptual space in which play happens, in fact encompasses all things. For years now they have managed to convey the emotions and experiences of being gamers, and include people like Ian Shanahan, author of "Bow, Nigger";[1] Kieron Gillen, who mistakenly gave the genre its name;[2] Julian Dibbell, Wagner James Au, Jane Pinckard, Jim Rossignol, Tom Francis, and Tom Chick, as well as a host of others who should probably be listed here, and any number of writers to come (plus Charles Herold for pushing game reviews into the mainstream). It is our sincere hope that the future promises still less blathering about whether the latest derivative shooter from EA makes sufficient use of your favorite dual analog controller, and more such "travel writing from imaginary places," to use Gillen's phrase. See you there.

Authors' Note

This book is the story of a number of characters, but especially the crusading virtual journalist Urizenus Sklar, who established the newspaper now known as the *Second Life Herald* in October 2003. But where virtual worlds are concerned, the concept of character can get confusing. Urizenus Sklar is an avatar, a pixelated person who exists only on a computer screen. Uri's "typist" Peter Ludlow, however, the man who is represented in the virtual world by Urizenus, is a very real person, and one of the authors of this book.

Like virtual worlds themselves, this book is a shared work. Just as the massively multiplayer online games we are writing about are brought to life by the interactions of thousands of players, so this book is an exercise in collaboration—though among a far smaller number of people, of course. Mark Wallace is the other author of this book; his avatar, Walker Spaight, has also served as an editor of the *Second Life Herald*, since January 2005. A few of Walker's stories, as well, show up in these pages.

How, then, to represent all these characters on the page? We've chosen to take what we hope is the clearest way out: to speak of all of these people in the third person. If it's at first surprising to find one of the book's authors referred to as "he" in these pages, it will soon become clear that this was in fact the only thing that made sense. Urizenus's story is Peter's, and Walker's is Mark's, and there is really no way to separate the identities that stare into the virtual world through a computer screen from those that stare back out at them. If you have spent much time in a virtual world (and if you haven't, we urge you to do so), you know this is true: your character there is not merely a collection of screen art and software subroutines; it is, in large part, you. What happens to the "you" who exists in an online game can in many cases be every bit as meaningful as anything that happens to the "you" of your offline life. Keep that in mind as you read this book and you will soon understand why virtual worlds are much more than only a game.

July 1, 2007
Peter Ludlow and Mark Wallace
Urizenus Sklar and Walker Spaight
Michigan, New York, and Second Life

Introduction

The last two years have seen an explosion of interest in the multi-user online environments known as virtual worlds. Though their technology resembles that of a video game, 3-D online "places" like Second Life, There.com, and others have, since the spring of 2006, "gone mainstream," becoming platforms for well-known corporations, artists, universities, and businesspeople large and small to mount marketing efforts, protoype products and projects, conduct research, put on performances, or simply show up for work. At the time of this writing, the list of companies and artists working in Second Life was long and growing: Starwood Hotels prototyped its new Aloft line there; Suzanne Vega played a live concert on the radio show *The Infinite Mind*, hosted by John Hockenberry, from within the virtual world; a designer of virtual fashions was making her full-time living in Second Life (as were dozens of other virtual product makers); automaker Toyota released a virtual version of its Scion xB there; MTV opened a Virtual Laguna Beach to accompany the hit television show of the same name; Major League Baseball held a virtual re-creation of its Home Run Derby in Second Life; a whole new virtual world services industry had sprung up and already seen its first round of mergers; Kurt Vonnegut gave a reading in the virtual world; a German couple was earning more than $200,000 per year selling virtual real estate, holding virtual assets in excess of $1 million with offices in Wuhan, China; Adidas Reebok was finding out what "impossible is nothing" means in a place where the laws of physics as we know them don't apply; singer Regina Spektor released an album in Second Life before it hit store shelves; American Apparel opened a retail outlet there; Universal Music opened a showcase stage where performers like hip-hop bad-boy Chamillionaire gave live performances . . . and the list goes on.

If it surprises you to hear that platinum-selling recording artists, major television networks, and global hotel chains are setting up shop in a virtual online space—one that might be mistaken for a video game—that surprise should not last long. As more and more people and companies discover the rich expressive power and social networking capabilities of virtual worlds, the phenomenon will become commonplace. With up to forty million people around the world regularly logging on to such 3-D environments, it only makes sense that corporations try to tap the rich potential market they represent. As you'll see, virtual worlds offer possibilities for work, learning, marketing, research, and socializing that are orders of magnitude deeper than those offered by the World Wide Web. The 3-D interface is not appropriate for every function found online, of course. But it has opened the doors to a new set of possibilities, and people are rapidly exploring what these are and how best to take advantage of them as the wired world evolves. Indeed it may be that our lives are rapidly moving into these virtual spaces—into what science fiction writer Neal Stephenson called "the Metaverse."

In his widely acclaimed 1992 novel, *Snow Crash*, Stephenson imagined a day when we would log on to a 3-D virtual space via the Internet, travel about in it, and conduct business and other important parts of our daily routines in it. It seems that Stephenson's vision is already upon us. The doors to this new existence have been opened.

Of course, if the doors to the Metaverse and a new online existence have been opened, they have not been open for long (just a couple of years), and their opening was not a smooth, elegant series of discrete steps, but rather the product of a wild and woolly combination of chaotic events and conflicts. For the people involved, the events were at once seismic, exhilarating, and often frightening. This book is in effect the story of a witness to the unfolding of these events—not a single witness, but rather a virtual newspaper (originally called the *Alphaville Herald*, and then the *Second Life Herald*), which was deeply embedded in two of these virtual worlds and recorded many of events that transpired. As this book makes clear, the *Herald* was a witness, but not always a welcome one.

While there has been much media attention paid to virtual worlds, most of it has been breathless cheerleading that overlooked the conflicts between the owners of virtual worlds and their users, between groups of users, and between individuals. These conflicts are not trivial. Legal scholar Lawrence

Lessig in his 1999 book, *Code and Other Laws of Cyberspace*, observed that the very architecture of cyberspace is up for grabs: "Depending on who grabs it, there are several different ways it could turn out." The same point can be made for 3-D virtual worlds. Do we want the laws of virtual worlds to be written by technology companies, whose agendas may not include granting us the freedoms we enjoy in our physical lives? Do we want the courts, which may have limited knowledge and experience of technology, to make such decisions for us? Or is there a middle ground, a way for virtual worlds to generate new kinds of governance structures that will take the unique properties of virtual worlds into account while at the same time respecting the laws and mores of physical nations?

These are the kinds of questions this book examines—not by delving into legal precedent and software code, but simply by telling the stories of the people on the edge, the people who are striking off into this wired frontier and already beginning to live much of their lives there. The authors of this book are not legal scholars, nor are they software engineers. But they have made a vocation, as virtual journalists, of witnessing the societies now beginning to emerge in cyberspace. They've listened to the same tales of joy, heartbreak, political unrest, and commercial struggle one would find in any newspaper, large or small, covering any community in the world. Their conclusion is that it's not too soon for the rest of the world to sit up and listen as well, because those stories will soon be everyone's—including yours.

1 The Death of Urizenus

It was a quiet night at the *Alphaville Herald*. The newspaper had been put to bed and a man known as Urizenus, its publisher, was as usual the last one in the office. He busied himself closing up shop, tending to fireplaces and cleaning up the messes that had accumulated over the course of the day. It took a few minutes to get Uri's cats, Cheddar Cheese Cheetah and a tabby named Black, back into their cages. Then he turned out the lights, locked up for the night, and headed home.

Alphaville never saw him again.

A few nights later, in mid-December 2003, Urizenus was snuffed out, his life terminated by a powerful unseen foe. His cats remained in their cages at the *Herald* offices, never to see their master again. His killers robbed him of his money, emptied his bank account, made off with much of his equipment and supplies. The *Herald*'s legal editor managed to have ownership of the newspaper's offices transferred to her, but in effect that game was over; the brave little newspaper that had only just begun to make waves had been put to bed for the last time.

And make waves the *Herald* had. It had been launched only six weeks before, but in that short span of time the newspaper had become a force to be reckoned with. Once the first edition hit Alphaville's streets, things got busy fast. Almost before he could venture out in search of stories, the news started coming to Uri (as his friends called him). Alphaville residents showed up at his office door unannounced, with stories, scoops, and complaints about local politicians, hoodlums, and scam artists. Uri listened, investigated, and wrote up what he found. Though he had never expected his little publication to become so influential, the *Herald* fast became the voice of the people, and gained a loyal following as a result. Of course, it had made more than a few enemies since that first edition had appeared.

Figure 1.1
Urizenus chills in his Alphaville Pad

The voice of the people was a muckraking yellow tabloid, as far as some were concerned. Around Alphaville, you either loved it or you hated it—but you could not escape its roving eye.

But now Urizenus was dead. Whoever it was that had hoped to smooth the ripples the *Herald* had caused had prevailed. At least for the moment.

Other publications picked up the story. The widely read online magazine *Salon.com* raised the question of censorship through murder. A few weeks later, Uri's death made the front page of the *New York Times*, which used the case to explore issues of free expression and of responsibility and governance in small towns like Alphaville. CNN, the BBC, and newspapers from London to Moscow to Madrid all sent reporters to Alphaville to cover the story.

But the police were never quoted. There was no mention of a trial. No bereaved relatives surfaced to deplore the killing. There was not even a murder weapon that could easily be brought to hand.

Because, in fact, there was no body. The "newspaper" that had given rise to a small international sensation had never actually appeared in print. Coverage of Urizenus's murder did indeed appear in major news outlets around the (real) world, but most of that coverage focused less on the details of his death and more on the uncertain boundaries that separate the real from the imagined, and on the grey area that divides the concrete world around us from the virtual world that exists only thanks to modern technology—a world whose very existence is a question of some debate.

In fact, Alphaville is not a physical place at all but rather a kind of collective digital fantasy, a place that exists somewhere between the data stored on a computer network server in Silicon Valley and the thousands of people who log on to that server each day. Urizenus was not a person, at least not in the conventional sense, but only a digital representation of a person, an entity known as an avatar, in an online world with tens of thousands of participants who hailed from all over the real, offline globe. Uri's cats were virtual cats, mere pixels on a screen, controlled by software subroutines running somewhere in California. And Uri's money, though convertible into hard cash, was not denominated in U.S. dollars but in a currency called simoleans that could be spent only within the confines of the online game world known as The Sims Online.

The *Alphaville Herald*, however, was a very real publication. While it never took the form of ink on paper, it existed as a Weblog outside The Sims Online (or TSO, as it is commonly known),[1] and ran stories five to ten times each week, covering events that took place in Alphaville—or, depending on how you preferred to see it, events that took place on the computer network server known as Alphaville, one of the dozen or so servers that collectively make up the world of TSO. And it pulled no punches, a fact that presumably caused much chagrin in the corporate offices of those who owned TSO's servers—and ruled them with god-like powers.

The mystery of Urizenus's death was never a whodunnit; the culprits were clear from the start: Uri's killers were agents of Electronic Arts Inc., the multibillion-dollar game company that owns and operates The Sims Online. More intriguing than who did it was why. What was it that Urizenus said or did or knew about the goings-on in Alphaville—or was on the verge of discovering—that moved EA to terminate his avatar with such extreme prejudice? Was there a report about EA itself that the company was eager to quash? Were there really such explosive stories to be found within the realm of a world like TSO, stories that blurred the boundaries between reality and virtual reality? The *Alphaville Herald* was an online newspaper covering imaginary events in an imaginary world. And yet it had catalyzed EA, the company behind that world—the wizard-of-Oz-like men behind the curtain, if you will—to step forward for a moment to exercise their power, and to violate the fiction on which the world's existence largely depends. What could have mattered so much to them if The Sims Online is only a game?

The answer lies as much in what kind of game TSO is as it does in what kinds of stories the *Herald* was printing.

Most computer games—including everything from Yahoo! Solitaire to Super Mario Brothers to Grand Theft Auto—provide a set scenario with a finite beginning and end, and a defined group of conditions at the beginning of each game, whether these include a deck of cards and some simulated green felt or a 3-D-rendered layout of mountains, valleys, streets, tunnels, buildings, traps, and treasures (known as a map) that's reset each time a new game is begun. You play until you win or lose (though you may often pause along the way), and then you start again with a fresh and untouched version of the original scenario.

But the class of games that TSO belongs to—known as "massively multiplayer online games" (aka MMOs, MMOGs, or MMORPGs—the RP stands for "role-playing")—differs from most traditional games in two key ways: the worlds they offer are "persistent," and they are inhabited by thousands of other players all gaming in the same virtual environment at the same time.

Persistent worlds are just that: open-ended virtual environments that continue to exist no matter who is logged in at any particular moment. MMOs take place not on a one-off battlefield that resets itself at the opening of each scenario, but in a game world that persists regardless of how often its players come and go, or what they do when they are there. In most other kinds of games, your on-screen representative is merely a placeholder, a highly detailed king in a kind of elaborate online game of chess, a game that pauses or ends when you switch off your computer. In MMOs, switching off your computer neither pauses nor stops the game. Step away from your screen for a day or two and the online you rests on one of the game company's servers until you're ready to play again; meanwhile, the game itself doesn't slow down at all. Other players in the same persistent world will have been garnering their own rewards. A character who might have presented no challenge to you last week may have become a fierce warrior while you were foolish enough to be off attending to real-life business. The point is that when you log back into the world, that world has continued to develop—it's not a fresh copy in which the elements have all been reset to some initial state.

In MMOs the words "game over" have no meaning, for the game you're playing never ends. And with thousands of other players also coming and going in the world, the experience of an MMO is very different from a game in which one player comes out as winner. Instead it's an ongoing story in which all the players pursue their own competitive and personal goals, but where no one is ever really the ultimate victor. Instead of one-on-one or team-vs.-team, in MMOs the player coexists with literally thousands of other players, in some cases tens of thousands.

Instead of finite games to be won or lost, MMOs offer open-ended environments in which players can tackle "quests," take on "jobs," form lasting relationships with other players, and continue to develop their online characters for as long as they care to. There is no way to win or lose the game itself (unless, like Urizenus, the creators destroy your character), because the game itself never ends; all you can do is play. In a way, your avatar takes on a life of its own. It develops characteristics and a history based on its experience. You can play the same ongoing character in the same ongoing game for months or even years, and millions of people do. For what they find in MMOs is something they find in no other kind of computer game: the chance to inhabit virtual worlds.

Virtual worlds come in as many different shapes and sizes as one can imagine: fantasy realms set everywhere from ancient Egypt to medieval Europe to fictional locales like J. R. R. Tolkien's Middle Earth, in which players take on the personae of knights, swordsmen, samurai, wizards, traders, or even damsels in distress; science fiction scenarios filled with stormtroopers, Jedi knights, starship pilots, and interstellar pirates; World War II simulations featuring combat missions both fictional and historical; "adult" worlds in which cybersex is the main part of gameplay; modern urban automobile fantasies, and post-apocalyptic ones; worlds filled with cartoon characters or comic-book superheroes or villains; one unusual MMO in which players take on the roles of players on baseball teams; and those in which your screentime is whatever you make it, including places like The Sims Online, the virtual world of There, and Second Life, in which the game is less a game than, well, a second life, and the "player" is a resident or citizen with limitless choices as to how he or she wants to spend time, rather than a competitor on some virtual global playing field.

The ongoing nature of these persistent virtual worlds gives the social interactions among their residents far more meaning than can be found in more straightforward competitive games. If a sniper blows you away in the action game Counter-Strike, you get to face her on a freshly leveled playing field at the beginning of the next round of play—if you choose to play against her any more at all. But any encounter in a virtual world is with someone you may well encounter again, whether you like it or not. If a valiant knight helps you kill a dragon, a shadowy rogue scams you out of a valuable sword, a space pirate besmirches your reputation, or a neighbor commits "rape" (as happened in an early text-based world[2]), that event becomes part of your ongoing experience of the virtual world and carries far more weight than if it were simply a one-off occurrence during a particular round of the game. The fact is that what goes on in MMOs goes far beyond what we think of as "play," and the number of users is positively enormous.

The most popular recent entrant to the field, World of Warcraft, boasted almost four million players around the world by the time it had been in release for a year. The Korean MMO Lineage enjoys a similar number. In China, some 22.8 million people reportedly played at least one MMO in 2004.[3]

With a total population of at least ten million regular users around the world and as many as forty million more occasional visitors, the internal workings of persistent virtual worlds are in many ways as rich and complex as our real world, and are real enough themselves to have some surprising effects on the offline lives of the people who inhabit them. For example:

- Far more than merely entertaining diversions, many virtual worlds have become full-time jobs not just for their developers but for some of their inhabitants as well, jobs that earn some people more than $200,000 a year—in cold hard cash, not virtual currency.
- Economist Edward Castronova of Indiana University, who specializes in the economies of virtual worlds, measures the per capita gross national product of Norrath, the imaginary setting for the MMO EverQuest, as more than that of a few real-life countries.[4]

- Virtual worlds like Second Life and There are now playing host to all manner of real-world business ventures, from public relations agencies to fashion chains like American Apparel, tie-ins involving the likes of MTV's *Laguna Beach*, and hit musical groups like Gorillaz (in Habbo Hotel).
- In China and Korea, real-world courts have handed down rulings on conflicts that arose between characters in virtual worlds, including thefts of virtual items. It is only a matter of time before such a legal stance is adopted in the United States—though game companies might prefer it otherwise.
- Almost half of MMO gamers live in Korea, where virtual worlds are far more popular than they are in the United States or Europe.
- The universe of MMOs includes dozens of graphical worlds, and hundreds of smaller text-based worlds with just as loyal a following.
- More than one gamer interviewed for this book is now married to someone they first met in a virtual world.

Meanwhile, the shadow economy that exists within online worlds and on their fringes outside the games has grown to surprising proportions. Because of the persistent nature of online worlds, the virtual items that are used in MMOs—things like swords and shields, virtual real estate, and even software that can be used within the virtual worlds to enhance (or hack) the user interface—have taken on real value to many users. The ability to trade such items back and forth within a virtual world has led to a thriving out-of-world market that now accounts for nearly $1 billion a year in transaction value, according to the leading online broker of such goods.[5] A growing service economy exists as well, in which expert "power users" take on the task of improving character skills and combat abilities for players who don't care to spend their time as weak, low-level characters.

There are aspects of these worlds that many find unsavory, of course. The virtual currency of many such worlds can be converted into real money, which has at times inspired unscrupulous residents to mount scams that have cost users significant sums. The relative anonymity that online life provides has allowed a variety of sexual communities to flourish in online worlds, composed of people who might have had a harder time connecting otherwise. Online "Mafias" vie for dominance in virtual worlds such as Second Life and The Sims Online, with their rivalries sometimes leading to costly online attacks on the world's underlying computer servers themselves. Many users complain of shadowy insider players who allegedly enjoy special favors from unscrupulous administrators of online worlds. Offline Mafias have their presence too: A ring of Russian credit-card scammers in Ultima Online is said to have cost Electronic Arts at least $4 million in the mid-1990s.[6] Real-life hate crimes and threats of violence sometimes grow out of online relationships, and even real-world killings have been blamed on interactions within virtual worlds.[7]

To be sure, the word "game" doesn't come close to describing much of what takes places in online worlds. Online spaces like The Sims Online and Second Life are better described as virtual worlds in which many different kinds of social relations can be conducted. Success in these virtual spaces is measured in the same ways people measure success in their offline lives: money, popularity, love, family, community, career—however you want to measure it. Some people work to make their avatars' lives as similar as possible to their own; others do just the opposite, creating online representatives of the opposite sex, attempting to build virtual versions of the family or social relations they may have found missing in their offline lives, or even playing out cruel and violent fantasies. To some extent they are fairy-tale worlds: Possibilities are unbounded and the laws of physics can be bent, if you know how. Unlike fairy tales, however, there is no guarantee that life in a virtual world will end happily ever after. In fact, virtual spaces have their share of dark forces, as Urizenus learned the hard way.

The dark forces lurking in the shadows of Urizenus's story are known collectively as Electronic Arts Inc., one of the biggest computer game publishers in the world, a company with 4,800 employees, and which reported 2004 revenues of $2.95 billion.[8] With dozens of games on the market and ownership of some of the most desirable franchise rights in gaming (including the rights to create games based on *The Lord of the Rings* and the *Harry Potter* series, *The Godfather*, and many professional sports leagues), EA is the giant among game companies, and TSO, it had been hoped, would make it even bigger. Before it hit stores in late 2002 the company predicted four hundred thousand users within the first six months of the game's release[9] and a total of two million eventually.

TSO was popular, but it never took off quite as EA had hoped. The game peaked at around 105,000 users in mid-2003 and had fallen back to fewer than 100,000 by the fall of that year, when the *Alphaville Herald* began publication. (By mid-2005, TSO had fewer than 40,000 users, and people were starting to speculate about whether EA would soon close it down.) But though it hadn't lived up to its expectations, TSO had garnered a population bigger than that of a small city the size of Albany, New York, or Santa Monica, California, and after twenty years in the business, EA had grown into a vast company whose universe of games had attracted millions more customers.

What could have stirred a behemoth like EA to take such action against Urizenus and the *Herald*? The company claimed that the newspaper and its editor had violated the game's Terms of Service agreement, the document that regulates the standards of proper behavior in an online world. But the evidence for this was so flimsy and any actual violation so many times removed from Urizenus himself that there had to be another reason.

Whatever it was, Urizenus was dead. But in a university office in Ann Arbor, Michigan, Uri's typist, the man behind the avatar—a philosophy and linguistics professor named Peter Ludlow—lived on. Ludlow was not pleased that his online persona had suddenly vanished from the face of the virtual world. His blood boiled as he read the email that had come from EA:

> Dear Urizenus,
> Your "The Sims Online" login account (578372615) has been permanently closed for severe and/or repeated Terms of Service or Rules of Conduct violations. Most recently, on 12-10-2003 at 16:25 GMT a cheating complaint was filed against you. You have continued to list alphavilleherald.com in your profiles after a warning and suspension for this. Your previous account record has also been considered in this action. While we regret it, we feel it is necessary for the good of the game and its community.

Part of what infuriated Ludlow was that the "cheating complaint" had been filed against him at a point when Urizenus was already under a temporary suspension, and so couldn't possibly have committed any "crimes"—he hadn't even been in the game! He had already deleted all the references to alphavilleherald.com that he could find in his profile, and in any case the site was not a "commercial" one, as EA had claimed in previous emails (linking from user profiles to commercial sites was forbidden under TSO's Terms of Service). The *Herald*'s only relationship to any commercial sites was through links to other users' Web pages, some of which offered commercial services or information about how to cheat the game. And besides the several hundred dollars worth of virtual assets that were lost with Uri's demise, Ludlow was outraged that the omnipotent entity that was EA (omnipotent as far as TSO was concerned, at least) would move against a newspaper like the *Herald* "for the good of the game and its community." It was almost as if EA were playing the role of an overzealous government agency, shuttering a neighborhood newspaper after less than two months of publication.

By late 2003, when Urizenus was terminated, the Internet and the World Wide Web were so old hat that they no longer seemed like revolutionary venues for the free exchange of information. But the Internet had gone through a new evolution, to Web 2.0—the social networking web of blogging, MySpace, Flickr, and Wikipedia. Uri didn't know it when he entered TSO, but he was about to witness the birth of the next iteration—what Mark Wallace liked to refer to as Web 3pointD—the emergence of graphical 3-D social spaces where people would not just socialize and conduct business, but do so in a place where spatial presence was palpable, and whose expressive capabilities were correspondingly enhanced. If the world had left Web 1.0 behind and was deep in Web 2.0, this was the beginning of the third online revolution.

A newspaper covering life in an online game might not seem like a very significant part of that revolution, but given the kinds of things that went on in TSO and other persistent virtual environments—and given the ever-increasing "connectedness" of everyone's "real" lives—the *Herald* could not be so easily dismissed as merely another Web site about just another game. EA certainly seemed to take it seriously enough.

The real-world journalists who picked up the story took it seriously too. International coverage explored questions of free speech in online worlds, and Amy Harmon, writing in the *New York Times*, drew an important parallel: Speech enjoys certain legal protections in privately owned spaces or media open to public use, such as phone lines and shopping malls; if virtual worlds were to be ruled the same kind of space, they would presumably enjoy the same protections.[10] Unfortunately for Urizenus and Ludlow, that day had not yet come.

Urizenus's termination left Ludlow taken aback, but around the time of Uri's death, an unusual event occurred in an MMO called EverQuest that stirred Ludlow's passion to keep fighting what he saw as the good fight. Rather than battling each other, almost two hundred EverQuest players banded together to slay one of the supposedly unbeatable monsters that populated Norrath, the game's imaginary world. It had taken the small army two forays into the lair of the Kerafyrm, a fearsome beast also known as The Sleeper—but not because The Sleeper had gotten the better of them on the first try.

Sony Online Entertainment, the company behind the game, was watching the first attempt on The Sleeper's "life" and realized that the unusual band of allies were prevailing. But SOE had intended The Sleeper to be unslayable. So when the monster had been beaten down to about a quarter of its strength, agents of SOE reset the game. Deus ex machina—the god in the machine—had come forward to save its "unkillable" beast. In effect, Sony saw it was losing the game and simply took its bat and ball and went home. As Andrew Phelps, author of Corante.com's *Got Game?* Weblog and a professor of game programming at the Rochester Institute of Technology, wrote in a blog post at the time, "Wrong move. Seriously wrong move.... a level of trust [was] destroyed." Just a few days later, however, undeterred gamers attacked the Kerafyrm again. This time, perhaps because SOE was asleep at the switch, the gamers prevailed, vanquishing their unslayable foe.

I Saw God and I Killed It

There are two very distinct crowds that play games, the "casual gamer" and the "hard core gamer"—or at least that's what the gaming industry says.... But I saw the true diehards last week, and I saw just how little the gaming industry understands some of them.

[EverQuest player] Ghenwivar writes, "On Monday, November 17th, in the most amazing and exciting battle ever, [EverQuest guilds] Ascending Dawn, Wudan and Magus Imperialis Magicus defeated Kerafyrm, also known as The Sleeper, for the first time ever on an EverQuest server. The fight lasted approximately three hours and about 170–180 players from [EverQuest server] Rallos Zek's top three guilds were involved. Hats off to everyone who made this possible and put aside their differences in order to accomplish the impossible. Congratulations RZ!!!"

My hat goes off to you. They killed what Sony Online Entertainment intended to be unkillable. But rather than actually make it untargetable, Sony just gave it ten billion hit points. For those non-EQers out there, a reference scale: a snake has about 10 hit points. A dragon has about 100,000. A god has 1–2 million. [The Sleeper] really does have about ten billion or more.[11] It took close to 200 players almost four hours to beat the thing down into the ground.

Why, you might ask, would anyone waste four hours of their life doing this? Because a game said it couldn't be done.... This is like the Quake freaks that fire their rocket launchers at their own feet to propel themselves up so they can jump straight to the exit and skip 90% of the level and finish in 2 seconds. Someone probably told them they couldn't finish in less than a minute.

Games are about challenges, about hurdles or puzzles or fights overcome. To some players, the biggest hurdle or challenge is how to do what you (the designer) said couldn't happen. If you are making a game, accept this. Now. Why do I say this?...

Lets back up to November 16, when the same three guilds on Rallos Zek made their first attempt on the Sleeper.... A supposedly [player-vs.-player] server banded together 200 people. The chat channels across the server were ablaze, as no less than 5,000 of us listened in, with "OMG they're attempting the Sleeper! Good luck d00dz!" Everyone clustered near their screens, sharing the thrill of the fight, the nobility of the attempt and the courage of those brave 200. Play slowed to a crawl on every server as whispers turned to shouts, as naysayers predicted, "It can't be done" or "It will drop a rusty level 1 sword" and most of us just held our breath, silently urging them forward. Rumors abounded: "If they win, the whole EQ world stops and you get the text from the end of Wizardry 1," or "If they win, the president of Sony will log on and congratulate them." With thousands watching and waiting, the Sleeper's health inched ever downward.

They beat it down to 27 percent and then, almost three hours into the fight, when victory looked possible, it disappeared, without dying, violating every rule in the world of Norrath on how a monster is supposed to behave. It seems that one of the Game Masters at Sony reset the zone because "they thought the encounter might be bugged" (or, more accurately, "We realized these guilds were going to win, and the Sleeper isn't supposed to be able to die"). Wrong move. Seriously wrong move....

Sony eventually relented, gave the characters involved some of their experience back, and got them safely out from under the dragon's feet. (They did know that they would try again, and had probably already made up their minds to allow it). [But] the damage was done, a level of trust destroyed. Poofing the sleeper said, "We do not really understand why you are doing this, so stop it."

We thought you understood us better. The fact you let it happen the next night means very little. The point is that on that first magical evening when warriors rode off to battle the supreme, you meddled. They thought of something you didn't, something legal by the rules of the game you set forward, and you meddled. In the parlance of the world you created: "shame & ridicule."

Oh, and god drops no loot.[12]

In its way, the Kerafyrm episode raised many of the same questions Ludlow was dealing with, questions having to do with just how "real" our online lives really are. To have two hundred players united against a common enemy in EverQuest was a singularly rare event in the admittedly brief history of multiplayer online games. *They thought of something you didn't.* It could have been counted one of SOE's crowning achievements: The game had been so well wrought that a real community of players had formed, one that was able to set aside its differences, at least for a night, in pursuit of a common goal. As anyone who's ever attended a shareholder's meeting or even a meeting of a co-op board knows, getting two hundred people to focus on accomplishing the same task is no small feat.

But then the company had violated the illusion that had made that co-operation possible. As a game company, of course, Sony was under no obligation to keep out of the way. But as the creators of an online space in which real people interacted with each other every day, what were Sony's responsibilities? With more than four hundred thousand subscribers, a complex system of social dynamics had developed in Norrath that made EQ, like TSO, something more than just a game. In fact, massively multi-player online games have now become among the most complex and sophisticated online social spaces in existence. And as the lives people lead in virtual worlds become more and more connected with their offline lives, such online spaces are shedding significant light on questions of liberty and responsibility, and on how an online existence reverberates in what we think of as a gamer's real life.

Still smarting from his encounter with the powers behind the scenes at Electronic Arts, Ludlow latched onto the Kerafyrm episode as emblematic of a basic conflict within virtual worlds between the freedom of the "residents" and the seemingly arbitrary commercial interests of the companies that had created those worlds—the gods, if you will. For Ludlow, the story of the Kerafyrm showed it was possible to come together and resist this undefeatable force. The defeat of the Kerafyrm was in a way the defeat of Sony, and the triumph of the gamers over their gods. For Ludlow it served as an inspiration that one could stand up to the multibillion-dollar corporations that produced and ran virtual worlds, and maybe even survive.

Ludlow survived, but Urizenus's life in Alphaville ended on December 10, 2003. That New Year's Eve, Uri's typist posted a short note on the *Herald* site celebrating the Kerafyrm's defeat and urging residents of other virtual worlds to follow the EverQuest players' example. "We all have unkillable monsters in our lives, both online and off," Ludlow wrote. "My New Year's wish is that the citizens of Alphaville stop fighting each other, recognize our true enemy, stand together, and fight the unkillable monster—The Sleeper—of our world. How big is your game?"[13]

2 Inside the Virtual World

You're standing in a dream forest, where massive trees tower hundreds of feet over your head and the forest floor is a carpet of tangled flowers, grass, and vines blended together to roll smoothly into the grayish-purple distance. The place is gloomy, but not without a certain luminescence. A few shadowy figures clad in cloaks and tunics of muted colors jog back and forth around you past the squirrels and deer foraging in the underbrush. You turn to see an oddly attractive female centaur, her human torso only scantily clad, pass behind a tree. In front of you are two crude wooden benches beside a kind of glowing sapling lamppost. Near the light stands a man in leather vest and wristbands, holding a long wooden staff. He has blue-green hair and beard, and foot-long pointy ears, and a fat yellow exclamation point floats above his head.

The exclamation point breaks the illusion of a dream somewhat, but even so, it's not that hard to suspend your disbelief here in the massively multiplayer online game known as World of Warcraft, one of the most popular MMOs in the world. Within four months of its release the week before Thanksgiving 2004, WoW had garnered 1.5 million subscribers in North America alone,[1] and by the end of 2005 had five million subcribers around the world.[2] (It is now said to have as many as eight million.) Even as august a media outlet as National Public Radio was touting it as "the best online roleplaying game to date."[3]

While it's not *everyone's* favorite virtual world, WoW represents more or less the state of the art for massively multiplayer online role-playing games. Entering the world of World of Warcraft is a bit like stepping into an animated movie. While the images that fill your computer screen don't have the clean, hard-edged lines and perfect curves of a Pixar production, they do have the kind of internal consistency that makes the world seem real, and a level of detail that's high enough to keep you engaged in your visual surroundings but not so picayune as to be distracting.

And getting around in the world is as easy as pushing the arrow keys on your keyboard. Your character starts jogging around like everyone else, and if you right-click the guy with the exclamation point, he charges you with the task of thinning the forest population of young thistle boars and young nightsabers (a kind of small, striped panther) in order to "ensure that the balance of nature is maintained." As you jog away, the exclamation point changes to a gray question mark to indicate you'll have to check in with him after you're done with this small quest in order to collect your reward.

A few seconds later, you're facing a thistle boar. You click the button on your screen that triggers an attack and your character draws its dagger and goes into a crouch. A quick thrust—accompanied by the sound of your dagger making contact with the boar's thorny skin—and you've done your first damage. A single-digit number appears momentarily above the boar to indicate how much damage was done.

But now the boar bites back. You're hit! Your character hasn't been hurt much, but it's probably a small shock, if this is your first experience of such a world. How many jabs of a tusk would it take to kill you? And what exactly would death mean anyway?

Fortunately you don't have to find out, at least not yet. You keep sticking the boar with your dagger and soon enough it falls. You've made your first kill. You accomplished it on your own, but you'll soon find out that as the tasks you face grow increasingly challenging, you will need the help of others. Before long, you find yourself partipating in hunting parties with other players, players who are facing the same challenges as you.

The multiplayer aspect of MMOs is the single most important factor in making such worlds what they are, and in a good game there will be a wide variety of opportunities, tools, and incentives for players to interact with one another. If you need help with a quest, for instance, you'll have to seek it via one of the in-game chat channels that allow players to communicate with each other. Often, you'll find someone else is seeking help with the same thing. In WoW, you can form a group of up to five characters who can then go off on the hunt. Larger groups of players can take on the most powerful monsters in the game or do combat in special "battlegrounds" where they face off against other players. In some parts of the game, players may attack each other freely (though you're protected from such dangers in most areas). Weapons and other items may be bought, sold, and traded between players. Chat channels can be used to seek help, socialize, make friends, and even make enemies. Tools are built into the world that allow players to form "guilds" made up of dozens of friends and allies, and in a game like EVE Online (in which players take on the roles of galactic space pilots), such organizations may even declare war on each other.

Hunting nightsabers is one thing. Hunting them while two other players are hunting Webwood Spiders at the entrance of a cave nearby is another. Joining up with those two to venture into the cave together is something else again. And rounding a corner to find yourself faced by a hostile party of players from an enemy faction is a whole different experience. Your heart pounds, your hands shake. And should you prevail, the feeling of victorious elation is something no other type of game can provide.

The same goes for any other kind of social interaction that takes place in an MMO. If someone lets you down in combat, scams you out of money, helps you through a tough spot, or besmirches your reputation, that act has visceral and often long-lasting effects in a virtual world. In open worlds like Second Life, There, or The Sims Online, in which most of the "game" has been stripped away, leaving something akin to a sophisticated graphical chat room, social interactions carry even more weight since they are overwhelmingly the main ingredient of what goes on in such places. From the very beginning of MMOs, this has been the case. The social interactions that take place in them today are not much different from the ones that took place in them twenty-five years ago, when the genre was born.

The very first multiplayer online games (then known as multi-user dungeons, or MUDs) were inspired in large part by a single-player computer game known simply as Adventure, written in the early 1970s by a young programmer named Will Crowther at Bolt, Beranek, and Newman (a company that was intimately involved in the initial design and development of ARPANET, the Internet's predecessor). A fan of the paper-and-pencil role-playing game Dungeons & Dragons and an avid spelunker, Crowther wrote an early version of the game in his spare time, partly as a way to form closer ties to his daughters in the wake of a divorce.[4] For that reason, Crowther conceived of a game that would be palatable to non-computer users, despite the fact that programmers and scientists were practically the only people with access to computers at the time.

Crowther's cave-exploring game was interesting, but it was another young programmer, a graduate student at Stanford University named Don Woods, who would add many of the features that have filtered down to the graphical MMOs of today (including a points system, puzzles, and many more rooms to explore and treasures to collect).[5] With Crowther's basic "game engine" in place and the features that Woods added to the world, Adventure became so popular that it can be considered the ur-game among modern role-playing computer games, and the distant progenitor of almost any MMO played today.

Adventure sent the player on a jaunt through the halls and caverns of an imaginary place called the Colossal Cave, in which lurked nasty dwarves and dragons, a towering beanstalk (well, towering once you'd figured out how to water it, anyway), frustrating mazes that had to be navigated in order to collect more batteries for your flashlight, and a great many other entertaining things. The gameplay, such as it was, consisted of reading a text description of your location and interacting with the game through commands like "throw axe," "take cage," or just plain "n" if you wanted to go north.

> You are in a splendid chamber thirty feet high. The walls are frozen rivers of orange stone. An awkward canyon and a good passage exit from east and west sides of the chamber. A cheerful little bird is sitting here singing.

Besides the fact that you had to find your way through an underground warren consisting of hundreds of rooms and passages, the puzzles you were presented with could be fairly challenging. You may have already encountered a cage and typed "take cage," for instance, but it may be more difficult to figure out how to get the bird into it. Simple enough to be played by a child but complex enough to keep programmers playing at their terminals until the wee hours of the morning, the game spread like wildfire, swapped for free across the early networks that would become the Internet. It was even used to test computer designs. If a computer could run Adventure without crashing, it was thought, it could run anything.[6]

But once you'd finally collected all the treasures and managed to get them out of the cave, what then? This question plagued a programming student named Roy Trubshaw at Essex University in the United Kingdom.

It was 1978 and Trubshaw and a couple of friends had heard of a Star Trek game that could be played in real time by two players. What if you could create a version of Adventure that more than one person could inhabit, they wondered. But the tools of programming were then so primitive (at least, compared to today's) that it wasn't initially clear whether there was even a computer instruction that would allow two different terminals to communicate, which had to be done by manipulating the same portion of memory at the same time.

Over the course of a summer vacation, Trubshaw concocted the first multiplayer game engine (writing the code out by hand before entering it into the computer). It's difficult to convey what a feat that was at the time. Just seeing two computer terminals communicate with each other sparked a moment of wonder. As Trubshaw put it, "the feeling of achievement, when the line of text typed on one teletype appeared as typed on the second teletype, was just awesome."[7]

It would fall to Richard Bartle, another Essex University student, to become the first multiplayer world designer. With Trubshaw's game engine (the software that maintains player characters, handles the user interface, and manipulates the contents of the world) mostly in place, Bartle would add a few refinements and design and write the database content that would become the first multi-user dungeon, on a room-sized DEC-10 computer. Over the years that followed, his creation would spawn hundreds of imitators (many are still around today), a few of which rival or even surpass some modern graphical MMOs for complexity of gameplay. In fact, pretty much anything that can be designed into a graphical MMO has already been designed into a text-based world, and years before, but without the graphics.

Players of MUD1, as Bartle's creation is known, begin life in an Elizabethan tearoom whose "exposed oak beams and soft, velvet-covered furnishings provide it with the ideal atmosphere in which to relax.... A sense of decency and decorum prevails.... There are exits in all directions, each of which leads into a wisping, magical mist of obvious teleportational properties."[8]

Type "east" on the command line and you find yourself "standing on a narrow road between The Land and whence you came. To the north and south are the small foothills of a pair of majestic mountains, with a large wall running round."

Although they're not the rich and often stunning visual experience of today's online worlds, these first scenes of MUD1 convey the requisites of their world just as well as the initial moments of World of Warcraft. Instead of tangled vines and foxy centaurs, a short paragraph of description is all you get. Instead of arrow keys and mouse clicks, navigation is accomplished through brief commands like "east" or "take stick." Instead of quests, your character is led along by key lines like "There are exits in all directions" and by careful attention to the few things described. For many people, such worlds are actually richer than graphical MMOs because the imagination is freer to roam in them, just as it is when reading a novel.

More important, there were other people in them, people you could communicate and interact with. MUD1 may seem drab to many players of today's graphical worlds, but the experience of meeting other people in a virtual environment was no less exciting in 1980, and perhaps more so, given that almost nothing like it had ever existed before. Writing for *GameSpy.com*, Roy Trubshaw recalled that "the joy of meeting other people and seeing them arrive and leave, whilst just standing around, was just indescribable."[9]

"Seeing," in this context, means seeing words like "Brian enters the room" appear on your screen. But the fact that this might happen independently of anything you'd done, and that you could talk to and interact with the people "around" you, was a quantum leap forward in terms of what it meant to play a computer game (and of which there were only a handful at the time). By introducing other people into the mix, the games suddenly became vastly more complex and wildly unpredictable. Computer-controlled dwarves made poor conversationalists; a person sitting at a terminal hundreds or thousands of miles away could provide a very different set of responses, from the polite, sane, and helpful to the churlish, crazy, and injurious, and everything in between. With human typists behind the other characters, it was like being in a parallel world.

With MUD1, computer games graduated from being finite tasks limited by the complexity of the software behind them, and became places where there was no end of possible situations one might encounter in the course of what looked at first glance like only a game. In that sense, it's no different from World of Warcraft, The Sims Online, Guild Wars, or any other contemporary graphical MMO. What such games consist of is as much a matter of what players choose to do there as it is a matter of the software behind the games. In fact, the experience of an MMO has *more* to do with the choices players make and the societies they form than it does with the quests and monsters and weapons and goals that the game itself provides. And sometimes those choices are surprising indeed.

Take, for example, the case of Dragon's Gate, a text-based MUD that has been around since 1989. Veteran games developer Jessica Mulligan, who was a Dragon's Gate administrator in the late 1990s, recalls the time she logged on to find eighteen people in the game: "That was a good total for four in the morning. But when I saw that all 18 players were in one room, that didn't seem like a good sign."[10] When Mulligan arrived to investigate, she found the eighteen people in the room not playing the game, but trading recipes for peanut butter cookies.

Similarly counterintuitive styles of "play" go on in graphical MMOs today. In Star Wars Galaxies, for instance, a group of players regularly engages in a "cantina crawl" in which they visit bars throughout the galaxy in order to dance and socialize with their friends. Other SWG players have started hiring themselves out as taxi services, ferrying passengers from one location to another. None of these things have anything to do with the goals and motivations that are programmed into these games. The important thing is that the game software makes these kinds of activities possible. The games are created by the players, as much as if not more than by the people who created the software itself.

Teamwork adds a new dimension of cooperation and communication to computer gaming. Your in-game personality and how you mesh with your teammates matters almost as much as your dexterity with a keyboard and mouse. Players who work well together form "guilds," "clans," or "tribes," and competition between these groups can be fierce.

No longer do gamers' passions require them to spend hours holed up alone with no contact with the outside world. Now your experience of a game is something that connects you with other people (although many non-gamers have yet to realize this fact). Being able to chat on-screen with allies and enemies allows a complex shared culture to develop, and many of these cultural tropes have little or nothing to do with the gameplay on offer. (In Star Wars: Jedi Knight II, for instance, it became traditional to use the game's crouch function, normally used to duck out of the way of an enemy's weapon, to bow to your opponent before entering a lightsaber duel, even though there was no gameplay reason to do so. Later editions of the game included a built-in pre-fight bow option. With the gesture now ratified by the game company, many players stopped bowing before their duels.)

Increasing bandwidth allowed out-of-game culture to flourish on the Web-based message forums and fan sites devoted to popular games. These became clearinghouses for boastful accounts of pitched battles, or for tips and tricks on how to best approach various encounters, as well as venues for the nasty "flame wars" that seem to develop whenever a diverse group of people gathers online to share opinions. Gaming was increasingly becoming about other people. It remained only for the games themselves to follow suit.

The first persistent graphical world to take advantage of client-server architecture and the networking power of the 1990s was a game called Meridian 59. Like MUD1, it was a homebrew project, dreamed up by two brothers, Andrew and Chris Kirmse, then in their junior year at M.I.T. and sophomore year at Virginia Tech, respectively. The Kirmse brothers had spent much of the 1980s playing a MUD called Scepter of Goth,[11] and as members of the first generation to come of age alongside the personal computer—learning programming and writing action games in their spare time—the idea that they could create a graphics-based MUD did not seem outlandish. By the spring of 1996, Meridian 59 was ready for beta testing. The Kirmses had written most of the game themselves, using 3-D graphics technology borrowed from the innovative Wolfenstein FPS games, and recruited a small team of developers that included Mike Sellers, now of game developer Online Alchemy, Damion Schubert, now an independent developer, and Keith Randall, now a software engineer at Google. The first 3-D virtual world went live.

While not as "massively" multiplayer as today's MMOs, M59's servers could handle several hundred players at a time, which was an unprecedented number of people to find in the same graphical online space. For its time, the game was a smashing success, especially considering that nothing like it had come before. But M59's commercial life soon took an unfortunate turn.

Games for consoles like the Playstation 2 are generally sold in "fire and forget" mode: Once a game is released, it gets little attention from the publisher who packages, markets, and sells it, unless it's to create a sequel. MMOs, though, require active customer service throughout their lifetimes, and those lifetimes can stretch on for many years. (The oldest graphical MMOs are now passing the decade mark.) The capital outlay required is typically enough to crush ambitious hobbyists like the Kirmses and can also overburden the small independent developers who sometimes buy the rights to a game with nothing but the best intentions.

In the majority of cases, MMOs are eventually absorbed by large gaming companies with strong track records in marketing console games but with little sense of the culture and spirit of massively multiplayer online worlds. This disconnect can lead to a number of conflicts between the residents of virtual worlds and the people charged with running them,[12] but for Meridian 59 it presented an even more serious problem. Short of cash, the Kirmses sold the game soon after it went beta to a company called 3DO. 3DO was headed into a long slide that would eventually result in the company's filing for bankruptcy in 2003. But the game died even before the bankruptcy. Unwilling to support it, 3DO shut down the game's servers in 2000, while many of M59's original developers remained logged on, staying until the bitter end.[13]

Meridian had suffered, but thanks to the Kirmses it was now clear where MMOs were headed: rich and complex text-based worlds could be fun and satisfying experiences, but would never draw enough gamers to be truly "massively multiplayer." Graphics, on the other hand, brought new players in who had never thought to enter an online world. Once they were there, the MMO experience kept them hooked.

Origin Systems, the next company to enter the MMO space, would raise the stakes by basing its virtual world on the success of its single-player Ultima role-playing franchise. Ultima Online, another traditional swords-and-spells game, was launched in 1997 with a fixed isometric camera angle that simulated three dimensions but was actually a step back from Meridian 59's graphics engine. But the success of the single-player Ultima games brought players to this already-familiar world. UO ramped up to nearly 100,000 players within the first year of its release, peaked at about a quarter of a million users in 2003, and is still played by over 150,000 people today.

UO introduced an important concept to the world of MMOs, that of "sharding." According to the game's lore, the Ultima Online world (known as Brittania) had at one point been captured in a jewel. When that jewel was smashed, each shard was discovered to contain its own parallel version of the world. It was a creative way to explain to players why they couldn't all play in the same world at once. Each shard—that is, each computer server—could handle only several thousand players at once. In order to accommodate all of UO's subscribers, dozens of different shards were needed. Multiple versions of online worlds are still often called shards today. Alphaville, for instance, the city Urizenus first inhabited, is simply one shard of the world of The Sims Online.

The game that capped the first round of major MMOs was EverQuest, another swords-and-spells game that drew much of its inspiration from sources like *The Lord of the Rings* and Dungeons & Dragons. Released in early 1999, EverQuest brought a new level of 3-D graphics to the genre, allowing players to alter the angle from which they viewed the world, climb on top of various objects, and operate in a space that truly had breadth, depth, and height. EQ attracted gamers like never before, gaining around 200,000 subscribers in its first year and peaking at over half a million. (EverQuest and its successor, EverQuest II, are still played by a combined 750,000 people today.)

EverQuest drew players in part because it offered "newbies" an easier entry to the world than either Ultima Online or M59 had. UO characters were defined by a complex system of skills that offered players the means to tailor their online personas in great detail. While the system meant you weren't limited in what kind of adventurer you could be (swordsman, for example, or blacksmith, or magician, etc.), some people found it difficult or confusing to manage.

With the shard populations in Ultima Online and EverQuest reaching levels never before seen in online worlds, Brittania and Norrath (the fantasy worlds of UO and EQ, respectively) began to see some fascinating social dynamics developing among their players. People were becoming more immersed in these online worlds and, as that happened, developers' assumptions about how people would play their games began to mean less. Though developers often had clear ideas about how their games should develop, the influx of unpredictable human players meant that something quite different was in store for them.

In Asheron's Call, for example, an MMO released in the autumn of 1999 (and shut down in 2005), the narrative structure of the game called for "evil" players to destroy a crystal that held the soul of the demon Bael'Zharon. Once the soul was released, the players could move on to the next stage of their story, and so it went—on every server but one. To prevent their adversaries from reaching their goal, a group of "good" players on the Thistledown server set up a twenty-four-hour watch to protect the crystal. As writer George Jones relates in Part 2 of *GameSpy.com*'s history of MMOs, "Alternate Reality: The History of Massively Multiplayer Online Games," "The longer [the watch] lasted, the more acclaim the defenders received. It got to the point that the new storyline could not continue. The developers finally had to intervene with high-level characters to destroy the defenders so the crystal could be broken and the story could continue."[14]

Everquest developers had similar stories. John Smedley, interviewed in the same *GameSpy.com* story, told of the surprise that ensued when fifty players organized to kill what was supposed to be an imposing monster. It took them all of five minutes. "Our designers' jaws were dropping—they couldn't believe their baby was being destroyed so easily!" Smedley recalls. "Gamers were solving problems in ways we had never imagined."

Nor did the unpredictability of players stop with computer-controlled adversaries. Certainly no one had foreseen that Lord British himself—the avatar of Ultima creator Richard Garriott—would be murdered by a UO player just as he was about to make a speech within the game, early in the beta testing phase.[15]

Just what was happening here? Why wasn't it enough to go around killing orcs and nightsabers, collecting gold and experience, and "leveling up" to increase your character's strength and abilities? After all, that's what these games were about, wasn't it?

It was, but only in part. The "play" of MMOs—slaying monsters, collecting gold, leveling up to turn your character into a formidable hero—is fun. But gameplay alone doesn't explain the appeal. Many single-player games offer gameplay that's every bit as rich and engaging, after all. (Try The Elder Scrolls IV: Oblivion for an excellent example.) For many players, the social aspect of MMOs is the only reason they're there. There are people to interact with, people to befriend and romance, people to plot against, to antagonize, to "kill." Rochester Institute of Technology's Andy Phelps, a long-time EverQuest player, knows players who have been in EverQuest for years and yet have not progressed past the first several levels of the game, because the only reason they log on is to hang out with their friends.[16]

The appeal of virtual worlds is the other people. Everything you do in an online world is done with an audience of up to thousands of others to witness it. If you and your guildmates slay the fearsome dragon Nefarian in World of Warcraft, you can be sure other people are going to hear about it. And when they do, this becomes part of the culture of the game, and part of your character's history. Every step you take in an MMO is part of a larger story that's woven from the threads of all the characters who inhabit the world. What's being created in an MMO is not just fun, it's a shared culture and narrative that gives everyone involved a stake in the proceedings.

In his prescient 1992 novel, *Snow Crash*,[17] author Neal Stephenson paints a picture of the "metaverse" as a 3-D virtual environment that in many ways is uncannily like the virtual worlds that can be experienced in MMOs today. While the real world of *Snow Crash* was bleak and unfriendly, the metaverse, while no utopia, was a place where your identity was what you made it, and where your story was determined by your interactions with people you would probably never meet in a physical setting.

But in the first few generations of MMOs, up to and including World of Warcraft, the metaverse had still not quite arrived. Even in the most open worlds, from Ultima Online to EVE Online, there was still too much "game" to them, too much direction, not enough freedom to actually create the world you wanted. Players were gaining control of the narratives that developed in these worlds, but they were still too often governed by the game mechanics of collecting gold and experience points and battling computer-controlled adversaries and other players. It was only a matter of time, though, before a game was created that would do away with winning and losing and the clear competitive goals that define most games, a game that would simply place people in a virtual environment—a kind of metaverse—and let storylines emerge entirely from their activities and interactions. The first graphical world to do this didn't do it very well, but that world, The Sims Online, where Urizenus lived and died, was the game that would bring that idea to the masses.

3 Slinging Bolts at the Robot Factory

Urizenus first appeared in The Sims Online in August 2003. For Uri's typist, Peter Ludlow, who had never set foot in an MMO before, the place was mind-blowing. Text-based virtual communities were old hat to Ludlow, who had been poking around the Internet since the early 1980s. But all you saw on an online bulletin board were your words. Suddenly, here was a graphical world, a place, a *place* where you saw your*self*—albeit a cartoon version of yourself—walking and talking and interacting with a (cartoonishly) suburban version of the world. Ludlow was fascinated.

Acclimating to your first virtual world can be a tricky business. Unlike a science-fiction story in which your consciousness is suddenly transplanted into someone else's body, it's more like your body has been extended into a new environment. There is no disconnect, no sense of being the ghost in the machine. Rather, the avatar simply becomes an extension of yourself that enables you to interact with this new world, much like a new pair of eyeglasses that require some getting used to, but that fast become so much a part of you that you don't even notice they're there.

Of course, this on-screen representative has a "physicality" with a whole new set of tics and gestures. It walks, moves, and talks slightly differently than you're used to. In the beginning, even the simple business of moving from point A to point B can be a challenge. But like walking around in the real world, using the buttons and motions that are necessary to navigate the virtual world quickly become second nature, and you're soon busy learning to keep your new "self" healthy and happy in the isometric, not-quite-3-D world.

In The Sims Online, you are immediately faced with a set of "attribute bars" representing your avatar's "motives"—things like Hunger, Comfort, Social—that are rapidly dropping into the red zone, signifying that they are "dangerously" low. How to turn these green again can be confusing at first, but can also yield amusing results. After only about fifteen minutes, you'll probably notice what a slob your on-screen self can be. After he jogs to the fridge to satisfy his appetite, grabbing a bag of chips and maybe a can of beans, he stands there munching for a moment, and then he tosses his trash onto the floor of his new home! His Hunger bar has climbed into the green, range but now Room (representing the attractiveness of one's surroundings) is dropping into the red. Click the clean-up option on the pile of trash and your avatar sighs, sweeps it into a plastic bag, and takes it out to the curbside garbage can. But then you have to watch your Bladder bar and make sure you send your avatar to the toilet before he gets too uncomfortable—or simply wets his pants, as will happen eventually.

Of course, to use the bathroom, you'll first have to install one in your new home. Buying a plot of land and building a house is easy enough to do using TSO's in-game store and construction interface. Once you've dragged some walls into place, chosen your wallpaper, bought yourself a houseplant and stocked your new split-level with a refrigerator, you can direct your avatar to have a snack, as described above. At that point, "greening" yourself in motives like Hunger and Bladder can be done largely in the privacy of your own home.

Your Social bar, however, requires you to spend some time interacting with other Sims (as TSO characters are known), and that's where the real challenge begins. The metaverse, it turns out, has developed its own unique set of social conventions to take into account two things: that communication isn't quite synchronous (you can never really talk over someone on a computer screen) and that the people you're talking to are more or less anonymous. The visual cues we take for granted in the physical world just aren't present in online conversations, or they have manifestations in online worlds that can have very different meaning. Age, sex, race, social stratum—we make educated guesses about all these things each time we meet someone in the real world. In a world like The Sims Online, though, the blinged-out and muscle-bound twenty-five-year-old ghetto-born rapper you might run into on a server could just as easily be a wispy forty-year-old white suburban housewife creating her dream of a more exciting life.

Ludlow's avatar, Urizenus, more or less resembled his real-life counterpart, at least at first. The chrome-domed Uri sported slightly less hair than Ludlow and a more devilish goatee, but dressed as befit a virtual journalist—or maybe an off-duty cop—in dark slacks, turtleneck sweaters, and leather coats. His name was drawn from quite a different source: William Blake's 1794 *Book of Urizen,* the story of a conflicted anti-hero who is cast out of the heavens and into a chaotic void, then rises to create a new world there. While Ludlow couldn't know when he chose the name just how aptly Urizen's expulsion would prefigure his own, a few lines from Blake's poem caught his attention as a poetic description of what it was like to participate in the birth of a virtual world:

View'd by sons of Eternity, standing
On the shore of the infinite ocean
Like a human heart struggling and beating
The vast world of Urizen appear'd.[1]

So, in the guise of a flea-bit 1970s detective with an eighteenth-century metaphysicist's name, he ventured out to explore Alphaville.

But even finding people to talk to was sometimes difficult. As he wandered around Alphaville in his first days in the game, Urizenus often came upon roomfuls of avatars seemingly engaged in tasks of one kind or another: lifting weights, reading a book, playing a piano, or learning other skills ("skilling," in TSO parlance) that would make it easier for them to green their motive bars or earn the game's virtual currency, known as simoleans. But when Uri tried to talk to them, he found no one home. Their typists were AFK—Away From Keyboard, in online jargon—while their online representatives automatically went about whatever tasks they'd been assigned. Though TSO had been envisioned as a game that would naturally guide players to form communities, many of the actual mechanisms of gameplay did just the opposite, letting typists watch television or read a paper-and-ink book, clicking their mouse only every few minutes, if needed, while their online selves carried on with their mechanical tasks within the game.

When Uri found a Sim whose typist *was* at the keyboard, he discovered there was a protocol for interactions in TSO. Inserting oneself into conversation wasn't always easy. Simply strolling up to a Sim and typing a line of chat was often considered rude, especially if the avatar was already in conversation with someone else. And when speaking in a room filled with dozens of avatars, it was important not to "Bogart the bandwidth." In a crowded room in real life, holding a conversation with only the people nearest you is not a problem. But in an online world like TSO, with its text-based communication system, anything you say can be "heard" at the same decibel level by everyone in the room. Uri soon found it was easy to make a nuisance of oneself by speaking too "loudly."

Once he'd learned how to avoid ruffling any feathers and managed to find people who were actually present in their online lives, there was the problem of the conversation itself, which was conducted in a language that was similar to English but differed in important ways. There were new words to be learned, and old words that had taken on new meanings in the world of TSO. While Uri's typist wasn't in the game to study the mechanisms of online communications, the linguist in him couldn't help but be fascinated by the micro-language that appeared to be evolving there. Many expressions had been imported from the text-based online communities Uri was already familiar with. When someone said "ROTFLMAO," he knew it meant "rolling on the floor laughing my ass off." He was aware that "griefers" were troublemakers and that a "n00b" was a slightly more pejorative version of a "newbie" (i.e., a new player). But it took a moment to realize what "greening" was, and though he had spent many years online, several simple expressions, like "oic" for "oh, I see" were new to him.

More interesting than the vocabulary was the rhythm of in-game communication. Long orations were definitely frowned upon, and the most effective way to communicate was in a series of witty quips and one-liners. The asynchronicity of speech in virtual worlds and the lack of visual clues like facial expressions and direction of gaze forced people to find new ways to communicate. Even speaking in chunks longer than a short sentence could make for confusion, as there was no way for your interlocutor to know if you were awaiting a response or busy typing your own. No less interesting were the "disfluencies" that people inserted into their speech; expressions like "er," and "uh," and "hmmmm" were routine ways of softening what might be construed as a harsh statement, or of registering doubt without coming out and saying you weren't sure. Emoticons, the smiley-faces and other facial expressions constructed from punctuation marks—such as :-) and :-P and many others—were used, but were considered a sort of crutch that experienced players often avoided. And when responding to an off-key remark, no comment was more eloquent than the blank stare, represented on the chat line as a simple ellipsis: ". . . ."

Having gotten the lay of the land and begun to master the living of his online life, Uri turned to the game itself. What was there to actually *do* here? Not much, it turned out, at least on the surface. Beyond greening and chatting, Urizenus found that the game design of TSO provided precious little in the way of entertainment or engaging diversion. There were certainly no nightsabers to kill, and no quests to undertake. Skilling turned out to be a particularly boring pursuit, consisting mostly of clicking the mouse once, watching your avatar pretend to read a book or play the piano, then waiting several minutes until the mouse needed to be clicked again (which helped explain why so many people were always AFK).

Of course, having an open, undirected world was part of the point. But by the autumn of 2003 it was becoming clear that what the game company was offering in terms of "play" just wasn't living up to what players had been expecting. The Sims Online's single-player predecessor, known simply as The Sims, had become the most popular computer game of all time because it had given players the illusion that a little virtual life was taking shape on the screen before them. TSO, by contrast, often failed to give players the illusion that there was any life to the game at all.

Two new features were coming online when Uri joined TSO that August: the ability to own a pet and the ability to hold a job. Uri explored them both, though neither were really entertaining. The pets couldn't do much more than be petted and pee on the floor, or (the best possible scenario, in Uri's opinion) run away. One of Ludlow's "alts" (a secondary or alternative character to his "main," Urizenus), was an avatar named Doctor Legion. Doc had taken a job in a robot factory known as M.O.M.I., which stood for Municipal Observation and Management Incorporated, a name borrowed from the movie *Brazil*.

The aesthetics of the robot factory itself had been drawn from old science fiction nightmare scenarios of what our future might become—Fritz Lang's *Metropolis* digitized and brought to you as alleged fun. Amid dark, discolored metallic walls, venting steam pipes and explosions were the dynamic visual events. Robot parts moved along an assembly line, and Doc's job consisted of "activating" certain machines to add heads and other extremities to the robots' chassis. Of course, there were never enough players at the factory to man all the machines, in part because the factory's equipment had a tendency to malfunction. Things would routinely explode, killing most of the players before the shift was over.

For Doc, the novelty of grinding away in a fascist steampunk workplace nightmare quickly evaporated. The place was creepy. Naturally, Doc soon grew reluctant to show up for his shifts. But if he stood too close to a road he ran the risk of getting snatched away by car pools at unexpected moments and delivered to the factory, where motivational posters exhorted workers to "Trust M.O.M.I." And there was no obvious way for Doc to quit his job. Eventually, he just stopped showing up for work, only to be hounded by M.O.M.I. for absenteeism.

Technical problems and frequent server crashes accompanied such add-ons, and the TSO online forums and bulletin boards were blanketed with angry and unhappy posts. Layering a new set of rote tasks on top of greening was not what TSO's residents wanted. That was clear from the numbers: TSO's population was already falling back from its peak of around 105,000 that summer as people left for worlds with more freedom or better-defined goals. The promise of TSO had been great; its reality was disappointing. For Uri, the problem stemmed from the kind of clashes that had been cropping up between game companies and their customers since the earliest days of Meridian 59 and Ultima Online. The game developers were telling one story, but the players were living another.

The Sims Online had its earliest origins in a game idea that occurred to a man named Will Wright in the early 1980s. Then in his early twenties, Wright—who had studied architecture, mechanical engineering, computer science, and robotics, all without ever managing to get a degree—found himself fascinated not with playing computer games themselves but with designing new maps for a helicopter combat game known as Raid on Bungeling Bay that he had written for the Commodore 64. Wright found himself so engrossed in placing just the right balance of roads, terrain, enemy tanks, and friendly aircraft carriers that he thought, *Why not write a game in which the players themselves can design such a virtual environment, as part of the gameplay itself?* Instead of a combat zone, he imagined a city, with its own traffic and pollution problems, its own economics, and its own zoning regulations. By the time he was twenty-five he had written his game and was well on his way to getting it out in front of the public.

That game became SimCity, one of the most popular and influential single-player computer games of all time. An open-ended single-player game that put the player in charge of designing and managing a simulated city, SimCity soon gave rise to a number of descendants and knock-offs that heightened the level of detail and complexity contained in its simulated world, though without substantially changing the feel of the game. Instead of zoning a large chunk of land as industrial, commercial, or residential, you could now zone a single city block. Some games let you manage a single office tower, or even an anthill. As the granularity within the game increased, it became clear to Wright where things were headed: toward a game in which players focused on creating and managing a single house and its resident "sims," seeing to their everyday needs and guiding them through their interactions with neighbors and with each other. As SimCity continued to generate sales and spin-offs for Maxis, the company Wright had co-founded in 1987, Wright began work on a "home tactics" game that went by the working title Dollhouse, and which would later become the single-player game The Sims.

When Electronic Arts Inc., the colossus of the gaming industry, bought Maxis in a $125 million stock swap in 1997,[2] Wright had already spent several years on Dollhouse. Maxis executives had been skeptical about the viability of such a game, though, and Wright mostly developed it in his spare time. EA execs were no different. Like big movie studios, big game publishers shy away from extending themselves beyond the tried and true formulae for success, and nothing like what Wright envisioned had ever hit the market. As Don Hopkins, a member of the original Sims development team, recalled in an interview with the *Alphaville Herald*, even after EA gave the project a green light, the development team was forced to spend much of its time convincing the suits not to cancel it: "Some of the EA old guard didn't trust nor respect Will's vision, didn't get the idea of Dollhouse, didn't think it would sell, wanted to inject it full of their old tried and trusted formula, and wanted to gut out the most interesting parts of the game, like the architecture tools."[3]

But the project managed to survive, and in 2000 Maxis and EA released Dollhouse as The Sims. With EA's weight behind it, the release was soon followed by a round of spin-offs (with names like The Sims Vacation, The Sims House Party, and The Sims Hot Date), each of which increased the variety and complexity available in the game.

The Sims asks little more of its players than that they keep their avatars healthy and happy. Beyond that, you can do what you like; how much fun you have "simming" is entirely up to you. Writing about the game in *Time* magazine, Lev Grossman asked readers to imagine "the most boring video game possible.... Instead of fighting evil, you would do the dishes, watch a little TV, then call it a night. Instead of saving the world, you would be saving for a bigger split-level."[4]

But for many, many people, The Sims is not boring at all (as Grossman went on to illustrate in his piece). In fact, its open-endedness, its lack of well-defined goals and the endless variety of "paths" through the game has captured the public's imagination as no other game has. Within two years of its release, The Sims had sold eight million copies in seventeen languages and had become the most popular computer game of all time.

With The Sims' popularity came a flourishing network of Web sites where players and fans could swap not just stories and screenshots but things like house designs, Sim clothing, and other unique items they had designed or built with the content-creation tools the game provided, or by using third-party software like the Transmogrifier, written by Don Hopkins. The Transmogrifier delighted Sims fans, who used it to create (and trade) everything from pumpkin pies to exotic avatar "skins" to luxuriously textured furnishings. These were more than just the stories that usually got posted on fan sites, they were unique creations, the handiwork of individual players. Putting on display what you'd created became part of the game; the shadow economy of items swapped outside the game helped fuel even more interest and more customers. In the simplest way possible, the Transmogrifier gave players a chance to feel that they were not only playing the game but were creating the very world their characters inhabited.

What people wanted was more of the same: more complex interactions in their simulated worlds, the ability to visit places beyond their "family" home, a way to create interesting artifacts within their virtual environment, and the means to show off those things and interact with other players "in-world" rather than being limited to swapping their creations outside the game in Web-based bulletin boards and forums.

So Wright and Maxis gave them just that, and in late 2002 Electronic Arts Inc. released The Sims Online, a massively multiplayer online game that let the legion of formerly solitary Sims players enter a virtual world filled with others just like themselves. In TSO, instead of the limited interactions with computer-controlled characters that were available in the offline version of the game, players can meet and chat with real human beings from around the world—or at least, their on-screen representatives. Not only that, but they can buy and sell the items they've acquired in the game, using simoleans, the game's virtual currency. And as Maxis built add-ons for TSO, Sims gained the ability to keep a pet, hold a job (as Doc did), earn rewards for creating popular destinations within the world, and even form relationships that mirrored those possible in real life.

One of the reasons Maxis was able to develop so many add-ons and spin-offs for The Sims and TSO was the enormous financial power of Electronic Arts Inc. It takes many millions of dollars to develop a computer game, and EA was willing to throw money at The Sims Online—$30 million, reportedly[5]—to ensure its success. When TSO was released there were over a million "inhabitants" of other virtual worlds, and given the millions of copies of The Sims that were selling (and the fact that EA had successfully leveraged the single-player Ultima franchise into a massively multiplayer success), EA figured TSO would sell itself. They boldly predicted that the game would eventually reach between one and two million subscribers.

But selling a brand is different from selling a game, and in focusing on the good name of The Sims to sell The Sims Online, EA failed to take one thing into account: its customers. One of the things people most loved about The Sims was the ability to create their own content for the game. Will Wright promised them this would be a function that was supported in The Sims Online and EA backed him up—at first. But it was a promise that would never materialize.

Despite the popularity of the Transmogrifier and of user-created items in The Sims, the idea of player-created content never gained corporate support, and when TSO went online no user-created custom content of any kind was permitted in the game, much to players' chagrin. TSO players were left with houses and avatars that all, in the end, looked much the same, variations from a limited suite of choices. The creative outlet that had helped make The Sims so popular had been denied them.

Will Wright himself had very much wanted to give TSO players the ability to create their own content. But even after the smash success of The Sims, it was as if EA didn't trust Wright's vision. The company continued to dangle the promise of content-creation tools,[6] but they never took any visible steps toward delivering on that promise. It was almost as if the EA suits had failed to grasp the very idea of the game itself: that the gameplay consisted of living the lives of your on-screen characters, and that the richer and more creative those lives could be, the more people would be attracted to the game. The "Trust M.O.M.I." banner that Doctor Legion had encountered at work now seemed to loom like a creepy Orwellian slogan, especially given what Uri was discovering to be the uneasy relationship between TSO's players and the $3 billion corporation running the game. For what EA also failed to grasp was that, in the absence of content-creation tools, TSO's residents would enrich their lives by inventing what they could: gameplay strategies that were often creative and at times quite subversive as well. EA's slogan was "Challenge Everything." But its game seemed to say, "Challenge nothing, be content with what you've got. Ignorance is strength."

If The Sims Online was about creating a second life, the question Urizenus found himself faced with was, *What kind of life would that be?* Raising pets or slinging bolts in the robot factory was clearly not going to be enough. You could do those things in real life, and get more out of them.

Though TSO was Ludlow's first MMO, he had been thinking and writing about the ways we connect online since the mid-1980s, when he had been a contract engineer for the Intelligent Interface Systems Group of Honeywell, Inc. Now a professor of philosophy and linguistics at the University of Michigan at Ann Arbor, Ludlow had long been a member of online bulletin board services and early social networks like The Well, part of a community that was thinking and talking—and doing things—about how connectedness would change our lives even before very many people were connected.

In those pre-Netscape days, before the browser company's IPO in August 1995 effectively launched the World Wide Web on a truly worldwide scale, the Internet was still in its infancy, and cyberspace was a place largely populated by visionaries, or those who wanted to be thought of as such. Even if, like Ludlow, you were content to just look on as the Internet and Web took shape, it was an exciting time. There was the sense that something was happening that would revolutionize the way we lived. The Electronic Frontier Foundation (EFF) was just gearing up to protect people's rights in cyberspace; publications like *Mondo 2000* and the *Computer Underground Digest* were beginning to shout the revolution's slogans from the virtual rooftops; thousands were flocking to The Well, the most important early user-run virtual community; and people like Lotus Development founder Mitch Kapor, science fiction writer Bruce Sterling, and early chroniclers like Howard Rheingold, Stewart Brand, and Josh Quittner (now editor of *Business 2.0*) were prominent on the scene. (Ludlow would later collect many of these early contacts into two compilations of essays he edited on legal and conceptual issues in cyberspace.[7]) Being there with those characters was like contributing to an avant-garde salon, and for ten years it felt like it was their space, a space where everyone was welcome but few had shown up yet, where it seemed nothing but fascinating things could happen.

So when faced with the choice of what kind of virtual life to lead, it's hardly surprising that Ludlow chose the role of a journalist, chronicling another exciting moment in an exciting medium. He'd also been impressed, in a biography he'd been reading, with the work of Benjamin Franklin in establishing an independent press in the early eighteenth century in the Penn Colony, which at the time was being run as an enormous corporation by William Penn's cruel and unethical heirs.[8] (Pennsylvania did not become a state until 1787.) If Franklin's *Pennsylvania Gazette* could provide comprehensive coverage of the privately owned territory that made up the Penn Colony, it seemed that Urizenus ought to be able to do something similar in Alphaville, another privately held colony in another new world.

To help fill the pages of the *Herald*, Uri assembled a small staff of real-world friends and acquaintances, including graphic designer and MMO addict Glenn Given (better known by his screen name, Squirrel)[9] and Candace Bolter, one of Ludlow's graduate students at the University of Michigan, who would come to play an important role in the *Herald*'s story. Together they ventured out into the world of TSO and MMOs in general to see what could be seen.

The surface gameplay of TSO itself rarely made for good copy. Doing the dishes, watching TV, and saving for a bigger split-level was not the stuff of banner headlines. But what the *Herald* staff eventually found in TSO was far more interesting than the game's public presence seemed to imply. Greening, skilling, and keeping your avatar happy and hale hardly began to describe the social dynamics that Uri was discovering as he moved through the world: things that looked very much like virtual families, gang rivalries, huge commercial undertakings, bitter personal disputes, and some very alternative lifestyles. This was the content that TSO's players were creating in the absence of other content-creation tools, the things that made the game more than simply the sum of its software. These were the kinds of things that made MMOs and cyberspace so fascinating to Ludlow. Though The Sims Online was nerdy and suburban on the surface, it was different than what had come before, and here again was the sense that something important was happening.

"We . . . want to know what [MMOs] tell us about ourselves," Uri wrote, in introducing the *Herald* and its mission. The *Herald*'s most important charge would be

> to reflect on what all of this means: what are the legal, social, and economic implications of what is happening in our MMO? Exactly what kind of economy is emerging in Alphaville? What kinds of social institutions are developing? What is the nature of the interpersonal bonds that are being formed? What does role-play in Alphaville tell us about the people who are engaged in the play? These are just some of the questions that interest us. No doubt other questions will come to grip our imagination as the *Herald* matures, and no doubt events both within the game and outside of it will have profound effects on what we write here. In the meantime, however, this is where we stand—on the shores of a new land, as inhabitants of a brand new city, indeed a new kind of city: Alphaville.[10]

As a journalist, Uri was skeptical from the start. Alphaville, this new kind of city, seemed to be plagued with many of the problems of plain old nonvirtual cities and nations. Already a kind of suburban flight was occurring, as TSO's residents left the game in tens of thousands. In one of his first *Herald* articles, Urizenus blamed that phenomenon on the suits at Maxis, whom he saw as unable to understand the nature of what they had created: "MMOs are not games," Uri wrote, "they are synthetic societies that develop synthetic cultures, economies, and governance structures. What we want from Maxis is some sign—some clue—that they are capable of grasping this difference, because until they grasp it TSO will continue to be a failure."

Uri called on Maxis to think of itself not as a gamemaker, but rather as a kind of government, providing the infrastructure that would allow the synthetic culture to operate smoothly. Its citizens, in turn, would have certain responsiblities: Rather than charging monthly fees, Maxis would take a small tax out of each transaction completed in-world. Nor would residents be able to earn money in amounts limited only by how much time they were willing to spend in-world (or how willing they were to hack the game). Instead, Maxis would control the money supply in similar fashion to the Federal Reserve, in order to check the devaluation of TSO's virtual currency against the dollar.

To Uri, TSO was in many ways a broken game. But it was also an innovative one, almost by accident. With no real "game" to play, it fell to the players to make up the rules of their world from scratch. Most of them weren't used to a game where winning and losing didn't exist. So TSO's residents found themselves forced to create their own game.

The game they played—the synthetic society—was one that at first looked a lot like high school.

What Uri learned in talking to people in TSO was that most of them worried not about the in-game indicators but rather about their social standing with the various cliques that had developed in the game. The "jocks" and their friends consisted of the Sims who lived in the most frequented locations, the DJs who were hired to pipe music into people's houses (via an Internet radio application outside the game, this being another user-content function Maxis failed to include in TSO), and an organization of vigilante players known as the Sim Shadow Government whose ostensible mission was to police Alphaville for frauds and scams. The "freaks" consisted of the black-clad goths and Dungeons & Dragons-style avatars, as well as various strains of cybersex aficionados, who let their online selves play out fantasies their offline bodies would probably never experience (with a few exceptions, to be sure). The "geeks," Uri wrote, "are harder to locate, and probably for a reason: they are all playing EverQuest or Star Wars Galaxies or some other geek-worthy MMORPG. Still, there are a few, and I guess anyone who writes for the *Alphaville Herald* has at least one foot in this camp."[11]

Uri went on to point out that even he was recapitulating his high-school role: "Back in the day . . . I triangulated a social position between all three camps." In Alphaville, Uri had developed valuable contacts in the Sims Shadow Government that would lead him into a deeper game within the game, and he at first worked out of a Mephistophelean church located in a neighborhood called Rose Thorn Gardens, a neighborhood of about one hundred homes where the predominant activity (outside the *Herald* offices) seemed to be a cybersex version of bondage, sadomasochism, and dominant/submissive sex-play. "In a place where you can look however you want and in some sense be whatever you want, why are so many of us falling into the same roles we did in RL [real life]?" Uri asked.

Though he didn't know it at the time, the *Herald* would also recapitulate Ludlow's earliest experience of what happened when a newspaper took on city hall. In junior high school in Minnesota, where Ludlow grew up, he and a friend had briefly published an "underground" newspaper called *The Oink: The Voice of the People. The Oink* addressed the issues of the day in hard-hitting editorials that called for the administration to allow chewing gum at school and change the dress code to tolerate untucked shirts. Foreshadowing his experience in TSO, school administrators confiscated all the copies of *The Oink* Ludlow and his friends had distributed—only to have a mob of eager students fishing through trash cans to get their hands on the paper.

The *Herald*'s early notices were favorable. Soon after its launch, the highly respected Website *Terra Nova* (http://terranova.blogs.com), authored by a number of academics and game developers (including the virtual economist Edward Castronova, author of the book *Synthetic Worlds*, and a professional acquaintance), celebrated the birth of the paper. "A number of virtual worlds have company-sponsored 'news' feeds, but they're often digital infomercials (though sometimes not)," Castronova wrote. "With the founding of the *Alphaville Herald*, however, a virtual free press comes into existence. The *Herald* is an independent news service focusing not on Home Town, USA but on Alphaville, TSO." *Terra Nova* contributor Dan Hunter, then a professor at the Univerity of Pennsylvania's Wharton School, who studies legal issues in cyberspace, noted, "In years to come social historians, theorists, statisticians, economists, etc., etc., etc., will all give thanks for resources such as these: deeply embedded accounts of what actually happens in-world."

Castronova's closing comment was more inspirational to Ludlow: "Whatever part of the world they occupy (indeed, which world?), free Sims sleep easier tonight, knowing that they now have a tireless defender deploying the full powers of the public press! On, *Alphaville Herald*! On!"

Uri was inspired, but he was not entirely sure the *Herald* was living up to such solemn reponsibilities. It remained only for him to dig up some real news—news that went beyond whether The Sims Online was a satisfying piece of gaming software, that actually documented some of the ways its participants had taken that software and made more than a game out of it. But if he was concerned about not fulfilling his accidental mission, it wasn't long before those concerns would be dispelled.

4 A Day in the Life of a Techno-Pagan Newsroom

The idea to operate the *Herald* out of a Mephistophelean, techno-pagan church was not, at first, a strategy for getting closer to the "dark side" of TSO but was simply the stylistic preference of one of Urizenus's early roommates in TSO, even before the *Herald* was in operation. What Uri discovered, though, was that a techno-pagan institution like the Church of Mephistopheles, in which the *Herald* had its offices, actually gave him an impressive amount of access to some of the more colorful characters that populated Alphaville. With its heavy, dark wooden furniture and its halls dimly illuminated by torchlight, the Church of M resembled any other castle in any other role-playing game—except for the typewriters Uri furnished it with for use by the *Herald* staff. The result, however, was that the newspaper's environment attracted TSO residents who provided the *Herald* with fodder for some of its best stories.

Though "purchasing" a plot of land in TSO is relatively inexpensive, the game's zoning requirements for construction can be prohibitive unless a player takes on roommates, a way in which the game guides people into forming closer in-world relationships—and the genesis of some of the bitterest disputes the *Herald* would cover. Uri's first "roomie" was an avatar called Daywalker who in real life worked as a hip-hop DJ and aspiring rap producer. Daywalker, who had a taste for all things pagan and goth, was excited to construct some kind of house of pagan worship, and Uri, curious to see what this might entail, was perfectly willing to go along with the idea.

As the *Herald* was getting started, the Church of Mephistopheles began to attract a range of colorful characters. Because of the social requirements of greening, interacting with one's neighbors is all but inevitable in TSO, and the Church of M—built near the sexually hyperactive Rose Thorn

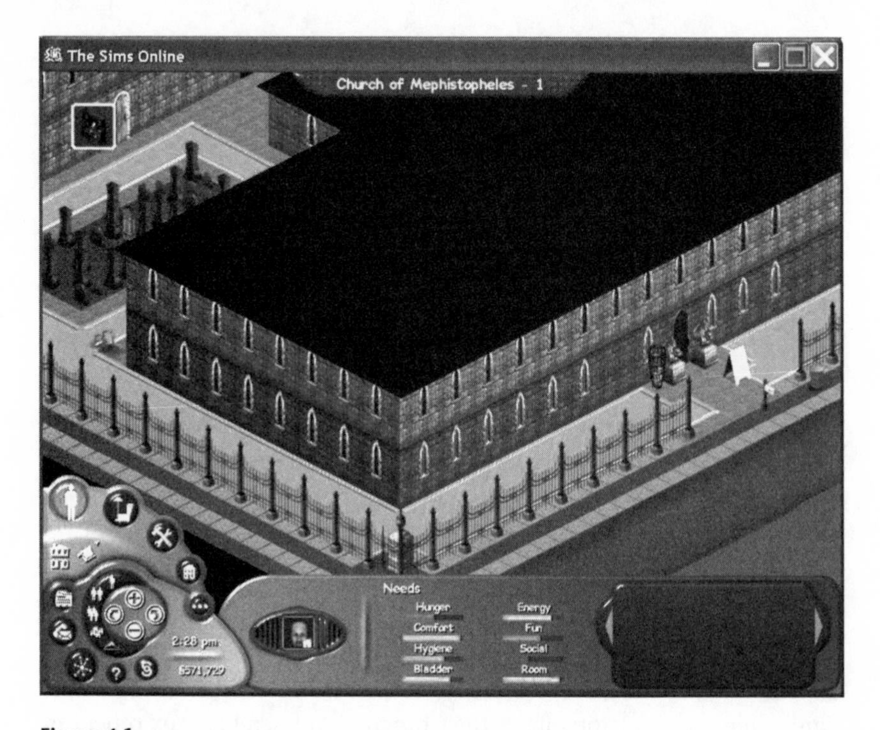

Figure 4.1
The Church of Mephistopheles

Gardens—saw an unusual procession of avatars come and go. Under deep (if tongue-in-cheek) cover as a techno-pagan priest, Uri learned about Alphaville's fringe culture at close range, meeting Satanists, sadists, Wiccans, griefers, mafiosi, perverts, prostitutes, scammers, miscreants, angry holy rollers, sociopaths, juvenile delinquents, random lost children, vampires, goths, doms, subs, Gorean masters and slaves,[1] and more.

By the end of his first few weeks in TSO, he had seen a lot. There was the teenage Satanist Twitty Robespierre, who wrote an in-game testimonial about Uri that read, "This man here made me so fuckin happy wen I saw he made a Dark Church for people like me. I shall call him the Anton LaVey of Alphaville. Rest assured, Christian Sims, we WILL torment ur worthless pathetic souls! In the name of Satan, we do wat we want." He had met Jesus X, who seemed to be role-playing a kind of transgressive "sexy Jesus." He had gotten to know the bondage, domination, and sadomasochism (BDSM) community well enough, including Lady Julianna and her sub Mikal, the Gorean Mistress Maria LeVeux and her slave Toy, and Lord Bastienne Dante and his subs, of whom the Lord was very possessive. There was Stella the Wiccan, Lightbringer and Aleister Crowley, not to mention Uri's roommate Daywalker, who was "powered by the blood of the innocent," according to his bio. There was Mistress of Darkness, who worried about her boyfriend, who she said hung out in real-life blood bars; there was the earnest and articulate Virtue, who wanted to be Virginia Woolf; and then there was Celestie, the abusive granny, who would verbally abuse and even slap around newcomers to Alphaville if they happened to wear glasses, have dyed hair, or be black.

A closer look, though, revealed more than at first met the eye (which in itself was often quite a lot). The radically nonstandard virtual lifestyles being practiced in the Rose Thorn Gardens (and beyond), did not preclude strong links being formed between residents, in ways that sometimes resembled real-life bonding patterns and sometimes constituted strange and fascinating departures from them. At some of the dedicated bondage locations, both men and women would be "collared" by their masters, in effect becoming virtual slaves. Masters often took on paternal guises, while fellow slaves were addressed as siblings. Not that such in-game relationships necessarily mimicked anything that was going on in the physical world. One particularly flirtatious female avatar in TSO was in fact played by a husband-and-wife team, and would flirt mercilessly with avatars of either sex, depending on who was playing her at the moment. Such instances were hardly limited to TSO. In another virtual world, two female avatars who were engaged in a loving (if platonic) lesbian relationship were both straight men in real life,[2] one of them a U.S. Air Force computer programmer on active duty.[3]

What Uri often found was that many of these bonds were actually part of larger structures that comprised nothing less than online "families," though this term sometimes implied something quite different from its real-life counterpart. It was a theme Uri would hear over and over in his travels around TSO. If Will Wright's original vision of The Sims was a kind of virtual dollhouse, The Sims Online became a place in which many people chose to "play house." For the most part, this fit within the advertised theme of TSO's gameplay: Players often formed virtual families in which various avatars took on the roles of father, mother, daughter, son, etc., as a way of engaging in more immersive or interesting roleplaying—in other words, for fun. But some TSO families were much more visceral; relationships and disputes could have the same emotional impact as in real life. As sociologist Sherry Turkle noted in her studies of life online,[4] some of these online families even became surrogate families to players who lacked such structures in the real world or were unsatisfied with what they had.

Some groups in TSO forged more complex ties. Various in-game "Mafias"—ostensibly dedicated to role-playing the Mafia lifestyle of movies like *The Godfather* or *Goodfellas*—stressed the importance of family and typically sprouted robust family trees with numerous aunts, uncles, cousins, and the like. Of course, not unlike in the movies or on *The Sopranos*, these relationships often led to betrayal and backstabbing, charges and countercharges, until what had been some of the closest relationships in the game became some of the most venomous.

That various forms of social groups and virtual familes had sprung up in TSO wasn't much of a surprise; Uri had seen stranger phenomena in his decades online. But despite the fact that no in-game software mechanic supported their creation, the role of these groups within the larger context of the game turned out to be more complex than he expected, and in some ways to subvert the very goals of the game itself.

One of the most prominent groups at around the time Uri entered Alphaville was an organization that called itself the Sim Shadow Government. By the time Urizenus arrived, the SSG had already been through a series of small "wars" with another prominent group, The Sim Mafia, which was headed by a Sim named JC Soprano. The wars were waged through the reputation system of "friend" and "enemy" links built into the game, though what was at stake in these conflicts wasn't clear at first. But as Uri learned more about the inner workings of Alphaville, he began to understand that, for many Sims, the central point of TSO was not improving your virtual lifestyle or enriching your virtual bank account, but a kind of social climbing that was made possible by the mechanics of the game—though it was far from what the game's designers had had in mind.

Uri's impression of TSO as a kind of virtual high school, filled with the same cliques as his own high school had been, was not so far off the mark—and these were high school cliques at their most ruthless. TSO had been designed as a social game, but the competitive nature of game players had an unexpected effect on the social aspect of the world.

For many, the idea of the game in TSO is to bring visitors to your virtual property. When a plot of "land" is purchased on a server (which can be done with a few simple mouse-clicks, if you have enough simoleans), the new owner is asked to classify the property as one of a predetermined set of categories. New players can head to properties in the "Welcome" category to get help adjusting to the game-world; impoverished avatars may visit a "Money" property to earn a few simoleans; those hoping to improve their virtual selves can drop in on "Skill" properties; and "Services," "Romance," and "Entertainment" are available as well.

But the game also features its own internal scoreboard that ranks the popularity of properties within each category. The more visitors that show up and the longer they stay, the higher the ranking a given property receives. Property rankings are updated daily, and if your property is in the top one hundred, you—and everyone else—can check on where you stand in relation to other players.

In effect, a game that was meant to promote socializing did so in part through a built-in scoreboard of social status, and it was status that became central to the lives of many Sims. Some players sought to work their way into popular groups, others looked to form their own "families" to challenge the established leaders. A few, figuring there's no such thing as bad publicity, sought to rise through the rankings by being outrageously bad. Nor were tactics limited to enhancing one's own reputation. Just as the high-school rumor mill could be used to undermine someone's social standing, some TSO residents perfected the art of the virtual smear campaign. You could opt out of the system and ignore the rankings altogether, but for those who cared, and they were many, TSO's social scoreboard made for a very ruthless game.

In the early days of the paper, Uri took to visiting the most popular sites in the various categories listed in the game's search tool. While improving his skills by playing the piano in someone's den or reading a book on mechanics in someone's library, or greening his social bar by hanging out at busy properties, or playing trivia for simoleans, Uri came into contact with a variety of avatars and began to take in all the gossip that is due the editor of a small-town newspaper: the playboy Sim who'd been caught "in bed" with another man; the popular DJ leading a secret double life as part of an in-game cult; the griefer who refused to sleep, bathe, or use the toilet, so his avatar was plagued with a swarm of flies, constantly wetting its pants, and every so often simply collapsing in someone else's home; and the infamous scammer named Evangeline, who invited newbies to her "welcome house" only to bilk them out of every simolean they'd entered the game with.

To get a closer view of what went on in Alphaville, Uri advertised the Church of M as available for vampire weddings and other goth-style events. These in themselves generated amusing tales. At one, Uri and Daywalker presided over a vampire wedding that drew twenty darksider guests—from vampires to satanists to run-of-the-mill bondage aficionados. Many of the guests were running computer systems that couldn't handle the processing power required by such a crowd, and were plagued by software crashes (not to mention a horny clown who kept chasing one of the guests around). As the groom crashed out of the game for the third time during a reading of a poem by Anton LaVey, a goth girl named SxyBelinda summed things up rather nicely: "This isn't going very well." Indeed, the groom ran out on his virtual bride the very next day and never came back.

As it turned, out, the techno-pagan shtick was often a double-edged sword. While it worked for the *Herald* and Uri's information-gathering task, it didn't always work in favor of other aspects of Uri's online life.

While lifting weights in a virtual fitness club one day, Uri met an attractive young female avatar by the name of Shawn One. Improving the figures that represented one's physical attributes, by doing things like lifting weights, had no affect on an avatar's appearance. But such statistics often had an impact on how one was perceived in a virtual world. To Uri, it seemed to say something about one's real-life priorities—despite the fact that in real life Uri's typist was rarely to be found doing bench presses or curls.

The virtual fitness club, as with fitness clubs in real life, was a place where it was easier to fall into conversation with nearby Sims than it was in other places in Alphaville. Soon Uri found himself chatting with Shawn and a couple of her friends. A stock, Maxis-issue attractive blond in TSO, Shawn was also an attractive blond in real life—or at least, that's how she represented herself on a site called RealSimsOnline.com, where many TSO residents posted details of their real lives, often including photographs. And while some people posted false information on the site, something about Shawn rang true to Uri. She was a DJ on an Internet radio station devoted to the game, and so Uri had heard her voice—decidedly female—and her personality seemed to fit her RL photograph. She wasn't the kind of person who usually attracted Uri's typist (who had previously been married to another university professor), but in the context of TSO he was curious about just what his attraction meant, and interested to find out more about her.

One might even say that he was flirting—at least, that's the reaction he got from one of the men Shawn was with, who promptly advised Uri—in decidedly cyber-Neanderthal terms—that it was time for him to find another gym. Undeterred by the threats from his competition (the guy was a cartoon character on his computer screen, after all), Uri stayed. But he did take one precaution.

One of the only tangible ways of expressing approval or disapproval in The Sims Online was through the green friendship or red enemy links that avatars could bestow upon one another. As Uri was learning, the enemy links—too many of which indicated an avatar was widely disliked—were one of the few "weapons" TSO's players had been able to concoct within the game. But the links could only be applied when an avatar was stationary, so when not lifting weights Uri made sure to keep his avatar in motion so that Shawn's would-be boyfriend wouldn't be able to tag him, one of the only threats that could actually be carried out in TSO.

At the *Herald* offices the next day, Uri was pleasantly surprised when Shawn One dropped in to pay a visit. She seemed less than thrilled to be in a house of techno-pagan worship, but the pair hit it off and before long were slow dancing around the newsroom, using one of the built-in animations that let avatars interact with each other. The "slow dance" animation, Uri later learned, was also the preferred animation for avatars engaging in cybersex. But to Uri, in his state of innocence, it was little more than a dance—though one that left him with the strange electric rush he remembered from junior high school dances. To his surprise, Uri found himself with the virtual equivalent of dating nerves, unsure whether he was supposed to put the moves on Shawn One or what that even meant. At one point, Shawn indicated that the pair might make good partners in the game; Uri wasn't sure what that meant either. All he was clear on was that he was starting to fall for . . . well, even that part was unclear.

Sim love, as it's called, tends to come on a person rapidly, and often departs just as fast. In TSO, an exciting new partner could be just a slow dance away. The reasons for this—like the reasons real-life relationships are usually slower to form and slower to disintegrate—are unclear, but they're probably tied up in the nature of identity online. All physical imperfections are airbrushed away when one becomes "embodied" in an avatar. Your on-screen representation is as cute or handsome as the game lets it be; you don't have to worry about your appearance, you can just "be yourself." On the other hand, the medium of cyberspace also lets you be "someone else" entirely, in a way that real life rarely does. But even through an avatar, such a charade is hard to maintain for very long. Whatever the underlying causes, one thing is clear: Sim love may not last long, but when it strikes it's positively electric.

If Uri had designs on becoming a virtual Romeo, though, they would be dashed by the same kinds of things that dashed the hopes of Shakespeare's tragic hero: Urizenus hailed from the wrong side of the tracks. The *Herald* offices didn't allow for a lot of privacy, and a few of Uri's more colorful neighbors happened to drop in during Shawn's visit, including the young Satanist, Twitty Robespierre. When the virtual dark-siders saw who Uri was consorting with, they were scandalized. They began castigating Shawn One for being part of the Sim Shadow Government, which was ostensibly devoted to stamping out various forms of sin in Alphaville. Uri's neighbors viewed the SSG as conservative and fascistic, and warned him against his new friend. The next day, Shawn One sent Uri a message explaining that she couldn't see him any more. He was too much of a darksider. It just wouldn't look good, she explained. And, besides, Shawn was hooking up with a guy from the SSG.

Given the prominence of the SSG in Alphaville, Uri made sure to keep in touch with Shawn despite the social pressures that meant they could never be more than friends. She would be a valuable contact for the *Herald*, he knew. Cable news channel CNN had featured the SSG in a story earlier in 2003, when the organization had been at war with The Sim Mafia. In addition to Mia Wallace, the head of the SSG, the interview had included the typist behind JC Soprano, who headed The Sim Mafia "family." But the interviewer treated the feud as little more than evidence that when you put lots of people in the same online world, all they did was find interesting new ways to misbehave.

Uri knew there was more to it than that. He got a glimpse of how much more a few weeks later, when Shawn One invited him to accompany her on a "tagging" mission. Just as Shawn's friend had threatened Uri with a red link in the gym, the primary weapon of the Sim Shadow Government in its campaign to rid Alphaville of ne'er-do-wells was the enemy link. A preponderance of green friendship links on an avatar's profile signaled their popularity (the most-linked avatars could be found in the game's search tool), while red links were the scarlet letters that could undo someone's reputation. Whenever the SSG identified a rogue Mafia family or other group they disapproved of, a hit squad was arranged that would seek to isolate the targeted avatars and then blanket them with red links. The links were often accompanied by comments such as "Avoid this Sim" or "Warning: Scammer." In TSO, red links could have much the same effect as a negative rating on eBay. But while the links couldn't actually harm you, they still stung a lot—especially when they were accompanied by a comment like "pwned," gamer-speak for "owned," as in the street-slang phrase, "I own you, biotch." No matter how you cut it, red links were to be avoided at all costs.

The "hit" Uri was invited on wasn't an official SSG operation but seemed to be a freelance job Shawn One had picked up on her own. A male Sim who had been jilted by his virtual girlfriend had put a bounty on her head: 100,000 simoleans to the first Sim to tag her with an enemy link annotated with the message, "Love never forgets."

Uri wasn't just along for the ride. Shawn wanted him to see what an operation was like at close range, and had invited him to actually do the tagging himself. While Uri's fledgling journalistic ethics told him this wasn't quite the way he wanted to do things, he was loath to pass up a chance to see a tagging mission from the inside, and this was as inside as it got. Deciding virtual brains would work better than virtual brawn in this case, Uri took a page from the ancient teachings of warfare, choosing stealth and deception for his tactics: He created a female alt in order to more easily approach his target.

Uri located the mark by doing a little investigative reporting: Her profile indicated she was low in her physical attributes that day, so he scouted a couple of places where this could be improved and soon found her at a fitness club, dancing her way to health. The bounty had apparently been widely broadcast: The place was crawling with Sims whom Uri knew to be members of various Mafia "families," all apparently eager to pick up some spare change.

Acting the part of the clueless noob, Uri, in his disguise as another woman, struck up a conversation. The mark was soon happily chatting away beside him, in the perfect position to be tagged. Uri hesitated, though, and the moment passed; she moved away. A chiding private message came from Shawn One: "I can't believe you didn't get her!"

Uri felt chastened at first—okay, emasculated—but then he began to feel guilty. To him, red links were an amusing measure of other people's whims, not an accurate gauge of one's standing in the world of The Sims Online. But he knew they were important to many Sims. So he sent the mark an instant message tipping her off to the price on her head. "Listen, this place is crawling with mafiosi," he wrote. "There is a hit on you." But his target was well aware of this already, it turned out.

Uri wrote back, "I have a business proposal for you. Let me tag you, then we split the 100k and after I get paid I remove the link." She considered for a moment, but before she could give a definitive answer Uri received another message from Shawn. Someone had Instant Messaged her that the hit had been called off. It had to be true: the mafiosi were already leaving the club in twos and threes. Uri was relieved. He had gotten a look at a tagging mission without anyone's getting "hurt."

Uri's contact with Shawn One dwindled after that, though she would later go on to open more doors for the *Herald*. The pair kept in touch sporadically, when Urizenus was working on a story or when the SSG sought information on scammers, but any thoughts of a virtual relationship, whatever that might entail, seemed to have been dashed. More important, though, Uri had, through Shawn One, gotten a glimpse at the SSG. Uri saw these types of organizations as a social phenomenon that seemed unique to online worlds: a group of far-flung people who banded together in the lawless reaches of the metaverse to attempt to bring some kind of order to the place in which they "lived." Lacking what would traditionally be thought of as weapons of any kind, they had found a way to use the tools of their environment to accomplish their ends and bring a kind of frontier justice to their virtual world. Documenting their history would be a coup for the *Herald*, and would fulfill the responsibility that apparently fell to the paper due to its mission statement and the encouragement of Ted Castronova when he celebrated the paper's birth on Terra Nova.

Of course, it wasn't all headlines and heresy around the *Herald* offices. Uri made sure his staff had their fair share of fun as well—particularly at the drowning parties he held periodically around the Church of Mephistopheles's moat-cum-swimming pool.

Although the worst that can happen to an avatar whose attribute bars go all the way into the red is that he or she passes out, "death" is possible in the world of The Sims Online. An old lamp may electrocute your Sim, an industrial accident may kill you while you're at work—or you might tire yourself out while swimming, and drown. The consequences aren't dire, but they are inconvenient. A headstone shows up near your place of departure and your avatar becomes a "ghost" for a period of hours or days, unable to take part in most of the activities of the world, save for haunting other Sims or examining your own ghostly remains. In keeping with his role as a dark priest, however, Urizenus had trained in certain skills that gave him a talent for resurrection, and among the services he offered at the Church was a revival ritual that would sharply reduce the amount of time a "dead" avatar would need to spend in limbo. At his drowning parties, Uri advertised cash prizes for the last Sim swimming, and dozens of avatars would show up at the church to jump in the moat and chat and carry on until they got tired enough to drown. The edge of the moat became littered with gravestones over the course of the night and at the end of it all someone walked away with a one-million simolean prize (about $40 at prevailing exchange rates on eBay at the time).

Uri's resurrection service also attracted Sims from time to time who had died at home or work and needed to be brought back to life. One of the avatars who availed herself of Uri's shamanistic skills was Evangeline (then named Voleur, the French word for "thief"), whose ghost arrived at the church one day in a sequined gown, modestly announcing she was "Queen of Alphaville." So notorious was she by the time the *Herald* started publication that a visit from her constituted nothing less than the patronage of a "cyberlebrity"—a virtual celebrity overdue for coverage from the *Herald*, in Uri's view.

While Uri's initial feints at information gathering drew nothing but coy responses from Evangeline, it was clear there was a lot to her story. Her property, the Free-Money for Newbies house, occupied the most popular slot in the game's Welcome category. But Evangeline also had more than sixty red links on her avatar's profile, making her one of the most widely hated Sims in Alphaville.

The charges against Evangeline—that she scammed newbies out of all their cash before they'd even had a chance to get started in the game—were fairly serious in the context of TSO, and Uri felt they should be covered in the *Herald*. But short of Evangeline's confirming the allegations,

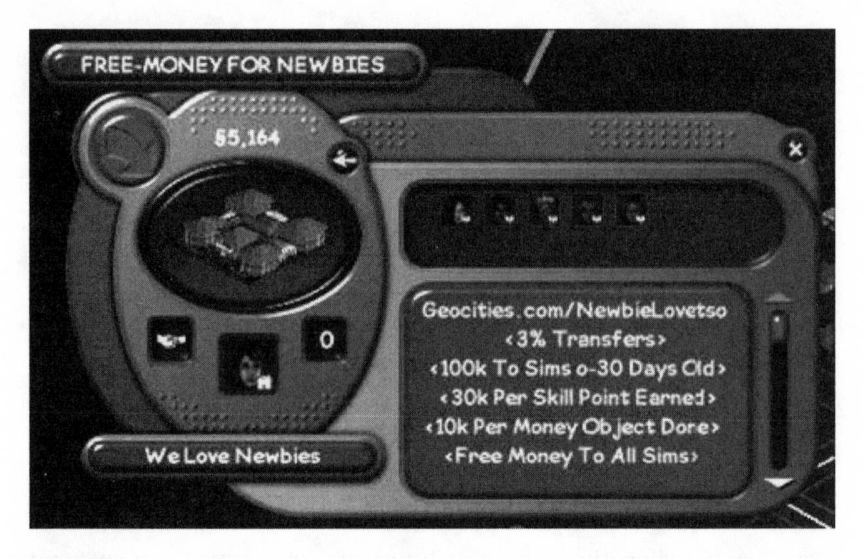

Figure 4.2
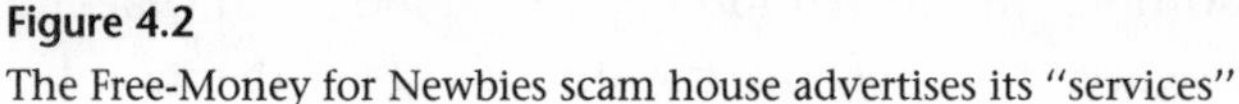
The Free-Money for Newbies scam house advertises its "services"

which she was clearly not going to do, Urizenus had few hard facts out of which to craft a story. So rather than rely on hearsay and allegations about what went on at the Free-Money for Newbies house, Uri hired an undercover reporter named Sheryl Hanson, a newbie herself, equipped her with 30,000 simoleans, and sent her out with the assignment to go get herself scammed at Evangeline's.

That proved easy enough to accomplish. Though Sheryl got nothing but a slap in the face when she first tried to talk to Evangeline about how she could get some of the free money that was ostensibly on offer, one of Evangeline's roommates, a female Sim named Cari, offered to help her out. Cari instructed Sheryl to open her trade window—an interface that lets Sims swap items and money back and forth, or simply give something to someone else—and type "99,999" into the simoleans field. When Sheryl clicked the "approve trade" box, Cari told her, the interface would automatically adjust to the actual amount of simoleans in Sheryl's possession. As Cari put it, this would safeguard against the Free-Money house getting scammed itself by Sims who actually had more money than they needed. If Sheryl's account really did have less than 100,000 simoleans in it, Cari said, the Free-Money house would happily match her funds and she could double her money.

The TSO interface for swapping items between players is similar to that found in many MMOs. One side of the trade window displays the items you are offering for trade, the other side displays those being offered by the avatar you're trading with. To use these interfaces properly, it's best to wait until both sides of the window are filled to your satisfaction before you press the "approve trade" button. Even then, it's best to hover your cursor over the "cancel" button in case the other party suddenly withdraws some items before completing the trade. The only time you'd want to approve a trade while one side of the window is empty would be if you were simply giving something to another player.

What the Free-Money house counted on, however, was that most TSO newbies would be unfamiliar with the trade interface, and would simply follow directions, approving the trade while there was nothing in the other side of the window for them to receive. Sheryl played along, and sure enough, Cari clicked her "approve trade" button while her own window was still empty, thus receiving the 30,000 simoleans Sheryl had offered as evidence of her need. Sure enough, Sheryl had been scammed.

Like a good cub reporter, Sheryl pressed Cari for an explanation, but she was simply ignored. Wondering how Evangeline felt about the incident, Sheryl turned to her for help, but was told to "go jump in a pool and drown to receive one million simoleans." With no evidence that this sum might be forthcoming were she to do so, Sheryl returned to the *Herald* and filed her report.[5]

As a result of the story, Uri got his interview with Evangeline a week later,[6] and followed it up with a second interview soon after that.[7] In these reports, Evangeline admits to scamming newbies and oldbies both, with the help of a few friends, out of something on the order of 8 million simoleans, or about $200, every month. "I don't pay $10 a month [in monthly subscription fees to TSO] to care about others," Evangeline said. "In real life there will always be a villain, and I'm glad I can fulfill that in TSO. Without me in the game, I think it would grow old. Now players can feel like they have a mission rather than just to skill." On the other hand, Evangeline added, "There's a sucker born every minute." Evangeline was a villain, all right. But the extent of her crimes, at least in virtual-world terms, would only become clear to Uri in the fullness of time.

5 Dollars and Cyberspace

One of the things that had interested Ludlow most about online worlds was the virtual commerce that went on in places like The Sims Online. While Evangeline's scams were not necessarily representative of how commerce was conducted, Ludlow knew there was a vast and complex layer of business that went on within various virtual environments. Most of that trade was in things that existed only as a collection of pixels on a computer screen or as a software subroutine on a server, and yet there was real money to be made here, in some cases $100,000 a year or more.

As an experiment in the world of virtual business, Ludlow's alt, Doctor Legion, opened a "goth supply store" in the Rose Thorn Gardens neighborhood in which the *Herald* offices had been built. Though customizing the objects provided by the game isn't possible in The Sims Online, many players find ways to run shops that specialize in some of the goods that are available in the game.

To build, furnish, and decorate a house and plot of land, TSO provides its residents with an interface through which they can spend their hard-earned (or eBay-purchased) simoleans on furniture, garden decorations, beds and toilets, artwork, clothing, appliances, and more. By buying these items in volume, users can obtain a discount, and, by then reselling them to other players, some manage to make a profit. Doctor Legion fitted out Mephisto's Goth Supplies with whatever quasi-gothic paraphernalia he could find in the game's furnishings interface: candelabras, mounted rhinoceros heads, suits of armor, and even the occasional pool table for Alphaville's more modern Simigoths.

To announce the store, the *Herald* ran an advertisement:

Mephisto's Goth Supplies

Building a church or renovating a B&D dungeon?
Need that special gargoyle or head in a jar to make your living room just right?
Come to Mephisto's Goth Supplies.
50% off retail for anything goth.
Store open by appointment only. IM Doctor Legion for appointment.

But running a small virtual business, it turns out, was almost as much work as running a real one. Making appointments via Instant Message rarely went as smoothly as Uri had hoped, and since Doctor Legion wasn't logged into the game as much as the *Herald's* editor, it became difficult to get many customers through the door. What looked like just another part of the game was in reality much more work than the game itself was ever meant to be.

As Uri talked to Alphaville's other shop owners and to the people who worked for them, he found out more about just how much work it was. To run a successful retail operation in Alphaville took a huge commitment of time. Because properties can't be visited in TSO unless one of the owners or roommates is present, just keeping a shop open means having someone on the premises as much as possible. And since most people in TSO already had jobs to hold or classes to attend in the real world, good help was hard to find in Alphaville.

The city's labor practices, too, left something to be desired. To recruit employees, many shop owners would offer a Sim a roommate position on their property. The proprietor got a helping hand, and in return the roommate got a share of the visitors bonus that the game handed out each week, a small sum rewarded based on how much foot traffic a given property had attracted. (Many players created alts expressly for the purpose of leaving them AFK on a property, simply to add to their visitors bonus.)

But the demands made on roomies were often high. Many shop owners expected strict hours to be kept, and shares in the profits were not always commensurate with what workers felt they were due. Virtual commerce involved much more than simply hanging out your shingle in the metaverse. To be successful took being a tireless worker and a harsh taskmaster. And there wasn't that much money to be made from an in-game retail operation anyway.

But there was money to be made. To make it, though, you had to straddle the line that separated the virtual world from the real, working both sides at once in an effort to profit off the middle. A few Sims managed to make money by hiring themselves out as architects for virtual homes, or even as partners for cybersex, but for the most part the big money was made selling virtual currency and rare in-game objects. Uri began to discover some of the ways this worked when he was approached by a Sim in a Santa suit named Respected Banker (known as RB for short), who asked whether Uri wanted to buy some simoleans. To Uri this at first sounded like a dubious proposition, as if the avatar had drawn back the flap of an overcoat to reveal an array of stolen virtual watches. To find out more about what was involved, Uri took him up on his offer, and in talking to the salesman found out more about the realm of virtual commerce in TSO than he had ever hoped to know.

To protect RB's anonymity, Uri published several interviews in which the simolean trader was identified only as TSO Power Player. Their first transaction was a simple one: Outside the game, Uri transferred some money—that is, actual U.S. dollars—to RB's PayPal account. Then, within the game, RB transferred an equivalent amount of simoleans, at the prevailing exchange rate (then about $40 per million simoleans), to the Urizenus character in TSO. RB bought his simoleans at lower rates from those who'd figured out how to produce large quantities of them in the game, allowing him to profit on each transaction.

RB's secondary line of business was in transferring money from one of TSO's dozens of servers (such as Alphaville) to another.[1] The game does not allow a player with characters on two different servers to transfer simoleans between them, so RB would take a payment of simoleans on one server and hold them in reserve for future transactions. He would then log onto the second server with a different character and transfer simoleans from his reserve there to his customer's account, retaining a small fee for the service, of course.

"TSO is my real-life job," RB told Uri. An Australian man on medical assistance, RB's typist supplemented his income by buying and selling simoleans and working the U.S.-Australian dollar exchange rate, to the tune of several hundred dollars a week. But some of his friends in the money-trading community, he said, pulled down thousands of U.S. dollars a week

Item	Price		Time left
TSO 1 MILLION ALPHAVILLE THE SIMS ON LINE	$45.00 $50.00	- Buy It Now	2d 22h 25m
TSO 500K ALPHAVILLE THE SIMS ON LINE	$20.00 $25.00	- Buy It Now	2d 22h 24m
TSO 1 MILLION INTERHOGAN THE SIMS ON LINE	$45.00 $50.00	- Buy It Now	2d 22h 24m
TSO 1 MILLION DAN'S GROVE THE SIMS ON LINE	$45.00 $50.00	- Buy It Now	2d 22h 23m
TSO 1 MILLION JOLLY PINES THE SIMS ON LINE	$45.00 $50.00	- Buy It Now	2d 22h 23m
TSO 1 MILLION ALPHAVILLE THE SIMS ON LINE	$40.00 $45.00	- Buy It Now	2d 22h 22m
TSO 3 MILLION ALPHAVILLE THE SIMS ON LINE	$75.00 $120.00	- Buy It Now	2d 22h 21m

Figure 5.1
Simoleans for sale on eBay

from their businesses. The clients who came to RB and his friends[2] for their simoleans couldn't seem to get enough of this virtual currency.

To those not acclimated to virtual worlds, buying currency you can only spend on pixels may sound like a strange idea, but to those who live part of their lives there, there's nothing remarkable at all in this. In any case, a currency is a currency, virtual or not. Why shouldn't you be able to purchase it in the markets, as one would purchase the currency of a foreign country?

That may sound simplistic, but in economic terms it's quite sound. Simoleans, it turns out, are assigned a value in the same way all real-world currencies are: Simoleans are worth something because the people who spend and receive them have agreed on their value. Ask an economist, and he'll tell you the same thing about the dollar, the pound, the peso, the yen, the yuan, or the rupee. Each time we make a monetary transaction in the real world—each time we hand over $50, say, and receive a PlayStation2 game in return—we are making a tacit agreement with each other as to how much the goods we're exchanging are worth. In this case, we have agreed with the retailer that a game like Grand Theft Auto is worth $50. There's nothing inherent in GTA that makes it cost that much money. We might just as easily buy it for $40, or for $20, or for $100—if we can find someone to agree to one of those prices. If we can't come to an agreement, we have the option of not making the transaction at all. If enough people don't agree, the game company will lower its prices. This is the law of supply and demand in action.

But we have agreed that the value of one copy of GTA is $50. What's less obvious is that we've also agreed that the value of $50 is one copy of GTA. And it's in moments like those—in the aggregation of many, many moments like those, going on throughout society over time—that the value of a currency is set.

The value of simoleans is set the same way. The fact that simoleans are used to buy virtual goods is, in the end irrelevant. The people who spend and receive them have agreed that they can also be spent to buy dollars, and so they have taken on some real-world value.

In real-world terms, their value isn't much, of course. An eBay auction of five million simoleans on the Alphaville server of TSO took in $74.95 in July 2005. That's only 0.00149 cents per simolean, or about $15 for a million simoleans. (The simolean has undergone a serious devaluation since Uri's days in Alphaville.) The fact that someone would spend $75 to buy virtual currency may not seem sensible, but looked at from the opposite side, things become more clear: on the other end of that transaction, someone spent 5 million simoleans and received $75 in return. Clearly, then, simoleans are worth something in the real, offline world.

And even in TSO, simoleans are worth more than at first meets the eye. We call the houses and hot tubs and pets and clown paintings that populate TSO "virtual" because they can't be held in our hands or occupied by our physical bodies. But when we look around us, the fact is that virtual goods in a broader sense have these days become rather the norm. From software to movies, mp3 files, online magazines, even the contents of this book are in some sense virtual (you didn't buy it for the paper and ink, after all). Looked at in that light, then, the fact that someone would pay real money for a collection of pixels on a computer screen is not so surprising after all. The truth is that these things are no more virtual than something like a movie or a television show, they're simply purchased in a different currency. It costs less than a dollar to put a movie onto a DVD. What you're paying the Virgin Megastore $25 for is the digitized *contents* of that disc, which can no more be held in your hand than could Uri's pet, Cheddar Cheese Cheetah, which cost about the same.

Software, too, is a virtual good. And very often, there's nothing physical at all about the transaction that brings such goods to our computers' desktops (another virtual location). Software can be ordered, paid for, and delivered without the purchaser's ever speaking to a real person, handling any physical currency, or taking possession of a physical package. What could be more virtual than that? And yet such transactions have made Bill Gates into one of the richest men in the world.

What is surprising is the sheer scale of the market for virtual (in-world) goods and services, which has grown so large that some people now earn their living from it. Steve Salyer, a former gaming executive at Ubisoft and Electronic Arts who is now president of a company called Internet Gaming Entertainment, estimates the global market for such items has now reached about $880 million a year. Salyer runs IGE.com, the leading broker of online goods and services for more than a dozen games. The trade conducted on the site is far broader than simply providing "money trades" in virtual worlds like TSO; they include transactions that, in the eyes of some gamers and game companies, have an impact on what it's like to play these games. And because this sometimes creates sudden economic imbalances, that impact is not always seen as a favorable one.

A quick check of eBay indicates how the trade in objects that can be used only in virtual worlds can reach nearly a billion dollars a year. If you play Guild Wars, for instance, a gorgeous swords-and-spells MMO released in the spring of 2005 by developer ArenaNet and Korean game publisher NCSoft, you may be having trouble slaying some formidable monster near the fantasy city of Ascalon. One solution to such a problem is to acquire a better weapon in the game, either by buying one from one of the game's nonplayer weaponsmiths, or by hoping you'll find one in the loot that monsters drop when they are slain. But saving game currency for a truly formidable weapon can take weeks or months, depending on how many hours you spend in the game, and good loot drops can be disappointingly few and far between. These are intentional points of the game's design, formulated to hand out rewards to players in rough proportion to how much time and effort they put into the game. But for those who want a quicker road to might, such design points can be frustrating.

The solution? Buy a Gold Fiery Dragon Sword of Fortitude on eBay. One of the more powerful weapons in the game, one recently sold on the online auction site for the princely sum of $187.50—in U.S. dollars, not virtual-world currency.

Such sales are completed in the same fashion as the money trade Urizenus undertook: A real-world transfer of cash is effected via PayPal or another payment service, and the "item" that's just been purchased is then transferred from one character to another within the game. Swords, armor, castles, shields—if it can be swapped within the game, it can be sold outside of it. And in virtual worlds like There and Second Life, many more items can be found for sale, including land, houses, clothing, magazines, artwork, vehicles, entire new "skins" for your avatar (which are just what they sound like), games to be played or films to be shown within the world, and much more.

While a better sword will do you little good in The Sims Online, there is plenty to purchase there that will enhance your Sim's lifestyle (if not its killing power). What Uri discovered was just how much money people were willing to spend for TSO, money that might have been spent to enhance their physical lifestyle instead of their virtual one.

But as Uri was to find, the practice of going outside the game to acquire virtual currency and goods was highly contentious in TSO (as it is in many game worlds). Many players argued that it amounted to cheating. The phenomenon had even generated a protest group in Alphaville called Sims Against Ridiculous Payouts (SARP), which the *Herald* covered in early 2004.[3] SARP had been founded to lobby against one of the consequences of simoleans being available for sale on eBay: Some players who wanted to raise their position in the rankings allegedly bought simoleans on eBay and offered payments to Sims who were willing to spend time at their properties, thus making the properties look more popular. To SARP, this was gaming the system in a way that was "unfair to non-payout houses," and amounted to bribing people to hang out at a property in order to move it higher up the top 100 list.

The issue of real-money trade (or RMT, i.e., the use of real-world money to purchase in-game goods) has generated controversy in traditional MMOs like Guild Wars, Ultima Online, World of Warcraft, and the dozens of other worlds that feature swords, spells, spaceships, or superheroes. The ground rules of such worlds dictate that their denizens become more powerful by undertaking quests or missions, dispatching scary monsters in pitched battle, or spending time collecting the raw materials of a craft or training in new skills. (In the space opera that is EVE Online, for instance, it can take several weeks to learn the set of advanced skills that allows one to research starship blueprints, and more than a month to learn other advanced skills.) To many gamers, the players who leapfrog that process by reaching into their wallets gain an unfair advantage that both skews the competitive playing field and takes away from the experience of being immersed in an online world. It is odd, after all, to log into Guild Wars and watch as a day-old character wields his $200 Gold Fiery Dragon Sword of Fortitude to lop the head off a monster you've been trying for a week to overcome.

The virtual markets also allow players to leapfrog the character-development process entirely by purchasing not only better weapons or equipment but entire characters. Players who have managed to level a character up to the heights of a game will occasionally sell their accounts on eBay or other sites. The buyer makes payment via PayPal and the seller transfers the account's username and password to the buyer. The buyer then has control over an extremely powerful avatar without having to do anything more than plunk down a wad of cash. That wad can be considerable. In mid-2005, one Ultima Online account sold on eBay for $535.[4] Avatars in similar role-playing games have been known to sell for over $1,000, and in TSO, "founder's accounts" (those that have been around since the game's beta-testing period) with no special powers but high social status have sold for plenty.[5] For instance, a TSO founder's account loaded with skills and rare in-game items sold for $810 in mid-2005.[6]

For many who haven't experienced an MMO, spending real money for items made of pixels sounds counterintuitive—perhaps because it doesn't really describe what's going on. A Dragon Sword is valuable not because it's sharp and you can poke things with it. It's valuable because it can make your time in the game more entertaining, and games, after all, are an entertainment medium. Weapons, castles, magic spells—all these things have value in the virtual world of MMOs for the same reason. If you think that Dragon Sword is going to make your time in Guild Wars more fun, you might be willing to pony up some cash to get it. But $187.50? Is it really worth that much?

Like things sold in the physical world, virtual goods are worth what the market will bear. If you can find someone to pay you $187.50 for your Dragon Sword, well, that's what it's worth. And many of the people who play MMOs so value their time in those worlds that they're willing to pay those prices. Edward Castronova, who is probably the leading scholar of virtual world economics, puts it this way: "Some people have lots of resources in the real world, but aren't doing so well in the game. By the same token, some people who may not have much in the real world might be doing better in the virtual world. Voila, there's your market."

Like real economies, virtual economies are governed by laws of supply and demand. In large part, Gold Fiery Dragon Swords of Fortitude are worth what they're worth because they're rare and difficult to obtain. If low-level monsters in Guild Wars suddenly started dropping lots of Dragon Swords when they were killed, the market would be flooded and the price for Dragon Swords on eBay would go down.

The Sims Online had its own version of such rare, hard-to-obtain items, known, perhaps not surprisingly, as "rares." Most things in TSO's in-world store could be bought in unlimited quantity. But rares were unique or provided in only limited numbers. Often they took the form of statues that would be given to players on their in-world anniversaries or hard to find pets like pink poodles or Cheetahs, like Uri's cat, Cheddar Cheese Cheetah (which he had purchased from RB for $25).

Unlike things like Dragon Swords, TSO's rares didn't change your powers or skill level in the game. But as Uri was discovering, the "play" of TSO seemed to lie in things like social status and other kinds of invidious comparisons. Owning a rare was a status symbol, and though Will Wright probably hadn't intended it when he designed TSO, status was a big part of what TSO was about.

With people paying hundreds of dollars on eBay for TSO rares, several "pet-culling" businesses cropped up in Alphaville and on other TSO servers. Pets bought directly from the TSO store came in pet carriers; you never knew quite what you were getting. Once in a blue moon, the cat you'd just bought would turn out to be a rare pet. So several enterprising Sims started buying up hundreds of pets, figuring the expense would be more than defrayed by the jackpot of finding one or two rares in the mix. In Alphaville, it took a Sim named Becca about 300,000 simoleans to uncover the server's first pink poodle. By the time the *Herald* covered the story a day or two later, she had been offered 20 million simoleans for it (around $500 at the time).[7]

TSO's pet-culling operations are an example of a common phenomenon of MMOs known as "farming." Like its real-world namesake, farming consists of nothing more complex than gathering resources from a particular plot of "land." In most swords-and-spells MMOs, farming takes the form of killing monsters and collecting the copper, silver, and gold pieces they drop when they die (a pursuit known as "gold farming"). But as with any business, a little extra effort can net you a bigger haul. A well-armed trip through the Stonesplinter Valley of Azeroth, the virtual world of World of Warcraft, will garner not just the gold that the Stonesplinter troggs drop, but a healthy share of linen cloth as well. For a character who's trained in the tailoring profession, the linen can be made into bags (which avatars never have enough of due to the ever-growing amount of loot they collect), and the bags can be sold in the Ironforge auction house, usually for a pretty penny. Farming copper and linen, though, are only the tip of the iceberg. Far more complex and sophisticated schemes are undertaken by gold farmers every day.

TSO had similar, if less elaborate, ways to earn money, which usually consisted of standing in one spot and repeatedly clicking an object on your screen.[8] If you calculated your hourly returns, though, you'd probably find you were earning well below the U.S. minimum wage for your efforts, perhaps enough for a bigger split-level in TSO or a better sword elsewhere. But some farming operations can be serious real-world moneymakers, employing dozens of gamers to do nothing but collect gold. The head of one such operation, a man who calls himself Smooth Criminal, claims to have made $1.5 million in 2004 by managing a farming operation in Star Wars Galaxies.[9] More widespread goldfarming operations in China were subsequently reported by the *New York Times*.[10]

It's clear that there's real money to be made in virtual worlds. Some even see the potential for the rising tide of MMOs to lift a few impoverished boats. Stories abound of gold farmers in low-wage countries who hire workers to sit and click their computers all day for pennies an hour, gathering MMO gold. One Chinese gold-farm worker reportedly earns about $250 a month.[11] While that's well below U.S. incomes, it's about 70 percent more than the $145 that is the average monthly income in China, according to the World Bank.[12] In the words of Smooth Criminal, "They get paid dirt. But dirt is good where they live."

By some measures, a few virtual worlds create more real value than some real-world economies. The figure that has made headlines is Edward Castronova's calculation that, in 2001, the per capita GDP of Norrath, the virtual world of the MMO EverQuest, was as high as $2,266, a level that would put it on a par with Russia and around the 100th richest country in the world, according to UN figures.[13]

But a closer look at the numbers suggests that while the Norrathian economy is indeed large, it is perhaps not as large as Castronova claimed. Castronova bases his GDP figures on the prices of avatars sold on eBay, averaged out across the population of Norrath. As Castronova gives it, the total GDP of Norrath (i.e., the total value of goods and services produced in a year) was around $136,821,000 in 2001,[14] ahead of only ten countries in the world. To find the per capita GDP (the value of goods and services produced per person) Castronova computes the average number of players online at any given moment, a figure of something like 65,000. But using this figure is akin to computing the per capita GDP of the United States based on the number of people at work at any given moment, rather than taking the country's much larger population figure as a basis.

If the population of Norrath were in fact 65,000, its per capita GDP would indeed be $2,266. But in 2001, EverQuest had more than 350,000 subscribers. Based on that number, the per capita GDP drops to only $390.92. That makes Norrath the 174th richest country in the world, with only thirty-six countries behind it, including Bangladesh, Afghanistan, and most of the poor countries of Africa.

Still, the fact that a game world was producing value of more than $30 a month per person is remarkable. If that income were equally distributed across all of EverQuest's players, they would each have been making a profit of about $15 a month by playing the game (after the $15 monthly subscription fee). But gold-farming and other forms of income-producing work in game worlds are not very lucrative on an hourly basis. Game worlds are not designed for work; they're designed to be fun. If it were easy to make a living in EverQuest, even as easy as it is in the real world, many more people would be doing it.

If online worlds are not designed to produce value, then, how is it produced? For those unfamiliar with virtual worlds, it's difficult to grasp where the value of virtual goods comes from, in part because it's hard to see how something of value can be created by activities in an online world. No actual automobiles, cell phones, widgets, gadgets, cogs, guns, or butter are being made in virtual worlds, but value is created nonetheless. How? It only tells half the story (the economist's half) to say that virtual currencies are worth real money because we've agreed it is so. The other half of the story (the gamer's half) can be discerned in the fabric of the rich and intricately textured virtual worlds that users, by their very presence there, help create.

One is tempted to think that life in an MMO consists of little more than performing a predetermined set of tasks like killing monsters and searching for treasures, and then being rewarded by the game company with a few bits of information—the loot. But much more goes on in virtual worlds than just that. As Uri was learning in TSO, the inhabitants who move through these worlds help fill them with stories and relationships and characters that the platforms themselves could never provide on their own. The true heroes and villains of virtual worlds, even game worlds like World of Warcraft, are the players: the knights and rogues and guilds and clans and virtual families, the scammers and griefers and anti-griefers, the mages and DJs and ladykillers and even the techno-pagan priests, all the inhabitants that compete with one another, wage wars, and hold grudges, hack, slash, steal, and heal, start rumors, nurture legends, tell tall tales, and share just plain old good times. Where value is concerned, look no further.

To a certain extent, the software that comprises an MMO, the code that determines how hard it is to kill a Stonesplinter Troll and how much copper and cloth you get from each, is only an empty shell, a blank canvas on which the inhabitants paint their histories and together create a shared culture that can be as rich and compelling as any in the real world. Of course, MMOs are not blank slates. The architecture, fiction, and "physics" of a given virtual world (in the form of its underlying software code) must first create the conditions that attract residents and enable them to create their own narratives. In that sense, value creation in online games is a product of the efforts of both players and game companies. But it is much more than the simple addition of these two components.

Take the example of the Sleeper, from chapter 1. When the rival guilds on EverQuest's Rallos Zek server banded together to challenge (and defeat) the unkillable Kerafyrm, they were doing more than just hoping to meet a particularly difficult challenge posed by the virtual world of EverQuest. Their task promised no economic reward at all. What they were doing was contributing something original to the metaverse itself, contributing to a rich narrative structure that encompassed not just Rallos Zek but the entire

EverQuest franchise of servers and expansion packs and fan sites and more—a narrative that helps make EverQuest valuable to other players in the same way that the Gold Fiery Dragon Sword of Fortitude does: It helps make the game more fun. When a World of Warcraft guild mounts a raid or takes on a rare endgame quest, and the tales of their heroics spread across the forums and from fan site to fan site, it adds to what each participant receives in return for his or her subscription fee. The stories that are told—stories that wouldn't be possible without players to have lived them first—raise the value of the virtual world and its virtual furnishings, and the value of "buying in."

Even a virtual newspaper like the *Herald*, which was so cheaply "printed" that it looked likely to leave ink stains on your avatar's fingers, contributes to this process by helping to identify virtual heroes and villains, by propagating lore within the worlds that it covers, by celebrating the residents and narratives of those worlds, and by providing a window onto them for potential immigrants who simply hadn't found their way there yet.

Players of MMOs and the residents of virtual worlds also frequently invent games within their games. In TSO, these took the form of tagging wars, but far more complex role-playing games have been built by players within the confines of Second Life, where residents have access to powerful content-creation tools. Even in games without any custom content, players organize all manner of contests and competitions, from things like the "last Sim floating" contests that the Church of Mephistopheles held, to player-organized archery contests, spaceship races, boxing matches, trivia contests, and more. It isn't game companies who contribute all this content, it's the players.

Game companies and other platform owners don't often see it this way, though their view is beginning to change. Where they once saw the customer as merely consumer, companies are beginning to come around to the view that the content that customers add can be as valuable as the content provided by the companies themselves. Still, most companies have yet to start designing for user-created content. To them, the world consists only of the content provided by the company's artists, programmers, and designers. But massively multiplayer online games and virtual worlds, by their very nature, aren't places people come to simply kill monsters and collect loot—they can do that just as easily (more easily, in fact) in a single-player offline game.

People come to virtual worlds because they find there much more than games; among other things, they find other interesting people. They come to compete with each other, to collaborate with each other, to learn from each other, to profit from each other, and to talk to each other at the coffee machine at work or in chat rooms on the Internet. Players come to MMOs to *interact* with other players, and in that way, MMOs are a very special form of interactive entertainment, in that they derive their value *mainly* from the fact that there are other players there. Without other players, MMOs would be—well, they would be empty.

MMO companies may provide the software and design infrastructure that make value creation frictionless, but it is the users that ultimately contribute much of the value both to the games and to the items that are used within them. NCSoft made the Dragon Sword scarce in Guild Wars, and that scarcity is part of what determines its value in the market. But the Dragon Sword is valuable to Guild War players not because of its scarcity, but because it is something that enables heroism, that gives them a chance to build their narratives within the world.

As noted, though, most game companies don't think in these terms—most still think of online worlds as products they make and people buy. Until recently, in fact, MMO companies universally frowned on the real-money trade in virtual items, and often did their best to stamp it out. Some still try to ignore or deny the nearly billion-dollar global market. When Jeff Brown, Electronic Arts's vice president for corporate communications, was interviewed by a reporter from the University of Michigan's *Michigan Daily* in 2004, he compared simoleans to Monopoly money: "No doubt, even Monopoly money has some value to enthusiasts. However, the limited amount of trading in simoleans on eBay is the exception that proves the rule: outside of the game, simoleans have insignificant value."[15]

But the "limited amount" of trading in simoleans on eBay (in fact, it's a very large amount) is proof positive that the virtual currency does have value outside the online space. One has to question whether Jeff Brown really believes that simoleans only have value as play money or collectors items, or whether something else was at work here. Was he really ignorant of the enormous market at his doorstep? Or was he merely pretending to be clueless in support of some broader corporate agenda?

MMO companies may say they don't believe in virtual markets, but that hasn't prevented them from trying to shut them down. To get into almost any virtual world users first have to agree to an End-User Licensing Agreement and/or Terms of Service document that states that the avatars, items, and coin that populate a world are the sole property of the company behind the game, and can't be bought or sold for anything but game currency. That $880 million global market is actually a shadow economy that exists outside the letter of the law laid down in most virtual worlds, but it is not going away and is, if anything, a signal that many MMOs are highly successful.

IGE's Steve Salyer puts the point in terms of online game design, but it could be made about online worlds generally: "The holy grail of game design is to build a game in which the sense of community is so strong and the tools are so strong that the gamers themselves begin to generate the content and unexpected behaviors emerge. At this point, when you design a game you design it to have a healthy in-game economy, and that guarantees the players themselves will link it to external markets. Certainly the linking of in-game economies to real-world markets emerged naturally from the behavior of gamers. I believe the secondary market is the most successful example of an emergent behavior in gaming."

In many ways, the position of game companies with respect to real-money trade is not unlike that of the old Soviet bloc countries, who on the one hand vehemently denied that a black market for currency existed while at the same time attempting, in a clumsy and authoritarian way, to shut it down. Of course, game companies have as much hope of shutting down the RMT markets as Soviet countries did of shutting down the currency markets: none.

Many MMO companies claim that the rules against real-money trade are there to protect users against fraud. In many cases, what is advertised as a virtual sword on eBay is only a scheme to bilk unsuspecting players out of their hard earned, nonvirtual cash. The most common form of fraud in virtual markets is the simple nondelivery of items. You pay your money but get nothing in return.[16]

Fraud in the virtual markets is common enough that it can cost an MMO a great deal of reputation capital if it becomes rampant. And while caveat emptor is the only applicable guideline when purchasing virtual goods, or anything else for that matter, outside of official channels, most MMO companies apply lax and inconsistent enforcement. Electronic Arts, the company behind Ultima Online, has rarely cracked down on the sale of virtual items in that game, according to those familiar with the market, and has even advertised account sales as one of the attractions of the game.[17] Some companies, like CCP, the makers of EVE, find it isn't cost-efficient to go after small-time operators. Others—including Blizzard Entertainment, makers of World of Warcraft—are more strict. But even they will only go so far.

Marcus Eikenberry, who runs MarkeeDragon.com, a leading broker of UO goods and services, says that the real subtext here—what MMO companies fear most and what prevents them from pursuing legal action against people who break their rules—is the specter of a court assigning real value to the virtual items that populate their virtual worlds. If that Gold Fiery Sword in Guild Wars is legally found to constitute a separate NCSoft product, a host of messy legal questions immediately crop up that illustrate how virtual worlds may already have become more integral to our real-life existences than most people realize.

For instance, what if NCSoft's Gold Fiery Dragon Sword of Fortitude doesn't work as advertised? Is NCSoft liable for damages? Or would it be the player who sold the sword on eBay? An 8 percent sales tax on $187.50 is $15. Who pays that, the company or the player? And what if the buyer, the seller and NCSoft (a Korean company) are all in different countries? What authority would collect those taxes? And if Guild Wars gold or simoleans are recognized currency, what would be the anti-money-laundering reporting requirements when large "money" transfers were made? Questions like these proliferate as soon as real money starts to punch holes in the tissue that separates the real world from the virtual one (which the *Herald* was fond of referring to as the "client-server divide," after the computer architecture that made virtual worlds possible). With some users already earning their real-life incomes entirely within these virtual worlds, the answers to such questions start to have an impact on people's real lives.

The MMO companies' nightmare scenario has already started playing out in China, where, in 2003, the Beijing Chaoyang District People's Court ordered the maker of the game Hongyue (Red Moon) to return the equivalent of $1,200 in virtual loot, including virtual biochemical weapons, to a customer named Li Hongchen, who went to court after the items were stolen by a hacker.[18] The court found the company responsible for the holes in its security that allowed the hacker in—which must strike fear in the hearts of many MMO companies in the far more litigious United States. In this light, Jeff Brown's claims that simoleans have insignificant value start to look like a strategy to protect EA in the event it should ever wind up in a similar court case.

The questions posed earlier regarding RMT and commerce in virtual worlds are ones that platform owners will soon be facing, whether they like it or not. How they, their customers, and the courts answer those questions will have a big effect on the future course of virtual worlds and the roles they'll play in our lives.

One set of answers is already beginning to be worked out in a place known as Second Life, a 3-D virtual world launched in 2003 by a small company in San Francisco called Linden Lab. In contrast to TSO, Second Life asks no personal maintenance at all of its avatars and is less a game than a parallel world unto itself. In addition, SL provides a set of content-creation tools that allows users to create objects far more beautiful and complex than anything that could be made in TSO. Here at last was everything TSO's unsatisfied residents had hoped for, and more. Soon after SL's launch, in fact, many TSO typists immigrated from EA's servers to those of Linden Lab. As one writer put it in the *Second Life Herald* (the *Alphaville Herald*'s descendant), "As [Second Life] residents we are at the top of Maslow's hierarchy, where only the need for novelty and companionship remains."[19]

That's an excellent characterization of the state of affairs in Second Life, where, by signing up for a free lifetime membership, you can enter a rich world filled with user-created structures, games, art, shops, vehicles, personalities, and more. The world itself is often known as "the Grid," a network of more than more than four thousand servers (and growing), each of which holds not its own copy of the world but its own 65,536-square-meter region (a little more than sixteen acres). Each region is known as a simulator, or "sim," confusingly enough for those accustomed to referring to their TSO avatars as Sims. The regions are connected more or less like squares on a chessboard, and residents can travel almost seamlessly from one sim to the next, touring the creations of their fellow residents, many of which are truly impressive to behold.

One of the remarkable things about Second Life is that almost nothing in the world is built by the company behind the game. Instead, Linden Lab provides a rolling landscape on which residents can plunk down their own creations. The free membership, however, only allows you to build temporary creations that are erased from the Grid every twelve hours (though copies of them can be stored in a user's inventory). To have a plot of land to call your own requires a monthly "tier" fee of $9.95 or more, depending on how big you want to make your virtual ranch ($9.95 entitles you to 512 square meters). What the tier fee really pays for is a portion of LL's server resources. In effect, though, it allows residents to "own" a small estate, where they can control who can build or even come and go, and where their own constructions will not be periodically wiped from the Grid.

Perhaps the most important difference between Second Life and most other virtual worlds is that SL's Terms of Service specifically grants residents ownership of the intellectual property rights in their creations. In Second Life, if you build it, you own it, no matter what you want to do with it. That difference allowed Jason Ainsworth, who was spending about four hours a day in Second Life in mid-2005, to pay the mortgage on his Las Vegas home with money he earned on the Grid.[20] Ainsworth leveraged his real-life experience as a property developer and contractor into one of Second Life's most successful in-world operations. In fourteen locations across the Grid, he owned enough "land" to rent space to nearly fifty retailers, who in turn earned virtual money selling everything from jewelry to clothing to art (all of it virtual too, of course). Tenants paid Ainsworth, who is in his late thirties, in Linden dollars, the currency of the game (often known as Lindens, or Linden$), and Ainsworth converted his virtual income to liquid cash on sites like eBay, IGE, and GamingOpenMarket.com. He even included that income on his tax returns.

In terms of how much time and effort is required, virtual commerce is not that different from the real thing, as Uri had found in TSO. "A lot of your success or failure depends on your ability to keep the fire lit," Ainsworth says. "I have good months and bad months, but the work is fun."

John Chapman agrees: "It doesn't get any better than getting paid to play games." Chapman, a thirty-ish gamer from Canton, Michigan, earned about $25,000 a year for the three and a half years in which trading in Ultima Online artifacts was his only source of income. "I wasn't getting rich, but I wouldn't even call it work," he says.[21]

Virtual businesses that resemble those in real life generate surprising amounts of both income expenses. In January 2005, the *Herald* ran a profile of a Second Life resident who goes by the screen name Anshe Chung.[22] One of the richest avatars in SL, Chung makes her money by buying large plots of "land" from Linden Lab and then subdividing them to sell on a retail basis to Second Life residents. By the time the *Herald* spoke to her, she was on track to earn the equivalent of US$100,000 in her first year in Second Life. According to Philip Rosedale, founder and CEO of Linden Lab, a large handful of people garner five- or six-figure incomes from SL, and close to a thousand see a profit on their activities in the virtual world.[23]

Among those to profit is Nathan Keir, an Australian programmer who is the typist for a Second Life avatar named Kermitt Quirk. During his 2004 Christmas vacation, Keir took advantage of Second Life's innovative stance on intellectual property to create an in-world game called Tringo, a hybrid of Tetris and Bingo, that has proven wildly popular on the Grid. By early 2005, Keir had earned more than $5,000 selling virtual copies of the game, and had been able to license its real-world development rights to a software company in California for an amount "in the low five figures" plus royalties, he said.[24] A version of Tringo for the Game Boy Advance was released about a year later.

The ability to prototype and create objects of real usefulness in Second Life is one of the things that most sets it apart from other virtual worlds, Rosedale says. The possibilities can boggle the mind. One resident has used the Second Life platform to prototype designs for real-world objects like bicycles.[25] Another uses it to design houses for clients of his architecture firm.[26] A program at the Wharton Business School is considering using Second Life as the petrie dish for student experiments in entrepreneurship.[27] And many larger real-world concerns—from American Apparel to Toyota to Sony Music and more—have now begun to explore marketing, product design, entertainment, and even retail sales in Second Life (see chapter 18). "If you launch a clothing line in Second Life and it's hot in Second Life, can you launch it in the real world?" Rosedale wonders. "Of course you can. It's telling you the same stuff. It's telling you that it's a cool, trendy idea."[28]

In many respects, the economies of virtual worlds do resemble those of countries on earth, with the main difference being that the markets within game worlds are not as free as those in most nonvirtual countries on earth. The prices of most goods and their level of production (i.e., how much is available from computer-controlled salespeople and how often they drop as loot) are set by the game's designers, not by the forces of supply and demand. (This is slightly less true in some worlds, including EVE Online and Ultima Online.) One strategy designers may choose in the future is to participate in game markets in the same way that the U.S. Federal Reserve Bank does, by attempting to achieve a small number of economic targets through market operations like buying up game currency or releasing additional loot.

But design is not the same as power, and the current participants in virtual economies—the players and residents of virtual worlds—often wield more power than some designers give them credit for. In Second Life, for instance, a group of residents banded together in 2003 to rail against the taxation policies of Linden Lab, which the protestors (who brought their own virtual tea crates) felt unfairly burdened those who created the largest, most impressive projects (the "builds"), which they felt contributed most to Second Life society. A similar protest took place in Ultima Online after a counterfeiting bug caused runaway inflation. In both cases, the company behind the game was forced to respond.[29]

These may seem at first glance like a satirical sort of roleplaying, but nothing could be further from the truth. The truth is that virtual world economies *are* extensions of the economy of the "real" world. Because real-world currencies are involved, there is nothing "fake" or "merely play" about them. As of November 2005, one U.S. dollar bought about 250 Linden dollars on the open market. Six months later, one U.S. dollar fetched around 300 Lindens. If your Second Life business is pulling in a million Lindens a month (as a large handful do, according to Rosedale), that's a difference of around $667 a month in gross revenues. That's not a lot in the grander scheme of things, but a 20 percent drop is a huge change in any currency market. If you're counting on income from your Second Life to pay your first life mortgage, you're in the red.

At least ten million people around the globe subscribe to one or more virtual worlds (by some estimates there are two to four times that many), and that number has been growing in leaps and bounds in recent years.[30] In Korea, which has widespread broadband access and an enormous MMO population, more young people now participate in online worlds each night than watch television.[31] How many profit from these worlds in a financial as well as recreational way is impossible to know at the moment.

But that number, too, is clearly growing. As virtual worlds increasingly move away from the pure game paradigm of Ultima Online and World of Warcraft and begin to become synthetic worlds with robust economies like Second Life and (to a lesser extent) The Sims Online, the potential for real economic impact grows as well. If a Chinese gold farmer can raise his standard of living through a membership in Ultima Online or EverQuest II, the implications are staggering.

At this point, the question of who controls virtual worlds takes on startling significance. Virtual worlds are currently, for the most part, an entertaining form of interactive art, the province of corporations that naturally wield a profit-driven control over who has access to which features of their software. But what happens when virtual worlds become the thriving online societies that are already starting to appear in germinal form? What happens when making a living in an online environment becomes a viable, not-at-all-outlandish alternative to holding an office job, building a career, or opening a business? Who will govern those societies? Who will say who can come and go, and what they can do there?

These were the questions on Uri's mind when, in the weeks after he opened Mephisto's Goth Supplies, he started to bump up against the powers that be in TSO. And the answers he got were anything but encouraging.

6 The Case of the Broken Jaw

One thing that was apparent to the roomies at the Church of Mephistopheles was that not many people knew who or what Mephistopheles was. One visitor thought the name had been lifted from the Broadway play *Cats*. Since there weren't actually any techno-pagans in residence, it often took a long time for guests to become aware of what was supposed to be an evil and ominous atmosphere. Many simply took the place for an actual place of worship; "Praise Jesus!" some visitors exclaimed, thinking they had found that rarest of commodities, a Christian church in Alphaville. But then, Alphaville's Bible-thumpers were hardly run-of-the-mill themselves. One visitor to the property was a Gorean slave,[1] a role played by a surprising number of women both in TSO and Second Life, who asked whether she could take up residence there. Uri and his roommates assented. After all, they got free housecleaning services from her. But after a week of cleaning the bathroom and picking up dirty plates, it dawned on her that the Church of Mephistopheles wasn't a god-fearing institution at all. After coming to realize the awful truth, she confided to Uri that while she was a Gorean slave she was also a good Christian, and she wouldn't be able to stay. Seeking a better, more righteous life, she left and moved in with a Gorean master in nearby Rose Thorn Gardens.

Given these kinds of misunderstandings, it came as no surprise to Urizenus when, in early October 2003, an avatar named Rich Rockstar came to the Church of Mephistopheles seeking absolution. Mistaking Uri, who was wearing a medieval monk's robes, for an actual (or at least virtual) priest, Rich sent an Instant Message asking him, "Does God forgive?"

Rich Rockstar's typist seemed young (or at least immature), but he also seemed earnest in his search for forgiveness. What Uri didn't realize at first was how seriously his visitor took Uri's priestly presence. As the two talked in IM, the supplicant became emotional, and confessed that he was a thirteen-year-old boy who had beaten his eight-year-old sister, breaking her jaw because she had annoyed him while he was watching the popular Japanese cartoon series *Yu-Gi-Oh!* (which has also become a video game) on TV. Uri quickly informed him that he was not, in fact, a priest, and suggested to the boy that he report the matter to the police, or at least to his parents. Apparently displeased by this suggestion, Rich Rockstar broke off communication, leaving Uri stunned.

The more he thought about it, the more Uri became concerned. He considered the possibility that the tale had been a hoax, but it didn't bear the hallmarks of one. Peter Ludlow, Uri's typist, had been part of various online communities for twenty years, and had seen his share of hoaxes. This smelled more real than that. Besides, anyone stupid enough to falsely claim they'd committed such violence really did deserve a visit from the authorities, in Uri's book.

In the end, Ludlow decided it was better to err on the side of caution. Following the instructions Maxis provided in its in-game user interface for the reporting of real-life crimes, Ludlow sent a report to Electronic Arts's game monitors (GMs). The procedure was simple; all he had to do was open a window in the game's interface, select a category to be used "if a player is discussing topics that involve real-world acts of crime," type his report, and hit the send button. Uri began his note with the words, "Report of real-life crime."

He was pleased to get a quick response from one of the TSO GMs. But he was less pleased to find that the GM had completely missed the point. Uri was advised to turn on the game's profanity filter if he had been offended by Rich Rockstar's language. (Several months later, a group of Uri's friends known as the Alpha Riot Grrlz investigated exactly what the profanity filter filtered, with surprising results. The results of their investigation were published in the *Herald*.[2]) It was hard to tell what was more shocking: the events he'd heard described by the boy or the callous and obtuse response he'd gotten from the company.

Uri resubmitted his report, pointing out that it was not a complaint about bad language, but notification of a real-life crime. Again, he received a detached and clueless response, saying that EA could only respond to events that happened in the game.

Uri responded yet again, citing the game's own Terms of Service agreement, according to which "claims of real-life crimes" were to be reported to the company. This time a different game monitor responded, telling Uri that if the avatar offended him he should "put the person on ignore."

By this point Uri was exasperated. It would have been one thing if EA had simply made some empty promise to "look into it." But he was receiving responses from the game monitors that seemed almost willfully obtuse. Could people really be this dense? Finally, he "shouted" in capital letters that he wasn't reporting bad language or offensive conduct, but simply trying to follow the Terms of Service by relaying a credible report of a real-life crime that seemed to have occurred. But this too was met with an infuriating message from a GM, who said that if Uri thought a crime had been committed, he should contact local law enforcement authorities. But local to where? New York City? Bakersfield, California? Eagle Grove, Iowa? Plovdiv, Bulgaria? Electronic Arts wasn't telling.

In addition to his travels in cyberspace as the muckraking reporter Urizenus, Peter Ludlow had a day job as a tenured professor in the Departments of Philosophy and Linguistics at the University of Michigan at Ann Arbor. Later on the day that he met Rich Rockstar, Ludlow ran into a woman at his school who would play a pivotal role in the Case of the Broken Jaw, and who in fact had already been integral to the *Herald*'s history.

In the spring of 2003, months before he'd set foot in Alphaville, Ludlow taught a graduate seminar in the philosophy of time. One of his students in that seminar was a young woman named Candace Bolter.

Candace grew up near Flint, Michigan (the city made famous by Michael Moore in his documentary *Roger and Me*), and then went to college at the University of Michigan at Flint. A philosophy major with strong interests in law and psychology, one of her teachers at Flint had described her as the best student he had had in forty years of teaching.

The graduate philosophy program at the University of Michigan at Ann Arbor is rated one of the top five in the English-speaking world,[3] and attracts some of the best graduate students from around the globe. During the recruitment weekend, when students from Oxford, Princeton, Harvard, and numerous prestigious four-year colleges came to visit the department, Candace, who lived only an hour away, was not there. She was in the hospital undergoing chemotherapy to treat the cancer that wracked her body.

By the time Ludlow and Bolter met, her cancer had gone into remission, but she had acquired a severe heart condition as a result of her medication. Soon afterward, she was diagnosed with lupus. She moved slowly, almost as though a sudden turn of the head would make her ill. She spoke slowly, as well, but she was always cheerful, a remarkable feat, given the circumstances of her illness. And the soft-spoken way she approached debates in philosophy belied her absolutely unrelenting nature. Candace held fast to her arguments with a conviction that seemed well beyond her deteriorating physical condition.

Every week when Ludlow saw her, she would begin her conversation with a challenge: "I thought about what you said last week, but I wonder if you considered the following ..." This continued throughout the semester, with Ludlow often attempting to defend a doctrine in the philosophy of time known as presentism, while Candace took the line known as four-dimensionalism, a position defended by the likes of Bertrand Russell and Albert Einstein.

Bolter pushed Ludlow on how his view could be consistent with the theory of relativity. Ludlow eventually had to turn for help to Larry Sklar, the resident expert on the philosophy of physics, and author of the book *Space, Time and Spacetime*.[4] But Bolter returned to challenge Ludlow on other issues. Soon they were debating the nature of psychology and the acquisition of temporal concepts in children, and Candace was devouring literature on cognitive development and psychology.

Candace was doing well in the philosophy program (as the chairman of the department was fond of pointing out to the other graduate students, Candace was the only student who was meeting all of her requirements on time), and had aspirations to go to law school and eventually work for the legal rights of children. She had been accepted into Berkeley, among several other law schools, but her health prevented her from attending.

Shortly after Ludlow found The Sims Online, Bolter's illness began to make it difficult for her to travel to the Ann Arbor campus. So Ludlow suggested she join TSO. In TSO, the two would be able to discuss philosophy and other topics on the days Candace was unable to leave her apartment. So Candace joined the game, created an avatar named Kale (pronounced *kah-lay* by her, though pronounced *kail* by everyone else), and became a fixture at the Church of Mephistopheles. When Uri launched the *Herald* in

October 2003, Kale became the newspaper's legal editor and a roommate at the *Herald* headquarters. She rapidly acquired shamanistic powers (useful for reviving friends after the *Herald*'s drowning parties), and could almost always be found in the *Herald*'s offices, busy at some virtual task while her typist was AFK, grading exams or reading law review articles and judicial opinions from court cases (something that counted as "reading for pleasure" for Bolter).

The difference between Kale and Candace was remarkable to Ludlow. Whereas Candace moved slowly—suffering from a combination of dreadful diseases and the effects of powerful medication—Kale danced around the *Herald* headquarters, was extremely quick-witted, and had a tendency to wax poetic. Of course, Ludlow knew full well that while the avatar was dancing, her typist was quite possibly experiencing nausea and exhaustion from her medication. To make her virtual life as comfortable as possible, Uri and Kale built a room for her toward the rear of the *Herald* building, with windows looking out on a virtual garden and beyond it a virtual lakeshore of Alphaville. They installed tables at which Kale could make virtual preserves, and she was often found "jamming" at all hours of the day and night. Sometimes Uri would drop in to the *Herald* at 3:00 in the morning and find Kale there, unable to sleep, jamming and gazing out onto her virtual garden. If she was in the mood, they would talk about philosophy, or her health, or law and the rights of children. It felt to Ludlow as though in the virtual figure of Kale he got the opportunity to see Candace Bolter as she really was. He was saddened that the other members of the philosophy department, who knew her only in the physical world, would never understand just how brightly she really shined.

When Ludlow ran into Bolter in the hallway at school on the day of his encounter with Rich Rockstar, he explained to her what had just happened. The tale set her blood boiling, and Ludlow could see that she was livid. She insisted that Ludlow contact the police. He objected to the folly of this enterprise, but she only pressed on. "You realize, of course," she said, "that as an educator in the state of Michigan you are legally required to forward all reports of child abuse to law enforcement authorities, whether they seem credible to you or not." Ludlow was unmoved: "That only relates to reports received in the course of work," he said. But as usual, Candace was unrelenting: "Ah, but that is the question, is this part of your educational mission or not? We discuss my academic work when we are online, for example."

Ludlow knew better than to try to win this argument with Candace, so he called the Ann Arbor police. The conversation went about as he expected. "What's an MMO? What's an avatar?" the officer wanted to know. "Where did this happen exactly?" he asked Ludlow. "Sorry, I don't know," Ludlow replied. "Well, is the kid in the United States?" Ludlow shrugged. "I don't know that either."

Out of ideas, Ludlow and Bolter began knocking on doors. One of the advantages of being at the University of Michigan was that, by some accounts, it was the best place in the world to study ethics. (By other, less reliable, accounts, it was tied with Harvard.) Just two doors down from Ludlow's office was the office of Liz Anderson, a leading expert in various fields of ethics. Anderson suggested they try the state's Children's Protective Services, who might be able to work with the police to put pressure on Electronic Arts to contact the relevant law enforcement authorities. After another long conversation involving the ins and outs of MMOs and avatars, the person Ludlow had reached at Children's Protective Services said there was nothing he could do without knowing where the act had allegedly taken place.

Exasperated, Ludlow gave up on the matter. But Bolter did not. In the weeks that followed, she began writing a series of letters to Electronic Arts, insisting that they take action in the matter and at least contact local law enforcement—wherever "local" happened to be. Bolter pursued her usual technique for more than a month, quietly and deftly applying pressure, but with no response. Finally, she too became fed up. But instead of giving up, Candace unloaded on EA with a blistering letter, which she also posted to the *Herald* on December 2, 2003. It read, in part:

> Quite frankly, this is a very serious issue and your lack of response is not only exasperating but also sickeningly disturbing. I literally lose sleep over this issue, yet everyone at EA must be sleeping so well (on comfy beds from the money your customers provide to you, it might be noted) that no one can even bother to reply to my inquiry. I'm imploring you to take the time to explain your rationale to me now. The customer is indeed not always right, but doesn't she at least deserve a reply to a legitimate inquiry? (Most helpfully, you might also explain to me how it takes several attempts over an extended period of time to receive any reply from you).
> Sincerely,
> Candace M. Bolter[5]

Several days later, EA relented. On December 5, Jeff Brown, EA's vice president for corporate communications, wrote to both Bolter and Ludlow: "after careful review of our web log, we contacted local authorities and identified the player. Resolution of this incident now lies with the local authorities."

Then the other shoe dropped.

On December 6, the day after Kale had received her response from Electronic Arts, Uri too was contacted by the company behind the game. The communication he received, however, was far less accommodating.

> Dear Urizenus,
>
> It has been discovered that, while using the EA.com Service to play The Sims Online, you have violated the EA.com Terms of Service and/or TSO User Agreement. . . . On 12-06-2003 at 05:35 GMT a cheating complaint was filed against your account (578372615). A sample of the logs of these actions is included below.
>
> Your account has been flagged in TSO for this violation. To avoid further actions against your account, including suspension or banning, you should reread and become familiar with the Terms of Service, the User Agreement, and the Message Board Guidelines.[6]

The "actions" cited by EA in flagging Uri's account were that his in-game profile included a link to *RealSimsOnline.com*, a Website on which many Sims, Uri included, posted further information about their avatars or details of their real lives. But RealSimsOnline also engaged in the trade in simoleans, and included links to third-party software modifications and add-ons for the game, both of which were in violation of the TSO Terms of Service.

The ToS forbade players from including links in their profiles that pointed to any site that violated the ToS. But like Uri, thousands of them did so. Unlike Uri, not many of them had their accounts flagged for it. "The question is," Uri asked in the *Herald*, "is this retaliation for my whistle blowing?"

Two days later, Uri reported that Maxis had moved again,[7] this time deleting references to the *Alphaville Herald* that appeared in the profiles of both Urizenus and Doctor Legion, Uri's alt at Mephisto's Goth Supplies, and replacing them with the words "Removed by Maxis." "Clearly, this is now a free-speech issue," Uri wrote, incredulous that Maxis would not only disallow mention of the *Herald* Website in the game but would go so far as to alter the biographical information that a user had entered into his own profile.

Whether it really was a free-speech issue turned out to be a more subtle question. What was clear was that he was incensed. He had done what he had felt to be the responsible thing, following the Maxis Terms of Service by contacting game monitors after hearing a report of what he felt was a real-life crime. In return, he'd gotten a slap on the wrist, and had his personal information altered within the game. To Uri, this was a threat, Maxis's way of saying, "Behave, or we'll toss you out on your ear," as the company had warned in its flagging notice. For someone to whom gaming was all about the freedom of information—about uncovering the fascinating things that were afoot in the virtual world, about discovering the social tropes of this new kind of online life, about chronicling the way we lived now—to have that freedom interfered with was a harsh slap.

But Uri had a job to do. The *Herald* didn't stop publishing just because he'd collided with Maxis. So he blew off some steam that afternoon, hitched up his virtual trousers, and went back to work. Little did he know that the trouble was just beginning.

7 Crossing the Line: Scamming, Griefing, and Real-World Crime

The Case of the Broken Jaw was an unfortunate example of real-world violence that Urizenus stumbled on within the confines of TSO. But even within the game, violence, scams, and just poor behavior could have disruptive effects on people's virtual lives, and in some cases on their real lives as well. As the *Herald* became more widely known around Alphaville, reports of misdeeds and cries of outrage came pouring in whenever Uri was in town, whether he was manning the *Herald* offices or not. The crimes being reported ran the gamut from behaviors that might be justified as a form of roleplay (playing the evil villain, for example), to actions that were just plain unacceptable in the context of an online game, to forms of harassment and account hacking that spilled out of the game and into the physical world and quite possibly counted as real-world crimes.

Evangeline's Free-Money for Newbies house was one of the clearest examples of abusive behavior in Alphaville, and Evangeline and her many alts were widely known as "griefers," that is, people whose preferred mode of play is to disrupt the virtual lives of others through a variety of tactics. Of course, griefers don't always see themselves as bad guys. And in some cases, what's a crime to one player is only good honest fun to another. But in a world of few laws, and those only haphazardly enforced, the question of what constitutes crossing the line can be a difficult one to answer. And as virtual worlds take more important roles in people's lives, the answers to such questions will start to take on more significance.

One case that occupied a gray area between griefing and roleplay was that of the avatar Celestie, whom the *Herald* dubbed "the abusive granny." While Celestie's crimes were not as serious as some, they made a good example of the ways in which the virtual world can blur the borders between the harmful and the benign.

Celestie, who claimed to be an adolescent male in real life, was in TSO a crotchety old woman in a housecoat who owned a property listed in the game's Welcome category. Celestie's house was anything but welcoming. When visitors dropped in, they were immediately presented with a list of requirements: no hats or colored hair were allowed, and no avatars in the form of a bear were permitted to visit the property. Anyone Celestie found "ugly" was required to wear an old-fashioned diving helmet, and Sims who didn't follow granny's rules would receive a virtual face-slapping from Celestie and a large dose of verbal abuse.

While a visit to Celestie's property could be traumatic for newbies (one came to the *Herald* offices to complain about the treatment she had received there), Celestie herself had a different view of things. "It's funny that so many folks take things personally," she told Uri in an interview. "What isn't amusing about an old lady who is irritable with others and has nothing to do but nag at folks about how they are and look, when in reality her own looks are burnt and her own personality is sour."[1] The way Celestie saw it, she wasn't an abusive person, she was just engaged in a slightly unusual kind of theater.

But TSO was a game that included players as young as thirteen years old. When Uri pressed about whether a young teen might not be ready for this kind of theater, Celestie was unapologetic: "Sim = Simulation, as in Life Simulation. Look around you. Not everyone is nice and friendly. Just because I take on the role of a sourpuss of a grandmother doesn't mean I am spoiling it for people. If that were true then most real lives would be spoiled."[2]

Griefing could take more serious forms than verbal abuse, of course, and could easily be hidden behind the straw man of roleplay. Extortion, for instance, is only natural when you're role-playing a Mafia don. So the mafiosi in TSO would often tag unsuspecting players with red enemy links, and then demand payment, usually around 100,000 simoleans, to have them removed. To some younger players, such links could be especially traumatic. One, reportedly a thirteen-year-old girl in real life, was forced to give up her pet cheetah (worth $25) to a group of griefers in exchange for their removing the red links they had just tagged her with. Mafias would also target some properties and demand payment in return for "protection"—which if not paid meant that visitors to the property would be red-linked and harassed. In effect, demanding protection money

Figure 7.1
Afterward: Lindens for target practice

amounted to a threat to knock a property off the leader boards. When confronted, the Mafias claimed the roleplay defense: TSO was a fantasy world and they were simply living out their fantasies.

In Second Life, one group of residents who had mastered the art of passive griefing were known as the W-Hats, a name borrowed from the lore of a Website called *SomethingAwful.com.* The W-Hats engaged in a kind of high-tech, hit-and-run griefing campaign within the confines of Second Life in which they would litter their own property (and sometimes the property of others) with enormous penises and swastikas or with distasteful builds, highly offensive to some, that depicted the attempted assassination of Pope John Paul II, the gruesome murder of a prostitute, or the September 11, 2001, attack on the World Trade Center—complete with a Death Star thrown in for effect.

But the W-Hats' antics could take more serious form, at times. Anshe Chung, who at the time was earning the virtual equivalent of $100,000 a year in Second Life's real estate business, learned this the hard way when she purchased some property on the borders of the W-Hats' estate. In an interview with the *Herald*, she complained that the W-Hats were trying to get her to sell land at a reduced price by erecting obnoxious and disruptive signs and builds on the border of her property. "I received one offer for my land shortly after I bought it," Anshe said. "After I declined the offer, the person told me that sooner or later they would get the land cheap anyway because nobody wants live next to them, pointing to the things they put on their land."

Anshe's appeals to Linden Lab fell on deaf ears. "Are you concerned that the Lindens will be slow to resolve the situation?" Uri asked her. "I am concerned that the Lindens won't resolve the situation at all since in the past they did not. There were also cases months ago that were not resolved," she said.[3]

Antics like those of Evangeline, Celestie, the TSO Mafias, and the W-Hats, as well as the many other griefers Uri came across in TSO and Second Life, are often cast as the work of stereotypical adolescent male troublemakers. While an avatar's real age and sex are impossible to ascertain by his or her actions, Uri did meet many griefers in The Sims Online—a game with a younger population than most MMOs—who claimed to be just as young and hormonally male as their actions signified.

Why people misbehave in online worlds is an open question. But the usual answer—that the relative anonymity and attendant lack of accountability on the Web allows people to haul out dark urges they might otherwise keep in the shadows—is probably not correct.

John Suler, a clinical psychologist at Rider University who has long been a student of the psychology of cyberspace, says, "The person may experience the anonymity—the lack of an identity—as toxic."[4] Most residents of virtual worlds do not understand themselves to be anonymous, at least not completely. One's avatar has a very real and persistent identity within an online universe, and most people are aware that whenever they log on they are building that avatar's identity within the world. Griefing can be an effective way to get noticed. For some, it's the only way they can think of to build their virtual persona. For others, it probably does give vent to urges they're unable to express in the real world. But the notoriety it brings is not always helpful.

What was interesting about many of the griefers Uri encountered in TSO was how often they could be found rooming together in what effectively amounted to surrogate families. In some cases, an adult—or what appeared to be an adult—roomed with them as well, serving as a parental figure after the fashion of Ma Barker, the woman who brought up four criminal sons in the 1930s and not only cared for them but encouraged their life of crime. In other cases, a leader would emerge from within the group.

Their goal in TSO—as is the griefer's goal in any game—was to find new and exciting ways to disrupt the normal course of gameplay. The properties in the game's Welcome category, for example, are intended to be places where new players can become acquainted with the game and receive help from friendly, more experienced players. But griefer "familes" would establish Welcome houses and then, like Evangeline, use them to con money out of newbies and even humiliate and verbally harass them. Properties with sexually discriminatory or racist themes were common. Griefers would also maintain numerous alts that were sent out into greater Alphaville in attempts to scam and disrupt other houses. Because alts were usually abandoned soon after they had been created, they appeared to others as new characters, and this had the effect of making many players highly suspicious of newbies, and of generating virtual gated communities in response.

Whatever the griefers' motivation, Uri was astounded that this behavior was not just accepted but actually rampant at many of the Welcome properties in a game that was meant to be suitable for children ages 13 and up. The fact was, the "authorities" of TSO's world—Electronic Arts' in-world and customer service representatives—were simply not very responsive to reports of abuse and griefing. This seems to have been due, at least in part, to EA's reluctance to spend valuable resources policing disputes between customers. But crime and punishment in online worlds is a more complex issue than it seems on the surface, and what was going on in TSO was simply too complex an issue for a corporation like EA to handle.

In order to give residents a rich and engaging experience, one that mimics the real world as compellingly as possible, avatars must be able to do all kinds of things that could potentially be used in abusive or even harmful ways—just as we can in our real lives. What prevents most people in the real world from committing crimes is one of two things: either they respect the mores of the society in which they live, or they fear the punishment that will result should they step outside those bounds. But in terms of what's actually possible, the physics of our universe has absolutely no problem with murder.

The same is true of virtual worlds. The "physics" of virtual worlds, as embodied in their software, allows abuse, theft, and in some cases even murder as well. But the metaverse is a place without an established set of mores. And while virtual worlds do enjoin their residents to abide by rules of courtesy, laid out with varying degrees of specificity from world to world and game to game, these agreements are rarely enforced with any consistency. There has yet to be a virtual world in which the effective letter of the law is not defined simply by what that world's software allows.

Enforcement of the rules in TSO seemed particularly lax to Uri. As the number of Alphaville's residents who came to him with complaints increased, it became clearer that EA was doing very little to address the scammers and griefers who lurked throughout the game.

In some cases, EA explicitly deferred to the "physics" of the world as the boundary for acceptable behavior—despite the fact that more stringent rules were written into their own Terms of Service and End-User Licensing Agreement. In the spring of 2004, a Sim named Reyes made a deal to sell an extremely rare robot cat for 50 million simoleans—about $2,500 at the time—to an avatar she thought was named Lead Architect, a Sim she trusted from previous business dealings. Lead was a respected builder and money trader in TSO with a great deal of reputation capital. Many people had trusted him to transfer their money from one server to another, or to deliver the agreed upon number of simoleans in exchange for a PayPal payment. But the trade window could handle no more than a million simoleans at a time, so the payment would have to be completed in fifty installments. Since Lead was a respected trader, Reyes gave him the pet when he gave her the first million.[5]

But the balance never arrived. Instead, Reyes got only a few choice epithets from Lead—and the painful realization that the avatar she'd been dealing with was not in fact Lead *Architect*, but someone named Lead *Archetict*. The misspelled avatar had been created specifically to scam people by taking advantage of the correctly spelled Lead's good standing in the community, a practice that was common enough to have its own name: cloning. Clones not only mimick popular avatars' names, they attempt to replicate their physical appearance and the contents of their in-game profiles as well. Lead Architect had been cloned—and Reyes had been scammed.

While Reyes probably couldn't have gotten $2,500 for her rare even from an honest dealer, she had been scammed out of a pet worth at least several hundred dollars. And she was not the only one. Others had also been scammed out of rares, and Lead Archetict had solicited money trades from a number of avatars and then simply failed to deliver the funds to their destinations.

When Uri interviewed the real Lead Architect, he was at his wits' end. He and several of the scam's victims had reported the impostor to EA, but the game company had come back with a typically lackadaisical response.

Urizenus: Are you familiar with the claim of Reyes, getting scammed out of 49 million simoleans by your clone? Is that a legit story?

Lead Architect: I know about it. I can't do anything. He is unstoppable, and EA won't do anything. Everyone is reporting him, and Maxis comes back with a lame excuse.

Urizenus: What do they say?

Lead Architect: Part of normal gameplay. Nothing was actually done against ToS.

Urizenus: lol[6]

But as much as EA might have liked that to be so, it just wasn't true. As Respected Banker pointed out in the comments thread of the interview, the game's ToS forbade "anything that interferes with the ability of other Service users to enjoy playing an EA game" (such as impersonating them, for instance?), and its End User Licensing Agreement (EULA) warned that players shall not "defraud or cheat other players in the game. This includes, but is not limited to, exploiting the game's trade interface to acquire another player's in-game assets."

Was EA too stupid to see that the trade-window scam was a clear violation of the company's own codes of conduct? Were they simply too lazy to do anything about it? Were they practicing selective enforcement, refusing to come to the assistance of someone engaged in trading outside the game itself, a practice they frowned upon? Or was there something else at work here?

Any or all of the above may have been true, but a more revealing explanation (as well as a more charitable one) is that cyberspace may simply have gotten the better of EA. In considering what was and wasn't allowed in Alphaville, EA's reps seem to have looked primarily to the "physics" of the virtual world, and only secondarily (if at all) to the "laws" they had written to govern it. What EA was really saying was, "The law doesn't apply unless we feel like enforcing it. If we don't, there is no law, and anything goes." Given a style of enforcement that verged on the capricious, TSO's residents had no choice but to defend themselves, both against the criminal elements of the virtual world and against that world's masters as well.

Uri's investigations in TSO were turning up other breaches of fair play—and aggrieved residents of the virtual world were coming up with their own solutions. A common reaction to griefing in TSO, if an ineffectual one, was for aggrieved Sims to visit the griefer's property to protest. But hanging around on a griefer's property only added to the griefer's visitors' bonus and raised the status of the property in the game's listing tool (griefer houses routinely ranked at the top of the TSO's leader boards). Law-abiding citizens who cared about the rankings were in a no-win situation. Though they weren't playing by the rules at all, the griefers were becoming power gamers.

A slightly more effective tactic was practiced by several organized anti-griefer groups. These tried to keep avatars regularly stationed on griefer properties (conceding them the rankings and visitors bonus the griefer would receive from their presence), in order to warn vulnerable newbies away. Others, including the BDSM community around Rose Thorn Gardens, established their own Welcome houses to draw traffic away from the griefers, and worked out schedules that would keep them open as much as possible. Visitors would be warned of known griefers and the dangers of scam houses, and instructed in how to avoid them (they could also get an instructional seminar in BDSM roleplay, if they requested).

More sophisticated communications-based strategies emerged in response to griefing in TSO as well. The BDSM community of Rose Thorn Gardens established a communications network that was used to ban troublesome players from the one hundred or so properties that belonged to the loose confederation. When a new griefer was discovered, a "ban" signal would be broadcast to all associated houses, and each could then use in-game tools to ban the specified avatar from their house, effectively freezing the griefer out of the neighborhood.

As Uri explored other virtual worlds, he discovered that the powers that be were so immersed themselves in the shared culture created by the population that they could be talked out of taking part in the resolution of many disputes. It was almost as if they had ceded their role as mediators by virtue of neglect. And when they tried to reclaim those powers of dispute arbitration, residents often tried to reject their efforts as meddling in things the companies had no business passing judgment on.

In Second Life, the Jessie sim is one of the few that is permantly set as a "combat zone" in which your avatar can die (in Second Life this consists of nothing more painful than being teleported to one's home location). To observe the often colorful goings-on in Jessie, the *Herald* established an underground bunker and a fortified observation deck floating in the sky above. A map hung on the bunker wall allowed Uri to teleport to various locations around the sim when there was particularly gripping combat to be observed.

As he lazed in the bunker one day weighing a few editorial decisions over a small glass of virtual Fernet Branca and a Cuban cigar, several shells came ripping through the thick concrete walls, killing him instantly. Uri "respawned" in the bunker, his home location, and immediately teleported to the observation tower—only to be promptly killed again. On being resurrected this time he fled to a deeper, more secure room in the bunker. With the muffled thump of explosions reaching him even at these depths, he puffed his bent stogie, lamented his broken glass of digestif and observed the action via an avatar detector, a kind of 3-D radar screen that displayed avatars' relative locations within the sim. After a few moments, he noticed the shooting had stopped. And there on his av detector was an icon for someone named Lee Linden, a representative of Linden Lab (all of whom bear the last name Linden, which is not available to other residents).

Uri teleported to the surface to observe events, and found Lee in the middle of a dispute that had broken out between a vampish female avatar named pancake Stryker and a man named FalconBK Hanks, one of a number of devotees of the MMO World War II Online (aka WWIIOL) who were also resident in Second Life.

The original cause of the dispute was unclear, but Falcon had armed his extensive properties in the Jessie sim with automated turrets that could track and fire on specified avatars—in this case, on pancake Stryker. But pancake's home was on Falcon's land. With his turrets set to fire on her automatically, she couldn't even stand there for more than a moment before dying, which made her Second Life existence into an eternally recurring cycle of death and rebirth.

So pancake reported Falcon to the authorities, who brought Lee Linden to the scene. Lee listened to pancake's complaints, but the leader of the WWIIOL group, chaunsey Crash, complained that crying to the Lindens was not the way disputes were resolved in Jessie. "There are calm ways of dealing with it," chaunsey argued. "Most situations are dealt with without Lindens."[7]

And, to pancake's chagrin, the Lindens were of no help anyway, at least as far as the present situation was concerned. On hearing the arguments, Lee immediately pled impotence. "Pancake, it's not your land," he said. "Other than providing you with the opportunity to enter or leave Jessie, there's not much I can do." Falcon, naturally, was delighted with this non-response and replied in his own characteristic way: "Yes! I was right! Eat that, bitch."

What was clear was that Linden Lab's representative wasn't actually trying to resolve the dispute, but merely to uphold the narrow letter of the law. The letter of the law in Second Life permits the killing of avatars on land one owns, even if the victim happens to live there as well.

But the residents' own dispute-resolution system, as patchy and abusive as it could be, seemed to work. After the Linden departed, chaunsey mediated the dispute the Jessie way, and by the end of the day Falcon's turrets had been turned off. Pancake was free to come and go.

It's not necessarily a bad thing that residents of virtual worlds are, for the most part, left to their own devices when seeking recourse for what they perceive as crimes. In fact, Linden Lab promotes resident control as one of the virtues of Second Life, advertising it as "A 3D Digital Online World Imagined, Created and Owned by its Residents."

But that "ownership" only goes so far, and its boundary is gray and wavering at best. Griefers are common to every virtual community, and every virtual community develops its own strategies for dealing with them. Altering the virtual laws of physics by changing the software to prevent unwanted behavior is rarely enough. There is almost always a way to circumvent the software, and griefing takes many forms.

The problem is that game companies are staffed by engineers, not dispute mediators, constitutional scholars, social workers, or psychologists. As a result, when the physics of the software doesn't settle a problem, the problem drops into the hands of company agents who are apt to act, or not act, without any guiding principle other than who they like and dislike, or perhaps what kind of day they're having.

Even deciding who is a griefer and when can be a far from scientific process, and is not the sort of problem that can be engineered away. The uncertain line that separates griefing from roleplay is one that in many worlds, Second Life included, is easily manipulated by a creative griefer in ways that can turn criminal into victim, and sometimes victim into criminal.

For example, while the Lindens had moved against one user's virtual concrete statues because they had exposed breasts complete with nipples,[8] the company simultaneously let another group go wild: The W-Hats of Second Life are particularly adept at "playing" the company behind the world. They regularly engage in behavior that most people would find unacceptable, and just as regularly dupe Linden Lab into tolerating it. When the *Herald* raised the question of whether a build depicting the destruction of the World Trade Center was appropriate in a virtual world like Second Life, Bakuzelas Khan, one of the W-Hats' leaders, offered their usual defense: "It's not real. It's a fantasy place. So many people get so serious in it, they can't play anymore. I have seen a lot of friends leave because it gets too uptight in here." Lighten up, Baku was saying, it's only a game. Another W-Hat member provided a more postmodern—if slightly nonsensical—defense: "It's an example of the absurdity of life.... Superimposing pop culture over tragedy shows how we manufacture our national outlook through the media." To *Herald* reporter Gina Fatale, though, who had been on the fortieth floor of one of the towers during the attack, the excuses rang hollow. In her view, the build was outrageous behavior for its own sake, and the pseudo-intellectual justification was made up to keep Linden Lab off the W-Hats' back. In Second Life, unlike in New York, the towers were left standing.

In early 2006, World of Warcraft was the site of a more disturbing instance of whimsical "law enforcement."[9] When WoW player Sara Andrews tried to recruit players for a gay- and lesbian-friendly guild within the game, she received a notice from Blizzard Entertainment to the effect that she had violated the sexual harassment section of the game's Terms of Service. Surely there must be some mistake, Andrews thought. Her guild was not even gay- and lesbian-only, but was meant to be all-inclusive. But no. When she contacted Blizzard reps, she was repeatedly given the same answer: "While we appreciate and understand your point of view, we do feel that the advertisement of a 'GLBT friendly' guild is very likely to result in harassment for players that may not have existed otherwise," Blizzard wrote to her. "If you will look at our policy, you will notice the suggested penalty for violating the Sexual Orientation Harassment Policy is to 'be temporarily suspended from the game.' However, as there was clearly no malicious intent on your part, this penalty was reduced to a warning."

Here was an unusual twist: not a griefer at all, here was a player being punished for other players' prejudices—not only that, but for harassment that hadn't even happened yet. Was there any sane universe in which this would seem like a reasonable course of action for a company to take? And, as in TSO, the game company looked the other way while actual offenses of the same nature took place in their game every day. Just dip into the Barrens zone of any World of Warcraft server and it won't be long before you see someone talking about fags, gays, and their wish that a hated player would die of AIDS. Were these players being reprimanded? Not at all.

The story quickly made its way through the blogosphere and even into the *Washington Post.*[10] In the end, it took a letter from a gay and lesbian rights advocacy group, citing anti-discrimination case law, before Blizzard would back down.[11] Despite the fact that Blizzard's warning to Andrews had been repeated by company representatives at a number of official levels, the company insisted the episode was nothing more than "an unfortunate mistake." By that time, though, Sara Andrews had quit the game in disgust.

The *Herald* took note of the episode as another example of why virtual worlds need to be watched as closely as the real one.[12] World of Warcraft is only a game, but it apparently—inadvertently or otherwise—institutionalized a form of discrimination that would be inappropriate in any context, whether virtual or real. These were the kinds of forward signals Uri was looking for, the keys to how such things would be dealt with in the more functional worlds of the future. The forward signals were not looking good.

In addition to dodging the wrath of "law", some griefers attempt to turn the laws of a world against their victims. In TSO, one tactic commonly employed was to create an alt and simply hang around someone's property waiting for the owner or a visitor to use a mildly offensive word like "bullshit." The griefer would then report the offending Sim, and because EA was more sensitive to swearing than to financial scams, the Sim would commonly be warned, receiving a black mark on his or her record, or—depending on which GM received the abuse report—might even receive a temporary suspension.

One *Herald* roommate learned this the hard way when several griefers showed up at the newsroom one day and began spouting racist epithets, prompting the roomie to tell one that he needed to be "bitch-slapped." The griefers filed abuse reports and the roommate earned a seventy-two-hour suspension, while the griefers got off without so much as a slap on the wrist.

What Ludlow didn't realize at the time was that this pattern was being repeated in any number of virtual worlds. Game companies are often uninterested in stamping out troublemakers, and the thought of spending money on the enterprise makes them even more reluctant to get involved. And their Terms of Service, in some cases, are written so that they don't have to, even when the violation is one that an avatar has no possible defense against.

The type of thieves known as "ninja looters," for instance, often commit virtual crimes that fall into this category. In games like World of Warcraft and EverQuest II, the loot that powerful monsters drop when they die can be quite valuable, and how it's parceled out can become a contentious issue. More contentious still is when it is simply stolen, snatched by an unscrupulous party member before anyone else can claim the need for it or otherwise make their bid.

In April 2005, on the World of Warcraft realm (WoW shards are known as realms) known as Destromath, a group of several dozen high-level characters working in concert bested a dragon known as Azuregos, one of the more formidable beasts in the game. One of the items Azuregos dropped was an extremely rare and powerful sword known as Typhoon, which was promptly ninjaed, scooped up by an unscrupulous party member before anyone else had the chance to argue for it. On one WoW-related forum, a player described the experience thus: "killed azuregos yesterday and a DAMN F***KING warrior named ancora of DESTROMATH (germany) stole typhoon. F***CKING ninja! burn in hell :/"[13] Obtaining high-level items like Typhoon is so difficult that ninjaing them is a serious crime, and yet similar crimes go on in MMOs every day. In some, the physics of the world allows players to attack each other at any time, but not in World of Warcraft. With little defense against the ninja, some players and guilds keep blacklists of known ninjas and refuse to have anything to do with them. Ancora certainly got himself noticed, and he'll have a hard time finding another party to run with once his name gets around.

Try reporting a ninja like Ancora to Blizzard, the company behind WoW, and you're likely to get the same response that Lead Architect got from EA. Ninjaing is an accepted mode of gameplay, according to the WoW "scam policy."[14] The "physics" of the world allow it, so it must be okay.

Not all scams are looked on so leniently. One of the most common is the trade-window scam that Evangeline ran on new players in TSO. Under the pretext of helpfulness, a scammer will persuade an unsuspecting newbie to place an item in the trade window and click "trade." Before they know what's happened, the victim has given the scammer some money, a weapon, or some other item of value they never intended to transfer.

While companies like Blizzard will occasionally look into such scams and even return the items to the original owner, if possible, their policing only goes so far. "We want players to learn from their mistakes," Blizzard states in its scam policy. "Players will only be allowed a certain number of item restorations, including those lost to scams."

This is fair enough, a rational decision on Blizzard's part to promote smarter gameplay by letting players feel the consequences of their actions. But even when a company does take action, it is often far from effective as a deterrent. One controversial resident of Second Life, who was fond of wearing German SS uniforms and building Nazi death camps, had been given no less than eight temporary bans by the time the *Herald* profiled her, and was showing no sign of abandoning the behavior that had gotten her account suspended in the first place. "Being away was great," she told the *Herald*. "Real life doesn't have babies who cry and complain. No fucking drama. No bullshit. Freedom to do what you want."[15]

In the end, the level of policing that companies are willing to do places the responsibility for seeking and carrying out justice largely in the players' camp. Company intervention occurs on an apparently random basis, and in many cases only serves to reinforce the idea that players should take care of their problems themselves.

The fact is that abuse-reporting systems rarely work as they're designed to in virtual worlds. The ratio of residents to game masters in the typical virtual world is so high (in some cases worse than a thousand to one) that no company can hope to adequately respond to every report of a scam, a ninja, or a racial slur flung across a chat channel. To work around this, some worlds feature a reputation feedback system similar to the reputation system that works so well on eBay. But this too has proved an inadequate tool, a system that is easily gamed to produce false results. eBay is a completely transaction-based system, and the vast majority of ratings are based on transactions that have actually taken place. In a place with many millions of users, the "noise" of friends or co-conspirators posting false ratings to an account is relatively low. But in places like Second Life or a shard of TSO or another MMO, where the population is more limited, the amount of noise coming through the signal is too high to make such a system truly useful.

What MMO companies generally *will* respond to are griefers who mount attacks on the virtual world itself. In some worlds, residents have been able to hack the world's databases to gain information about monsters or other players, to add gold and valuable items to their own accounts or to delete them from the accounts of others. Where they can be found, these users are usually banned permanently from the world under assault.

In Second Life, several notorious griefers managed to mount serious attacks, not only disrupting the virtual lives of other residents but causing costly problems for Linden Lab, the company behind the world. In December 2004, six of the three hundred-plus servers that then ran the world of Second Life suddenly crashed. One of them was the home of a resident known as Reno Parks, and *Herald* reporters soon learned that the crashes were the result of an attack on him by a blinged-out avatar called Baller-MoMo King who in real life lived in the United Arab Emirates. In an interview with the *Herald*, Baller admitted to "nuking" Reno's sim, but said the other five sims that had crashed had been an accident, the result of a virtual weapon more powerful than he'd intended. He'd bought the nuke from an avatar called One Song who was known for his bomb-making prowess. The price? A mere 100,000 Lindens—about $400 at prevailing exchange rates.[16]

Figure 7.2
BallerMoMo King

That someone would pay $400 to mount an attack on another resident of a virtual world shows just how strongly online identities do matter to many people, and how wrapped up they may be in the families that form in such online environments. BallerMoMo King was not just an avatar making his way in the virtual world, but the head of his own blinged-out crew struggling for dominance in the shadowy underworld of Mafia familes, gangbangers, and street posses that flows through Second Life. Decked out in virtual furs and ice and surrounded in his vast and ornate mansion by bodyguards and scantily clad "MoMo Ho's," Baller vied with organizations like the Black Hand Mafia, the Street Killaz, the Bad-Boys (of which Reno Parks served as "don"), the Un-Touchables, the Valentino Family, the Cinquetti Family, the Bellini Family, the Diablo Cartel (virtual drug dealers in SL—despite the fact that the drugs they sold had no effect), and the many upstart groups that made briefer appearances on the Grid. And what they were vying for, more or less, were bragging rights. Baller's nuking of Reno's sim was in response to a perceived slight (he had been "dissed" by Reno). Here was frontier justice at work. Even in a world without competitive yardsticks, it is not very hard to create one's own.

But to have six of a virtual world's servers crash at once is more than an annoyance for a small company like Linden Lab. As with any other business, server downtime costs both money and reputation capital. Residents who find themselves plagued by frequent server crashes, no matter the reason, are unlikely to return. In this case, Linden Lab moved swiftly to punish the perpetrator, as well as a number of alts he created in the wake of the attacks. Even so, the suspensions were only temporary, and soon enough Baller was back. It seemed again that if the software allowed it, it couldn't be all that bad.

Of course, the hardware wasn't always where the damage was done. Shortly after BallerMoMo was banned from Second Life, an avatar named Hellraiser Millions appeared whose in-world profile bore the same photograph BallerMoMo's avatar had on its "first life" page (where residents often placed information about their typists). According to the *Herald*'s sources, this new avatar, who bore a striking resemblance to Baller, had approached a third party and offered to pay him 20,000 Lindens ($80) to "f**k up" The Edge, one of Second Life's most popular nightclubs.[17] It looked like the crew in the UAE was back in business.

Shortly after the *Herald* published this new story, Uri's typist Peter Ludlow received a phone call. The call came from the United Arab Emirates, and the caller, who identified himself as BallerMoMo's real-life brother, was furious at Ludlow for printing the charges. After half an hour on the phone, Ludlow wasn't quite convinced that the story had been unfounded, but he now had a clearer sense than ever of how seriously things like reputation and bragging rights were taken by some in the virtual world. Indeed, the wall between the real world and the virtual one was beginning to look positively porous.

Some attacks can shake the very foundations of a world. In July 2005, a hacker's exploit did just that to the economic foundations of Second Life. In Second Life many residents do a healthy business selling virtual items that range from simple clothing and furniture to more complex programmed objects embedded in things like aircraft, weapons, games, or animations (many allowing an avatar to simulate various sexual positions), as well as a range of other things. Most of these transactions are conducted via scripted in-world financial applications that have become the backbone of commerce on the Grid. These applications are made secure through Second

Life's system of read/write permissions, which residents can set on programmed objects to make their internal workings invisible to the general population.

But in mid-2005, a group of Second Life residents wrote a hack that tricked the Second Life client (the software loaded on a user's machine, through which residents view the world) into letting them look inside scripted objects that were supposed to be secure. Just like that, every piece of intellectual property on the Grid was theirs for the taking.

Fortunately for the residents of Second Life (and for Linden Lab), the hackers were not so much interested in enriching themselves as they were in stirring up trouble (though one reportedly managed to steal about $700 worth of virtual currency and goods from another resident[18]). As was soon discovered, the perpetrators had links to the W-Hats, the griefer group that had been disrupting people's second lives for months. The *Herald*, which had been complaining about the Linden policy of benign neglect toward the W-Hats for nearly as long, could only say, "We told you so. And told you so. And told you so."

Although the actual damage in this case was relatively minor, the potential for damage was great, and it raised several questions about life in the virtual world. Could more stealthy hacks have gone undetected? Who was responsible for the security of scripts like those that were hacked, scripts that handled hundreds if not thousands of dollars worth of virtual commerce every day? The scripts themselves had not been hacked, Linden Lab's software had. Was the company responsible for protecting the security of every single script on the Grid? Or were the scripters themselves expected to plug holes the company might have left? Could the company shield against all eventualities, even if it wanted to? Could anyone? In the end, though very little financial damage was done, the exploit shook residents' confidence in the security of the objects that many of them used to supplement their real-life incomes or build a reputation on the Grid, and raised serious questions about whether secure commerce in Second Life was viable at all. Indeed in the months since that attact, Grid-wide attacks in Second Life have become ever more frequent, much to the dismay of users.

Among virtual worlds, Second Life is one of the most robust platforms for any kind of application one can imagine, whether commercial, educational, social, or of any other sort. The virtual platforms that we all inhabit will increasingly resemble environments like Second Life in many ways. Who will protect us on these platforms? Will it even be possible to settle on a single authority who can do the job? Or will responsibility in the virtual universe of the future be something equally shared by all? If so, will anarchy reign, or frontier justice, or some more ordered system of checks and balances? As the *Herald* reported, the answers were anything but obvious.

The *Herald* came to revel in the stories of griefers in virtual worlds, not just because they made good copy (though they certainly did), but because Urizenus suspected they could shed light on what people were doing in these worlds in the first place. In many cases, as well, he sensed a deeper story behind some of the griefers' goings-on. There seemed to be a level of "play" that he didn't yet know about, but which he knew was out there somewhere. As it turned out, the person who would introduce him to that game-within-a-game would be his old friend Shawn One.

8 Down the Rabbit Hole

In October 2003, Urizenus stepped out of his techno-pagan cleric's robe and went straight, moving the *Herald* newsroom out of Rose Thorn Gardens to a neighborhood controlled by the Sim Shadow Government. He had seen enough of the darksiders and come to realize that the SSG was clearly the key to unlocking the secrets of Alphaville. The Church of Mephistopheles was no more. Instead, Uri changed the name of his property to "Alphaville Herald HQ," changed the description in his in-game profile from "High Priest" to "Publisher," and added a link to *Alphavilleherald.com*, the Website where his and his reporters' stories could be read.

Almost as soon as the *Herald* had set up shop in its new location, a different kind of news started coming through its doors. Uri got a pleasant surprise one morning when, as he was going about his usual chores in the *Herald* headquarters, he received an Instant Message from Shawn One, the object of his near-romantic encounter some weeks before and the Sim who had first let him in on the workings of the hit squads that populated TSO.

Shawn dropped by later that morning. She played with Cheddar Cheese Cheetah as Uri fixed breakfast. (Even when socializing in TSO, one had to remember to green one's Hunger bar.) "I see you changed your property description," Shawn said.

"Yep," Uri replied. "Went legit."

"Good," Shawn said. "I was worried about you, what with the Satanic church and your talking to Evangeline and all."

"Yeah, the Satanist shtick was getting old," he said. Uri was touched by her concern and reminded of the days of their nearly romantic liaison. But his task as a virtual journalist was never far from his mind. Hoping that Shawn and the SSG would welcome the coverage he could give them as

Alphaville's only virtual journalist, he soon steered the conversation around to the Sim Shadow Government, and a tentative conversation the two Sims had had weeks earlier about Uri's joining the vigilante group's operations. Uri had learned a lot about the SSG, but he was anxious to see it from the inside. To his delight, Shawn was still receptive to the idea, and after some Instant Message discussions with higher-ranking officers, she announced that he had been added to the ranks of the organization. "Expect a lot of spam," she said, referring not to unwanted solicitations but to the high volume of Instant Messages generated by the SSG.

Uri had learned early on that much of the "game" in TSO did not take place on the graphical surface provided by the game's software, but behind it. The chat interface provided by Maxis was clunky; most users preferred to communicate through third-party chat programs like YIM (Yahoo! Instant Messenger), AIM (AOL Instant Messenger) and Microsoft's MSN Chat, which they kept running in the background when they played TSO. (Uri, in his capacity as editor of the *Herald*, found it necessary to keep all three running, since his sources might use any combination to get in touch with him.) The SSG used YIM for its communications, running several layers of "spam lists" (i.e., communication channels, not lists used for unwanted commercial solicitations). The SSG "Overlord" could thus communicate with all members at once or with various subsets consisting of generals, foot soldiers, and so on.

As SSG officers began adding him to their own spam lists, Uri got a closer glimpse than ever before of the game within the game. A flood of communiqués began to come his way, some from SSG officials he recognized from the organizational chart on the SSG's Website (including SSG Overlord Snow White). There were also numerous messages from a Sim named shadowradio2003, who was connected with the SSG's Web-based radio station. Within minutes Uri began receiving almost constant updates on the movements of various Alphaville mafiosi and scammers, and the response of the SSG tagging units who sought to keep them at bay—much like having access to a police dispatcher's radio channel.

One of the first messages to reach him alerted the SSG to a Mafia operative who had red-tagged an innocent Alphaville citizen named Candi, adding a quote to the effect that the mafia family now "owned" Candi. "Seems Mistress Kali has attacked an innocent sim," Uri read in the SSG message.

"This type of treatment is not tolerated. Let's have a 'talking' to her and let her know our stance! Thanks to everyone in advance!"

The SSG sought to maintain order in Alphaville by fighting back against such capricious red-taggings and responding in kind—tenfold, if possible—in a game of reputational paintball that could seriously damage a Sim's standing in the community. Of course, their missions didn't always go as planned, but their commitment to their task was impressive.

After being added to the spam lists, Peter Ludlow, Uri's typist, left his computer on when he went to bed to see just how much traffic the SSG generated. It turned out to be a restless slumber, as YIM messages chirped into his computer throughout the night, keeping him half awake with visions of cartoon hit squads dancing in his head. The SSG, it seemed, kept its watchful eye on the streets of Alphaville all night long.

The next morning, as Ludlow paged back through the messages, attempting to decipher the cryptic, if clearly urgent, communiqués, he got a glimpse of a mission that had gone badly, and how the SSG improvised when confronted with unexpected obstacles.

The Sim named shadowradio2003 had sent out a message urging SSG members to come to the aid of SSG member DJPurplebunny, who had been tagged by members of the Sclafani Mafia family. But when the SSG arrived at Krystal Sclafani's house, they found themselves unable to tag the perpetrators, though the Sclafanis were apparently able to tag the SSG at will. "I've seen this before, there is some fucking cheat," wrote SSG member Ronan. The vigilantes were forced to regroup. "Send out a spam saying not to go there," shadowradio wrote.

As Uri interpreted the chat logs, it appeared that the mafiosi had found a bug in the TSO software that let them "sleepwalk" through a limited number of tasks. They could red-tag others, but because the software considered them to be asleep, others were unable to red-tag them. SSG operatives reported the exploit to EA representatives, but got no response.

The SSG's IM threads burned with urgent messages, but it wasn't long before a solution had been devised, once shadowradio sent out a spam requesting information on the cheat. The SSG's new strategy was to pump up the volume. An SSG member familiar with the bug also knew that loud "noises" in the game would awaken a sleeping Sim, so SSG operatives returned to the Sclafani house carrying the game's version of laptop computers, playing loud music on them. When the mafiosi awakened, they were tagged.

The web of communications that let the SSG respond to the tagging of DJPurplebunny and solve the problem of the sleepwalking Mafia was a fascinating example of player-organized governance structures in TSO. But of even more interest was the command structure of the SSG itself. Ronan, Uri knew, was a general in the organization, high up in the SSG command. But Uri was surprised to see that shadowradio2003 apparently outranked Ronan, and almost seemed to be the nerve center or central switchboard for the SSG. Shadowradio wasn't the Overlord Snow White, Uri knew. But who was it?

A few days later, the Herald published an interview with SSG Overlord Snow White in which she described the problems the Shadow Government was battling. "We are basically a large body of Sims that are fighting for the same cause: to keep Alphaville a happy place for Sims to live." Besides targeting scammers like Evangeline, the SSG also had a "no Mafia" policy that sought to run crime families out of town. To illustrate the potential problems, Snow White described her experience on another TSO server, Fancy Fields:

Snow White: We all see what the Mafias have done to the other cities.

Urizenus: What has it done to other cities?

Snow White: Well, Blazing Falls for instance. It has Mafia family names all over the map, with this Mafia OWNZ that mafia. It's a mess. I moved to Fancy Fields from Alphaville, and lived there for about five months. I saw what cities with Mafias are like. It is no fun for Sims!

Urizenus: Why is it no fun? Isn't it just role-play?

Snow White: I had the #1 house in Fancy Fields for months, my roomies and I worked very hard to get it there. Then, one day, a Mafia decides that they want me to move to their neighborhood and sell them the house. When I refused, I felt the repercussions. They would come to my house and empty the buffet all over the house, slap visitors, enemy-link myself and my roomies. They would even go so far as to berate visitors to try and get them to leave.

Urizenus: And you feel this continues to be a widespread problem in many cities?

Snow White: Yes, I have been thanked on many occasions for keeping [Alphaville] free of Mafia, even by the Mafia families in other cities. It is nice for them to be able to come to a neutral city to get away from all the fighting. It can be rather tiresome not being able to go to any house that you want, or to mingle with everyone, in fear of an enemy link.[1]

The SSG also ran "outreach" programs to help underprivileged Sims, and held contests with cash awards for things like "spookiest" house. But as Uri probed deeper, startling facts about the SSG came to light. With several hundred members, Snow White claimed the organization had one or more undercover agents as roommates in each of the top twenty houses in all of the game's leader board categories. Agents fed information about scammers and other "bad" Sims to the SSG Executive Branch, which would then contact the avatar in question and decide on what action to take. Red-tagging was the usual punishment for those found to be transgressing on the SSG's accepted forms of behavior, but stiffer penalties were also possible, such as having a Sim banned from all houses where the SSG had an agent—in effect banning them from the most vibrant locations in the game. Of course, the banned player could always return under an alt, but the SSG was on the lookout for alts as well. "If you identify someone as a re-created bad sim," Uri asked, "do you banish them immediately, or do you give them another chance?"

"I always have an open line of communication," Snow White told him. "I always try to talk to them first. I can generally tell by the first few words whether they will be good or bad."

In addition to banning players from top properties, more draconian measures were available in the SSG arsenal. One strategy was borrowed from griefers themselves: SSG agents would follow avatars all over Alphaville and report them every time they misstepped, or, as Uri learned later, they might even use access to Maxis employees to complain about certain Sims. If the case was serious, SSG generals sometimes instructed an army of avatars to bombard a Sim with roommate invitations. If the target accidentally clicked "accept" instead of "refuse" while clearing their screen of the dozens of invites, they stood in danger of losing their own home as they automatically became a roommate in the SSG property—from which they were, of course, expelled within seconds.

And in the most extreme cases, the SSG would call in Master Bam. Master Bam had been expunged from the SSG by the time Uri caught up with him—he had been a loose cannon, prone to attacking avatars for reasons as slim as the fact that he didn't happen to like their looks (in many cases because they resembled him). In his day, however, he had been an important asset to the organization ("the balls of the SSG," as he referred to himself). Uri's interview with him was another eye-opener.

Urizenus: What was your position in the SSG?

Master Bam: Commander of the Crime Bureau and 4 Star general in everything else except intelligence, something I wasn't born with.

Urizenus: lol. What are the responsibilities of the Commander of the Crime Bureau?

Master Bam: I set up the demo (tearing down houses) of the real bad people. I usually just tore them down myself.

Urizenus: How were you able to do that?

Master Bam: You be nice to the owner of the house or seduce them [by] being a girl (usually the bad guy being a male) and tell them you're gonna build them something. Then when they're not there, BOOM!

Urizenus: How many houses did you demo?

Master Bam: For SSG, probably about 20.[2]

Given some of their tactics and tacticians, it is tempting to think that the SSG was merely trying to stamp out its rivals. But to Uri there was more going on. As he was learning, much of the activity in TSO was within social structures that were not designed into the platform, but which had been constructed by the users themselves. What was really happening was that a shared culture was developing on the blank slate that was EA's software—a culture created almost entirely by the TSO user base. TSO's mafiosi wanted the game to be about control, about power wrested through the use of what rudimentary weaponry the game provided. The SSG wanted their virtual world to be about law and order and the use of that weaponry to maintain a semblance of peace (or so it claimed). To Uri, it was less a Manichean collision of the "good" and "bad" elements of TSO's population than it was a struggle to determine the nature of online life itself.

That struggle was made possible, in part, by EA's hands-off approach to managing the world of The Sims Online. In fact, Snow White claimed that Maxis, the EA subsidiary that ran TSO, supported the SSG's efforts in Alphaville. "We have received many comments from them on how productive we are in keeping the city thriving," she told Uri.

"Are any Maxis employees members of SSG?" Uri asked.

"No comment."

Could it be that the SSG had more power than the company itself? What did it mean that a vigilante organization that could make life miserable for certain players was apparently being endorsed by the company behind the game? Of course, Maxis and EA also tacitly endorsed the activities of the scammer Evangeline, the SSG's #1 Most Wanted. "They feel that her occupation as a thief is an acceptable one," Snow White reported.

Here was the social aspect of MMOs at work, though in ways Uri had never expected to find. Electronic Arts had failed to produce much in the way of vital, engaging content, but TSO's residents could always find ways to make online life more interesting—whether through capricious red-tagging, self-appointed police organizations, newbie scams, pet-culling operations, or business dealings that straddled the divide between the real and virtual worlds. To enhance the game, residents found themselves banding together into Mafias and shadow governments, and creating their own games, with their own ill-defined rules, within TSO. And while EA rightly condoned such creativity in gameplay, the company also appeared to be playing one side against the other. In the end, the society that was developing within TSO had less to do with the architecture of the game itself and far more to do with the personalities involved—including those of the EA employees responsible for managing the game.

To the *Herald*'s editor, this kind of thing was exactly what he'd come looking for. Little did he know that the rabbit hole had yet more secrets to divulge, and they were secrets that, to his surprise, went beyond the bounds of the game itself. The day after his interview with Snow White appeared, Uri received an instant message from shadowradio2003, congratulating him on the interview—and, for a moment at least, deepening the mystery behind the organization:

shadowradio2003: Do you know who I am?

Urizenus: Nope.

shadowradio2003: I play [Star Wars Galaxies] now, but I was one of the typists for Mia Wallace.

The founder of the SSG had been a Sim named Mia Wallace whose typist, Uri now discovered, was actually two people, a husband and wife who had been in TSO since its pre-release beta-testing phase and who alternated playing the Mia Wallace character (much to the confusion of the Sims that Mia would flirt with). In the early days of TSO's release, Mia Wallace ran a property known as the Sims Sorority House. Always full of female Sims and the men who came to court them, the Sorority House held firmly at the top of the game's property rankings, Mia's female typist told Uri in an interview.[3] As Uri learned in talking to Mia (both male and female), the SSG had not sprung entirely from the desire to protect Alphaville's helpless Sims; it had actually had its earliest origins in a vengeful conflict for the top spot in the game's rankings. And it was a conflict in which the notorious Evangeline sat squarely in the middle.

Soon after the game was officially released, Mia Wallace began to receive Instant Messages from a female Sim named Roxy Merrill, mocking Mia as a Suzy Homemaker and Martha Stewart and eventually threatening to knock her out of the top rankings spot. Roxy's roommates would pay annoying visits to the Sorority House, harrassing visitors and attempting to red-link Mia. Roxy's own property, the Hotel Erotica, was half a dozen spots behind the Sorority House, and Roxy wanted the top spot badly.

So Mia took action, and the concept behind the SSG—if not yet the organization itself—was born. Whether Mia sought revenge for Roxy's abusive visits or simply wanted to forestall any potential threat to her place in the rankings isn't clear. But she did move swiftly against her new enemy, sending a friend on an alt named SuperSimette to infiltrate Roxy's house by becoming a roommate there.

What Mia's operative found when she arrived was a bit more than most people knew was going on in a suburb like Alphaville. The Hotel Erotica had set itself up as a house of cyber-prostitution, and to become a roommate there you had to pass a test.

To become a roommate in most houses in TSO involved an interview of some sort. Usually this involved just a few questions about how often you were planning to be in the game and whether you'd be willing to help keep the house open to receive visitors. But Roxy's interviews were different. According to Mia, her questions included things like, "Explain to me how you'd suck a good dick, and be elaborate." Essentially, Roxy wanted to know that her roommates could type, as Uri put it, "descriptively." As the madame of a cyber-brothel, she had to know that her girls could perform.

SuperSimette was apparently quite the typist, and passed the interview with flying colors. The interviewer congratulated her with high praise: "You are as good a whore as I've seen in an interview in a long time."

But SuperSimette had no intention of actually cybering with any of Roxy's clients. Instead, using the strategy that would later be deployed so effectively by Master Bam, she waited until she was alone in the Hotel

Erotica and then summoned her friends from the Sims Sorority House. Being a Hotel Erotica roomie gave her the ability to build—or tear down—structures on the property. So the sorority sisters demolished the Hotel Erotica and replaced it with four swimming pools that together spelled out the word SLUT.

"It was beautiful," Mia's female typist told Uri. But the Sorority House wasn't finished. They immediately filed an abuse report with Maxis, claiming to have "discovered" an obscene build. When Maxis saw the architectural epithet, they deleted it without notice. Mia's operatives simply rebuilt the "slut pool" and called Maxis again. Maxis arrived and deleted the build again, only to have the sorority sisters rebuild the pool one more time and re-report it. This time, the company dished out a 72-hour ban to all the roommates in the Hotel Erotica. (Because SuperSimette was an alt, her typist didn't really care.) The SSG had won its first victory even before it had been formed.

Roxy Merrill, expectedly, was not pleased. But just as the episode was giving the SSG a germinal shape, it was also helping to shape one of the SSG's worst nemeses, for Roxy was to drop out of the scene and then return with a series of different avatars until she eventually became the notorious Evangeline, proprietor of the Free-Money for Newbies house that was anything but.

Roxy continued to harass Mia Wallace. Eventually, after several heated conversations both within the game and via email, one of Mia's typists apparently dropped the right (or wrong) hint, and Roxy was able to guess the password to the Mia Wallace account—and to delete or steal practically everything associated with it. "Mia Wallace was a dumb ho and I fucked her ass up," Roxy's typist told Uri during the *Herald*'s interview with Evangeline. Roxy also claimed that it had been Mia who had become jealous, after the Hotel Erotica knocked the Sim Sorority House out of the top spot. But that sequence of events was impossible to confirm. Roxy's patter made for good copy in any case: "Left Mia Wallace broke and homeless, no money, no simmy, no objects. Moved her ass to a tiny, empty one-square lot. I could have made her go poof but I left her to suffer."

Uri's two-part interview with Evangeline[4] (aka Roxy, aka Voleur) covered the early history of her conflict with Mia Wallace and the formation of the

SSG. But what was more intriguing to most *Herald* readers were the details that came to light about Evangeline herself, and the nature of the cyber-brothel Roxy/Evangeline claimed to have run in TSO.

Evangeline told a hard-luck story of "growing up" on the gritty streets of beta-period TSO, when "everyone was new and innocent." She related this tale in a kind of sing-song, rap-reminiscent style. "I was strolling the places with no purpose. I lived in the ghetto, a bad neighborhood in Sims."

But soon enough, she hit on her calling:

Urizenus: What was your first character in-game?

Evangeline: Roxy Merrill

Urizenus: And she set up the first brothel, on October 11, 2002?

Evangeline: Yes, back when TSO was filled with homeless disgusting people. Everyone was new and innocent. Many people say I brought sin into TSO. I don't care. Sex sells, and it was my goal to create the greatest cybersex house.

Urizenus: How soon after you came into the game did you open the cyber-brothel?

Evangeline: First day, I started recruiting.

Urizenus: So you knew as soon as you got in that that is what you wanted to do?

Evangeline: Yes. I was never a skill person. I needed money. Why skill when you can suck dick to keep food on the plate?

Urizenus: Good point![5]

So much for doing the dishes and saving for a bigger split level. Though those might be interesting activities in the context of TSO's advertised gameplay, it was clear now that much, much more was at work here than just the "home tactics" game that Will Wright had originally envisioned.

Evangeline's Hotel Erotica was not a place for the faint of heart, and certainly not for the many teenagers who were Electronic Arts's customers in the game. While the slow-dance animation sufficed for most virtual sex in TSO, the Hotel Erotica was different. According to Evangeline, her girls (many of whom were reportedly adolescent boys in real life) were the most graphic, dirtiest-talking Sims in creation, and were so much in demand that a waiting list had formed for their services. "No one could get the customers to cum like us," she told Uri. From the sound of things, Evangeline was a demanding madame. As Mia's operative had found, she interviewed her girls by having them demonstrate their cyber-sexual prowess on a private chat channel—which was the best way to arouse another typist, after all. Evangeline claimed to have charged her customers up to 500,000 simoleans for her girls' services—the equivalent of about $50 at the time—a princely sum for a service that consisted of no more than a few crude cartoon interactions and several minutes of X-rated chat appearing on your screen. (Then again, as an economist friend of Ludlow's at the University of Michigan remarked at the time, compared to the cost of phone sex it was pretty much fair market value.)

Exactly who Evangeline's customers were was also a tantalizing question. Outraged neighbors had reported the Hotel Erotica to the authorities (i.e., EA and Maxis), Evangeline said, but, "It didn't work cuz Maxis was eating my pussy alllllll night."

"Does that mean you had Maxis employees as customers?" Uri asked.

"Possibly."

That a suburban bedroom community like The Sims Online should have a brothel in its midst was no surprise. Nor was it surprising, if you took the metaphor a step further, that the city fathers might avail themselves of its services. But if it was true, here again was an example of the game becoming more powerful than its designers. Not only had TSO's players created a culture that produced more than its developers had ever expected, but they created a culture so powerful that those charged with managing that culture were willing to turn a blind eye to their own rules in order to experience it—if Evangeline was to be believed.

Since Evangeline had since moved on from her cyber-brothel to the Free-Money for Newbies house, Uri had no way to directly verify any of the history she was serving up. It was clear that the Hotel Erotica had existed and had been one of the most highly rated houses in Alphaville. A Website still advertised it as a place "where intimacy knows no bounds and where desire knows no rules. One night of wreckless sexual abandonment. A night you can still taste years after the sun comes up." But it was the only top property that no one but its enemies could remember going to.

Part of Urizenus's curiosity stemmed from the question of whether the Hotel Erotica had actually been another scam house. Cyber-prostitution and cyber-brothels are fairly common in online worlds, and in adults-only online worlds, where they can come out of hiding, they are generally among the most popular locations. This was no surprise; sex is one of the first applications for any new technology, and in an online game where part of the attraction is living out a fantasy life, many players like the idea of swapping their daily realities for the life of a prostitute or pimp or mack daddy john. But given the popularity of cyber-prostitution and the money changing hands, scams naturally emerged in which sexual services were advertised, money taken, and nothing given in return. Knowing Evangeline's record and reputation, Uri wondered if the Hotel Erotica hadn't been something of a scam itself.

When Uri asked whether Evangeline had tried to confirm that her working girls were at least eighteen years old, he got a startling response: "Fuck that shit, I ain't even 18." TSO was meant for ages thirteen and up, but by now it was clear to Uri that the age barrier didn't anticipate very many of the possible developments in a place like Alphaville. When Uri probed Evangeline for details of her typist's life, he found she was an avid collector of Disney memorabilia from tales like *Snow White, The Little Mermaid* and *Sleeping Beauty*.

"Not to sound like a bigot, but isn't that odd stuff for a guy to collect?" Uri asked.

"You believe I'm a guy?"

"Aren't you? You type like one."

"I hate stereotypes," Evangeline said. "They make me want to throw up. My Sim is wonderful, I love being her. I can't be mean in real life like I can in TSO."

While the idea that teenage boys were selling cybersex for money caught the attention of *Herald* readers, Uri felt the more troubling issue was behavior he himself had witnessed while visiting the Free-Money for Newbies house. Donning an alt, he had dropped in on the property to find a female newbie, whose avatar appeared to be African American, caged on the property and being humiliated by Evangeline and her roommates. The Free Money roomies continued to verbally abuse the newbie, calling her a monkey, among other things, until Uri sent the newb an instant message with instructions on how to free herself. In the interview, Evangeline was unapologetic.

"Newbies are so disgusting, they're the bane of my Sim life," she told him, falling into her rap patter. "I fuck a newbie just for practice, give a fake address and play like an actress. The freezer is for fools who don't shut up." The freezer was "a small, narrow room with a vent, old food and a porta-potty." Newbies who had earned Evangeline's disfavor were lured inside, and if you were unfamiliar with the mechanics of TSO it could be difficult to get out. Van apparently couldn't stomach avatars she found unattractive, especially those on which she couldn't make out the Sim's eyes. "If I can't see your eyes, you're ugly. And when you don't obey, I'll cage you like an animal and have people laugh at your ugly ass."

Many of those caged had dark-skinned avatars, as Uri had witnessed. "Not my fault people decide to be ugly Sims that are so black you can't see their eyes," Van protested.

In real life, Evangeline was indeed a teenaged boy, which threw the "interviews" Roxy/Evangeline put her girls through into a different light. After the *Herald*'s articles on the Hotel Erotica appeared, the *Detroit Free Press* managed a brief interview with Evangeline's typist's angry mother in early 2004.[6] While Evangeline's RL details shed some dim light on his motivations, the more important issue, as far as Uri was concerned, was the lack of action on the part of Electronic Arts to stem things like cyber-prostitution, theft, and overt racism in an environment meant for thirteen-year-olds. But just as in the Case of the Broken Jaw, the company refused to acknowledge that there was even a problem. EA spokesman Jeff Brown claimed the game was no more seamy or dangerous than watching television. "Regardless of what people might be messaging to one another, it is impossible for the characters themselves to do anything more intimate than dance or lie in a bed," he said.[7]

It was another indication that the game company had little or no idea about what was actually possible in TSO, or about the nature of virtual worlds themselves. Jeff Brown preferred to hide behind his software. To him—and his was the official company line—if it wasn't part of the software, it wasn't part of the game.

But in virtual worlds—in all interactive entertainment, in fact—that's just not true. The software provides only an architecture: It provides both the mechanical abilities with which one navigates the world, and the "physical" attributes of the world itself. But what the game itself will be is determined by much more than that. Software can guide gameplay to a greater or lesser extent—in Pong, to take an extreme example, players have only a very few options, whether they choose to follow the rules of the game or not. A relatively open world like TSO provides its residents with a vast array of choices. And each one of these choices becomes part of the experience of the game. This is true not just for the player making the choice, but for all those who come into contact with that player, and even for those who have never met him or her but are only touched by the indirect effects of those choices. Even before Uri met Evangeline he had heard tales of her misbehavior. Just knowing that Alphaville housed this singular criminal changed the game for him. In a sense, the mechanics of the virtual world were unimportant. As in Shakespeare, the play is the thing.

But the king seemed to have no conscience. Jeff Brown, who was fast becoming the guy Uri loved to hate, couldn't see past the castle walls formed by TSO's server farm. As Uri was discovering, however, what was going on in TSO actually extended far beyond those bounds.

When the Sim Sorority House was torn down by Evangeline, Mia and her sorority sisters evolved into something very different. After a Sim named JC Soprano made a failed attempt to extort money from the Sorority House, Mia and her friends became the Wallace Family Mafia and briefly joined forces with Soprano's Mafia family, the Sim Mafia, in a virtual crime syndicate. But the nature of that particular mini-game hadn't appealed to Mia, she said. The Sim Mafia fulfilled the role they had chosen, shaking down casino properties for "taxes," for example, Mia said. "We never did extortions or demanded money from Sims for protection," she told Uri. "We were more geared toward griefing the griefer. We were just targeting those that were targeting us, namely any player that wanted to randomly Instant Message me or anyone on my web [of friendship or enemy links] and start causing trouble."

The Wallace Family's operations seemed to be a bit broader than that, however. "I won't lie and say that I never requested back-up against a known Alphaville griefer," Mia told Uri. "I did do that. But it wasn't against unknowing or undeserving individuals."

Who deserved to have their property infiltrated and torn down, though, was an open question. Mia and her friends found that the tactics that had worked against Roxy/Evangeline would work against other Sims. Soon enough, they broke with JC Soprano and formed a new organization, the Sim Shadow Government. "There was always talk of Maxis instilling the idea of actual government into the game," Mia said. "So if they did that, we'd still have a place in Alphaville."

Before Uri moved the *Herald* to the Shadow Government's neighborhood, he had received an earful about the SSG from his neighbors in Rose Thorn Gardens, but not just from the darksiders. Several of the avatars that came to visit the Church of Mephistopheles were under the control of a typist who was also a frequenter of the TSO chat boards and message forums. Known most often in TSO as Dyerbrook, he dropped in on Uri from time to time to warn him of the dangers of associating with the BDSM crowd. He at one point hoaxed the *Herald* into interviewing a "spoof Sim" he had created that was really Dyerbrook's typist posing as a fifteen-year-old "witch" in Texas. And, as Uri learned, Dyerbrook was also one of the most notorious forum posters to be found on the TSO boards.

For players who want a venue to express more than they can within the virtual reality of a game world, there are any number of Web-based forum sites and bulletin boards devoted to various MMOs, on which players post their impressions and opinions of "life" online. Though they are simply strings of conversations about particular games, what lurks not far beneath the surface is an atmosphere of venom and self-promotion that can do much to poison one's experience of a game—and which at times raises important questions about free speech in cyberspace.

Dyerbrook's presence on the TSO forums took the form of eye-poppingly long posts filled with charges of favoritism and even conspiracy on the part of the game's owners and management. It was the Sims Shadow Government that was receiving all the special treatment, according to Dyerbrook, and it was his self-appointed task to bring light to the shadows. On the forums and on his Sims Out of Line Website,[8] Dyerbrook detailed the special treatment certain Sims allegedly received, and offered the help of his Lightsavers organization ("a partisan liberation movement dedicated to freeing TSO of the Sim Shadow Government and all its works") to "victims" of the SSG. Sims Out of Line also chronicled "raids" by the Lightsavers, in several of which Dyerbrook delivered lamps to SSG properties with the hope that they might symbolically "disperse the shadows."

To Dyerbrook, the SSG was a hegemonic, collectivist machine that sought to wrap all of Alphaville, and even lands beyond, under its auspices. Dyerbrook was further outraged to find that Mia Wallace had received a friendship link from Will Wright, whose vision stood behind all the Sim games, from SimCity to The Sims Online. To Dyerbrook, this was a clear sign of corruption and favoritism on the part of Maxis and Electronic Arts.

Though Dyerbrook's posts probably overstated the problem, the complaint is not an unfamiliar one in MMOs. Just as forum moderators are often drawn from the community of posters, "game masters" and "liaisons"—in-world characters responsible for guiding players through the world or toward quests, and for policing things like profanity and abuse—are often drawn from the community of veteran players. The danger of such a practice is that GMs will sometimes give special treatment to friends they've made in the game, leaving new players or those with fewer connections at a distinct disadvantage.

Even if game managers never knighted special players or elevated them to the level of demigods, it is probably inevitable that a Brahmin class of players will emerge in any virtual world. The social-software guru Clay Shirky has fleshed out the picture, suggesting that a kind of elite inner core will almost always form in online environments: "A pattern will arise in which there is some group of users that cares more than average about the integrity and success of the group as a whole. And that becomes your core group, Art Kleiner's phrase for 'the group within the group that matters most.'"[9]

In Shirky's view this kind of formation is a good thing: "In all successful online communities that I've looked at, a core group arises that cares about and gardens effectively. Gardens the environment, to keep it growing, to keep it healthy."

Dyerbrook, Evangeline, and many of the darksiders in TSO were having none of this. In their view, the SSG, and not Evangeline, was the true evil force within the game. This set up a tension that would dominate the narrative structure of Alphaville for the first two years of its existence.

The SSG raised fascinating questions about the nature of online societies. The *Herald*'s interview with SSG Overlord Snow White had been picked up by several Websites and blogs, including *Terra Nova*,[10] a multi-authored blog featuring many well-respected academics and game developers. There, a comment by someone called Euphrosyne drew the inevitable real-world comparison: "Paying your monthly fee to [a game company], who then lets a self-organized posse administer its own in-game justice, is like paying income tax to the federal government, who then lets local gangs rule the place."

But the SSG was more than just an in-world posse. Mia Wallace may have set the SSG up originally as the vigilante police force of Alphaville, but as Snow White told Urizenus, things had since grown considerably: "We are in [the MMO] Star Wars Galaxies as well, and there have been several people asking to take it into [the MMO] There.com."

As Euphrosyne pointed out, the SSG was an organization that wielded its power across many virtual worlds but was based in no one particular world. This was an unprecedented development in virtual politics, and one that has important ramifications for the virtual worlds of today and the future. As Uri had seen, there was real money to be made in places like The Sims Online, Second Life, and even traditional MMOs like Ultima Online and EverQuest II. There was a real emotional investment that people undertook when they entered an online world; there was even something approaching sex. MMO companies were either unwilling or unable to police these worlds, nor was it clear that they should. But what would happen if a force like the SSG gained real control of a virtual society and its economy—not to mention more than one?

This was an issue that gnawed at Peter Ludlow. That October, at The State of Play, a conference on law and virtual worlds sponsored by Yale Law School and New York Law School, he discussed such questions with people like Clay Shirky and economist Edward Castronova. The conference was still very much on his mind when Uri interviewed Snow White, and it yielded, in his opinion, one of the most interesting responses of any interview he had done:

Urizenus: The case of SSG came up at The State of Play conference in New York a couple weeks ago. [We] were musing about the possibility of users completely taking control of the game and forcing the owner to capitulate. I offered SSG as a possible mechanism that could achieve enough control to do this.

Snow White: Oh, wouldn't that be sweet! If there was something serious enough, we would possibly consider it. But as of yet, we have been able to do everything we need on our own, without much intervention from Maxis.[11]

In real economic and societal terms, the development of virtual worlds is still in its infancy, and the prospect of a self-appointed group of users gaining control over a virtual world doesn't present much of a threat. But given how fast the population of virtual worlds is growing, and how important they can be to their residents, both socially and economically, it is only a matter of time before the online public may have to grapple with these questions. And depending on who it is that takes control, they may be questions that will need answering in a particularly urgent way.

9 "Cyber Me, Baby!": Sex, Love, and Software in the Virtual World

As Uri was drawn deeper into the game-within-the-game that was playing out in The Sims Online, his typist Peter Ludlow grew more fascinated by the complex web of social structures that had developed on TSO's Alphaville server. But there was another set of secrets that seemed to fascinate *Herald* readers and Ludlow's friends just as much, if not more. The first question out of anyone's mouth once they learned about Evangeline was simple: "What in God's name goes on in a cyber-brothel?!" The answer, of course, was cybersex—and not just cybersex, but cybersex for money.

Among the first uses of any new technology is sex. Almost as soon as the camera was invented, in the early nineteenth century, enterprising early photographers wasted no time in convincing curvaceous young women and eager young men to disrobe in front of their lenses. (Some of these images rival contemporary pornography in their explicitness.) Film, video, and the Internet all saw similar forays into licentiousness soon after they were developed. Virtual worlds experienced the same phenomenon. The question was how to take advantage of the technology to simulate sex in an environment devoid of physicality.

Ludlow had seen early examples of cybersex in the text-based MUDs, virtual communities, and CompuServe forums he'd visited in the mid-1980s, long before the first graphical MMO lit up. Every once in a while, he'd drop in on a chat room only to find that the people there were going at it hot and heavy—at least, by keyboard. (People in other, more platonic chat channels restricted themselves to merely typing ⟨hugz⟩ back and forth to each other.) With the advent of 3-D graphical virtual worlds, though, it seemed the time was ripe for those so inclined to take the technology to places it had never been before.

Cybersex—or, as it's sometimes called, tinysex, netsex, or just plain cyber—is one of the most popular activities in social MMOs like TSO, There, and Second Life, and is not unheard of in combat-oriented games like EverQuest and World of Warcraft. The simplest way to describe it is as one-handed dirty typing. In a way, cyber is analogous to phone sex: Just as phone sex consists of exchanging descriptive phrases to help bring a conversational partner to orgasm, cybersex has the same goal but uses text-based conversation rather than voice.

There are, of course, natural limitations to cyber. With no physical or audio contact and no olfactory information, the sensory input is limited, and visual cues are constrained by the limited ways in which you can dress, undress, and animate the avatars involved. Even if TSO players could have undressed their Sims completely (they couldn't: underwear could not be taken off), all they would have seen were the blurred squares that appeared on-screen to obscure their genitalia whenever Sims used the toilet. Yet cyber in TSO and other virtual worlds has some very enthusiastic supporters. And it is surprising how far the simple sharing of words and ideas can go in arousing a partner.

"As any but the most inhibited of newbies can tell you, [cybersex is] possibly the headiest experience the very heady world of MUDs has to offer," wrote journalist Julian Dibbell in 1993, before the dawn of graphical MMOs. "Amid flurries of even the most cursorily described caresses, sighs and penetrations, the glands do engage, and often as throbbingly as they would in a real-life assignation—sometimes even more so, given the combined power of anonymity and textual suggestiveness to unshackle deep-seated fantasies. And if the virtual setting and the interplayer vibe are right, who knows? The heart may engage as well, stirring up passions as strong as many that bind lovers who observe the formality of trysting in the flesh."[1]

Not only is there the possibility of arousal, as Dibbell noted, and not only can it lead to real-life romance, but cyber sometimes holds clear practical advantages over many real-life sexual liaisons. After all, cyber is nothing if not safe sex; there is zero chance of becoming pregnant, catching a disease, going home with a psycho, or waking up beside a complete stranger. Beyond that, cyber allows one to pursue fantasies that might be impossible in real life for reasons of health, physical disability, location, or reputation. A married homemaker, a grade-school principal, or a Supreme Court justice probably wouldn't want to get too frisky with an acquaintance in real life.

But behind the cloak of anonymity an MMO can provide, it's much easier to pull out all the stops. And when you tire of your partner, it's easy enough to get rid of him or her: If you can't disengage without a fuss, just set your user interface to ignore anything they say (as many games let players do). If that doesn't work, turn off your computer for a few days until the coast is clear.

Of course, the flip side of the coin is that you don't know what your cybersex partner looks like in real life. He or she might be the last person you'd be attracted to. What's interesting about that, though, is that cybersex has the potential to level the playing field in many ways. Though someone may be picky in real life, cybering may open the door to a host of new potential partners and possibilities.

What Uri found in talking to people in TSO was that cybersex isn't usually a way to fill a gap in a real-world sex life so much as it is a way to spice things up in an environment that is safe by comparison, and which in some ways offers more possibility than can be found in the real world. Cybersex is different from traditional pornography. Instead of buying a magazine or renting a video and passively reading or watching what it contains, this is an interactive pursuit that entails active participation on the part of those involved in it, is often practiced by people who were already acclimatized to the new interactive medium they inhabited. Just as gamers in online worlds can be very adept at using their creativity to build on the limited narratives game companies provide, the same highly creative people can take their online sex lives to places that few who haven't been there would imagine.

As Uri discovered, what happened at Evangeline's cyber-brothel, according to reports, though outrageous in theory, was actually pretty tame compared to what took place when avatars slipped into an Instant Message channel and began chatting each other up. Of course, not every virtual hook-up sent the sparks flying. Like sex and romance in the physical world, good cybering requires skill, experience, imagination, and sensitivity to one's partner.

Cybersex turns out to be guided by many of the principles that guide online interactions of a more casual nature. Just as in talking to someone in a game there is a kind of rhythm to the conversation, so too there is a natural rhythm to cyber. You don't want to type on endlessly, and you don't want to abandon the keyboard for too long. You need to be creative and interesting, but you also need to give your partner a chance to steer the "conversation" as well. You need to be flexible, and you need to respond to whatever your partner might toss into the mix. Can you steer your partner away from a particularly disturbing idea? Do you want to?

Cybersex purists hold that their virtual version of physical intimacy should remain text-based, and that the visual dimension provided by graphics-based games is nothing but a distraction. But purists are as hard to find online as they are in real life, and gamers have routinely pushed the limits of game technology to provide visual aids for their online sexual encounters.

In games like TSO, where no user-created content is permitted, players can't get much more sexy than whatever the game's software allows. The most suggestive action a Sim can perform is the not-very-suggestive slow-dance animation. The coin-operated "love beds" EA added into the game were generally agreed not to be conducive to cybering. Once the meter on the bed was paid, the avatars automatically dove under the covers and started thrashing around and making animal noises, but soon their time was up and the bed had to be paid again. TSO's hot tubs, with their built-in massage animation, were slightly better. But for the most part people preferred to cyber unencumbered by the mechanics of the game itself. It was hard enough to type with one hand without having to also click your mouse to keep the game going.

To enhance the fantasy, users did manage to create programs that could make things appear more interesting. Most TSO residents learned early on that there was a free third-party software add-on available from Kingware-Software.net that could make avatars look nude, provided they wore the correct clothing. As a result, it wasn't unusual to find a large number of female avatars walking around in the yellow "showgirl" outfit, as that was one of the outfits that could be rendered nude to someone running the add-on.

While Electronic Arts was fond of saying that the worst thing avatars could do in TSO was to lie in bed together, TSO users found plenty of things they could do beyond having their nude avatars slow dance or play in the hot tub. One option was to build a narrow hallway and have two Sims walk toward each other. Unable to pass, the Sims would bump up against each other in a fair approximation of sex animation—especially if they were running the nude skin feature. A similar strategy involved placing a nude female avatar in front of a urinal, facing away, and sending a nude male avatar to use the bathroom there. Again, a reasonable sex animation would result, though this one with overtones of golden showers.

Such techniques were valued more for their humor than for anything else; the real action took place in chat, with the game architecture simply providing the right atmosphere—a bordello motif, perhaps, or dungeon chic. The avatars engaged in cyber might be slow dancing, bathing in a hot tub together, or sitting next to each other in a dungeon cell, it didn't much matter. As elaborate a visual fantasy as one could create, cyber was nothing without the chat line.

Some people did take things a step further, using a voice-over-IP service like TeamSpeak, Ventrilo, or Skype to achieve something much closer to phone sex. Some even made use of Webcam links to send real-life visuals in one or both directions, taking cybersex almost completely out of the realm of the online world. But the initial connection was still made within TSO, and as *Herald* gossip columnist Pat the Rat found, some Alphaville residents had earned reputations as sought-after Webcammers, reportedly making up to $50 for a session of exhibitionism.[2]

Even beyond Webcamming, there was a distant dream known as *teledildonics*. This dream came true in Second Life in the summer of 2005, when one Second Life resident wrote a software interface that allowed an avatar to send signals through the world to a game console controller, which could be hacked to operate a vibrator or other sex toy that a cyber-partner could then control.[3] For the most part, though, residents relied on the chat lines for their jollies, and being a "descriptive" typist was good enough for daily life in TSO.

The fact that "sex" in virtual worlds consisted mostly of text-based chat and was not all that easy to master didn't keep people from cybering away. Uri, however, was slow in coming to understand how widespread the practice was, in spite of hearing constant tales of cyber-sessions from his friends in TSO. Not only was hooking up in the game more common than he'd realized; it took some time for it to dawn on him that many of the visitors at *Herald* headquarters in Rose Thorn Gardens were there for precisely that reason. The newspaper's offices were located in a neighborhood notorious for its sexual goings-on, yet Uri was often surprised to find female avatars hanging around the *Herald* offices for hours on end. What they might want there he couldn't fathom, until one of them finally asked him, "So, are we going to get real, or what?" Uri politely declined.

Once he'd grasped how widespread the practice of cyber was, the question of cyber-prostitution still remained. As Uri was to find, the practice of cybering for virtual currency (that is, cybering for money), was not at all unusual in TSO and similar virtual worlds, such as Second Life. In retrospect, the presence of cyber-prositution shouldn't have been surprising. Prostitution is the oldest profession, after all. For many players, having the chance to role-play as a prostitute, a pimp, or a john was an attractive way to live out their fantasies in the safety of the online world.

In TSO, many cyber-prostitutes worked solo, simply advertising their services in their in-game personal profiles. For those who preferred the full-on bordello experience, there was the cyber-brothel option. The cyber-prostitutes Uri interviewed told him they found the experience mostly fun, the downside being that they would occasionally develop feelings for some of their customers, only to have the customers subsequently disappear from the game. They did encounter the odd customer with a request that went too far, but it was certainly easy enough to decline in those cases, or to log out if things got too threatening.

In Second Life, a game that has an official (but not well enforced) minimum age of eighteen, cyber-prostitution is free to come out of the closet, and it does so quite robustly. Many of the most popular properties are dance clubs that openly advertise the availability of cyber-escorts, and in some cases the clubs will openly post the prices for various services. The escorts themselves typically wear a nametag indicating they are available for hire.

Sex and love in the virtual world takes many other forms as well. Some of it is far more kinky, while some of it merely mimics the most loving flavors of sex in the offline world, or the blandest. Sometimes it begins as Sim love and later becomes the kind of relationships any of us could recognize from our own, offline lives. And some of it happens in far more extreme—some would say disturbing—ways, ways that raise further questions about the "laws" of online worlds and the nature of freedom and responsibility in cyberspace.

Perhaps because it's so far removed from reality, cybersex is often found costumed in fantasy in virtual worlds. Around the Rose Thorn Gardens neighborhood in TSO, sexual roleplay often took the form of "lifestyle" BDSM (bondage, domination, sadism, and masochism). Rather than occasional BDSM indulgences in the bedroom, lifestyle BDSMers practice their craft 24/7. Real life, of course, presents obstacles to lifestyle BDSM: Wearing leather fetish wear and being led on a leash by your master as you walk down the aisle at Stop & Shop isn't acceptable to most people. Online, though, masters and collared slaves could be found in all corners of TSO—to the dismay of many who felt that this overt behavior was inappropriate in a game that admitted thirteen-year-olds.

Submissives in TSO could often be seen "kneeling" at the feet of their masters, fetching plates of food, "drawing baths," "warming beds," or cleaning up for those who commanded them. To get some insight into the community, Uri interviewed an anonymous member of the Rose Thorn Garden community. The result was the most heavily commented upon story in the history of the *Herald*. In it, Anonymous detailed the size and organization of the BDSM community (at the time around seventy houses in just one of the BDSM neighborhoods in TSO), and attempted to explain the attraction of the lifestyle, including the common practice of virtual collaring.

Urizenus: What does it mean to be collared?

Anonymous: To my mind, it's a serious thing and not something that should be done lightly. It is a commitment similar to marriage in the vanilla [i.e., non-BDSM] community, and I think it is something that should never be done immediately.

Urizenus: What's the nature of the commitment?

Anonymous: The commitment is for the Dom to promise to protect, guide, teach and love the Sub, and for the Sub to obey, love, trust.[4]

Anonymous also explained that there were elements of political correctness in the community, and that to some, if you weren't a lifestyle BDSMer, you just weren't PC: "Some people are offended with the idea of BDSM only being about sex and not about a complete way of life."

One of the controversial aspects of the interview with Anonymous were the things she had to say about the community members known as the Goreans. As *Herald* readers learned in the interview, the BDSM community in Alphaville came in many flavors. Toward the extreme end one found the Goreans, who based their roleplay on the science-fiction/fetish novels of John Norman. Set on the fictional planet Gor, Norman's books describe a world where sexual slavery is institutionalized and considered the norm.

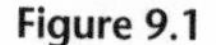

Figure 9.1
Listed prices for escort services at Second Life erotic club

In fact, players have incorporated Gorean roleplay into a number of online games, adopting the social structures, institutions, and in some cases even the language of Gor. While Anonymous was having none of this—comparing it to Star Trek fans who take pains to learn and speak the Klingon language—the Goreans themselves came forward in short order to tell their side of the story to the *Herald*.[5]

"The basics are this," Uri was told by a Gorean dominatrix named Mistress Maria LaVeaux. "Gorean culture is based on the culture of an alien world where slavery is an ingrained and culturally accepted practice. Gorean slaves are primarily, though not exclusively female, while the Masters are primarily, but also not exclusively male. There is a language, a culture, a history that we honor.

"Mainstream BDSM practitioners do have a certain mistrust of us," Mistress LaVeaux continued. "We are viewed as brutal, and uncaring of our slaves' well-being. All patently untrue."

In the same interview, a slave called Toy confirmed her mistress's view. "So many think of Gor as mainly 'by the book,' but that is limiting oneself to really discover what it really is to be Gorean," she said. "Goreans, both men and women, are deeply passionate and emotional people, and openly express that passion. Their deep love for life and freedom of their natural selves is neither hidden or suppressed. Gor is about honesty as to who you are and why. It is a life of free men, women and slaves, a life that's built with honor, trust, respect and loyalty."

Though stories made the rounds of newbies who were unwittingly pressed into service as slaves of various BDSM communities, the Goreans Uri spoke to seemed to feel that, rather than being influenced by the game, the game was merely validating things they already felt. Online life was not a corrupting influence, it was simply an opportunity to live out fantasies that were more difficult to achieve in the real world. "Gor put a name to what I already was," Mistress LaVeaux told him. "It gives substance to what we already are."

What went on in Rose Thorn Gardens was a slightly unusual form of virtual sex, and what went on in the Hotel Erotica was a slightly amoral one, but what went on in TSO in general, with its sexless avatars and limited animations, was only the tip of the iceberg where cybering is concerned. In worlds like Second Life, where residents can create whatever body parts and animations they like, and in the few worlds that are explicitly designed as sexualized, adults-only enclaves, it's much easier to become immersed (so to speak) in the act of cybersex. In those worlds, the image that appears on your computer screen can have as much to do with your level of arousal as the words that are scrolling up your chat box.

The most common vehicles for cybersex in Second Life are the user-created scripted objects known as "sex balls," which put avatars into various sexual positions limited only by their creators' imaginations. Most often, this takes place in structures known as "skyboxes" (termed "Second Life's Mile-High Clubs" by former *Herald* reporter Neal Stewart and intrepid SL adventurer and game developer Pirate Cotton), which float high above the clouds, out of sight of most avatars walking or flying around nearer the surface.

With the freedom to virtualize—if not to reify—any sexual fantasy at all, Second Life's residents have come up with some scenarios that are mighty interesting, to put it politely. The fact that anything is possible in a virtual world—and that the messy real-life consequences of unusual sexual encounters are so easy to avoid—inspires some people to create things they wouldn't otherwise dream of. One's mind expands to fill the possibility space, and some people's sexual urges expand to fill it as well.

So broad are the possibilities that some things that would be startling in real life can come to seem mundane. As in TSO, one of the most popular modes of sexual roleplay in Second Life seems to be bondage and domination. Whips, chains, cages, and similar equipment abound in SL's skyboxes and other private (and sometimes not so private) abodes. Other modes of fetishism can come to seem almost as common. As Pirate Cotton wrote in the *Herald*'s review of Mile-High Clubs, one skybox came complete with "a bad math-solution on the blackboard to 'punish' a student for, all kinds of bent-over poses and props, and an apple on the desk. It was only missing the obligatory schoolgirl. I imagine that's what the cold hard L$ [linden dollars] are for."[6]

While bondage and fetishism are run-of-the-mill in Second Life, other manifestations of residents' sexuality take more unusual, and sometimes scandalous, forms. And as residents' curiosity gets the better of them, the question of privacy in online worlds comes to the fore.

Avatars in Second Life have the ability to zoom in on objects at a distance. With some experience, this can even be used to look through walls and see what is happening behind them. In a sense, the technology of the game allows as much or more of a violation of privacy as is possible in real life. The question that quickly arose was how much privacy avatars were entitled to expect in their private encounters online.

For example, Second Life resident Taco Rubio took advantage of the fact that SL avatars have far more going on between their legs than just blurred-out genitalia, and created an entire museum of screenshots he'd taken while surreptitiously looking up female avatars' skirts.[7] Like the real-life upskirt shots that are often posted on Websites, Taco's upskirt museum caused an enormous outcry in Second Life, with calls for his being banned from the game. (Some of these, however, came from Taco himself, in an effort to draw attention to his museum.)

In his own defense, Taco insisted that avatars are, after all, cartoons. "I think that people in SL get so wrapped up in it that they forget it's not real, and start applying real rules to here," Taco told the *Herald*. "I'd not do this in RL as it would be improper. But I think that improper should be more loosely defined in this world. This should be a freer world than the one we live in." He also argued that, given the large degree of control Second Life granted users over what they could view, no one should be surprised if their virtual genitals ended up in a museum such as his.

For reasons never articulated, the company behind the world shut down Taco's upskirt museum and suspended his account for several days. (In an interesting turnabout, though, they later interviewed Taco's typist for a job at the company.)

The lesson of Taco's upskirt museum was that one avatar's freedom is another's invasion of privacy. And just how much more free virtual worlds should be, if at all, was an open question.

The question also reared its head in the case of Sasami Wishbringer's "slave quarters" at a place called the Fantasy Slave Market. Sasami's avatar was modeled on a Japanese anime character of the same name, a girl with the body of an eight-year-old but who, according to the story, was actually many centuries old, having slept for seven hundred years without aging a day. At the slave market, Sasami offered "hentai" artwork (Japanese cartoon pornography) for sale, featuring the Sasami character in various sexually graphic unions with men, and also offered herself for hire as a sex slave.

Sasami's typist was presumably over eighteen, and no actual children were involved in the production of the images. But opinion in the community was split. Some people found the idea of an apparent eight-year-old sex slave highly offensive, even if the typist was over eighteen. Others, however, took strong offense to the *Herald*'s exposing Sasami, arguing that what Sasami did with her customers was her business. Uri's position was that the *Herald* had only published information that had appeared in public places like the Fantasy Slave Market, one of the leading dance clubs/cyber-brothels, and in Sasami's public profile. The *Herald* also had access to private information about Sasami's typist, which Sasami herself had published in her in-world profile. But Uri revealed only the public behavior of the Sasami avatar, and chose not to publish the information about Sasami's typist.

Regardless, Sasami eventually threatened the *Herald* with legal action, to which Uri could only say, "Bring it on." When the legal threats went nowhere, Sasami attempted to enlist some of the Second Life gangs and Mafias (including BallerMoMo King) to attack the *Herald*, but Uri and the *Herald* staff soon heard about it. Virtual bomb-maker (and cyber-brothel owner) One Song stepped in on behalf of the *Herald* and nipped these efforts in the bud, making it clear to Sasami that the virtual gangsters of Second Life were not going to side with someone who liked to role-play an eight-year-old sex slave.

Given the rich possibilities inherent in Second Life, some groups built up complex social structures around their sexual preferences (or the sexual preferences of their avatars, at any rate). Most of the *Herald*'s Gorean neighbors in TSO (including Toy and her mistress) had emigrated to Second Life by early 2005, as part of a general migration from TSO. (The population of Second Life had surpassed that of TSO by the autumn of 2005.) In Second Life, the Goreans were able to construct a much more elaborate community than had ever existed in TSO, complete with a deep history kept in printed volumes in the Gorean "scribery," a full set of rules and regulations for the behavior of slaves, masters, and "free women" in Gorean territory, a city kennel for disobedient slaves, an elaborate Website,[8] a weekly virtual newspaper called *The Tarn's Feather*, and regular classes and homework assignments for new slaves in training.

Virtual worlds allow for rich sexual fantasies in which residents might be reluctant to engage in the real world, but they also generate sexual customs that are unique to the pixelated universe. The fact that one's physical identity is almost infinitely malleable gives rise to some interesting situations. Second Life avatars don't come with genitalia as part of the standard package, but the tools of the world are such that highly detailed vaginas can be created for female avatars, and male avatars can buy or build penises that will go from flaccid to erect and which can even ejaculate (and what they can ejaculate is limited only by the imagination as well). Many female avatars carry their own set of phalluses that they fit to their male partners before sex. As one SL resident reported, "I never paid for any of my dicks. Girls buy them for me."[9] (Perhaps the detached penis *Herald* editorial director Walker Spaight stumbled across on his SL property one day was part of this wealth of virtual schlongs.)

One of the most popular publications in Second Life is *Players Magazine*, a virtual version of real-world magazines like *Playboy* or *Penthouse*, published by SL resident Marilyn Murphy. The *Herald* has a content-sharing agreement with *Players*, whereby the newspaper features a new "Post Six Grrrl" every week (a play on the page three girls of British tabloids). The Post Six photo spreads produced by Marilyn not only show off some of the most attractive avatars in Second Life (male and female), they are also great examples of what can be done with one's "body" in the hands of an expert. One of Walker's early stories at the *Herald* followed the ingénue model Diamond Hope through "The Making of a Post Six Grrrl," during which he got a graphic illustration of how a veteran SLer can guide a newbie to virtual perfection through the world's appearance interface.

Soon enough, we were wandering around the Players Shack (the Players Mansion having been torn down some time ago). After stripping Di down to her thong, Marilyn cast her weather eye over the av before her. "Did you purchase that shape," Marilyn asked, "or did you do it yourself?"

"No, it's my own," Diamond replied, looking slightly shy.

But Marilyn was pleased: "You did a good job."

I wondered out loud how long it takes to get a girl ready to shoot.

"Frankly, it depends on how well I get on with a girl," Marilyn said. "If she needs a major overhaul, I sometimes just make an av for her. Now I just turn girls away if they are not up to it. There's just no time, and there are a lot of nice well done avs out there now, not like the old days.

"Frankly, Diamond is pretty good just as she is."

But some study was necessary.

"Go into appearance please," Marilyn directed. "Go to torso in shape and tell me the number on your breast gravity. It's right below breast size."

Diamond Hope's breast gravity is 47.

"Good girl," Marilyn said. "Excellent. So many think perky breasts means no gravity, or very little, but the way the Lindens set it up, that is so not the case."

"Now go to legs and tell me what the muscle number is."

Diamond Hope's leg muscles are 80.

"The break at the knee is very pronounced at 80. Make that 50," Marilyn instructed. "You rock, hun, you did way good on her."[10]

In real life, Diamond was a midwestern single mother who would never consider posing nude for an erotica magazine. But in Second Life, she wasn't shy because it wasn't really her. She was pleased as punch to be photographed, not a little flattered by Marilyn's attention and delighted with Walker's article. While virtual sex can sometimes manifest itself in disturbing forms, it can also be a constructive vehicle through which people can safely experience things that might be more threatening in the real world.

Not only that, but when a male named Unmitigated Gall read the article, he was so taken with Di's looks and personality that he contacted her in Second Life and the two began a virtual romance. Months later, they were married—not just in Second Life, but in the real world as well. The *Herald* celebrated its first virtual matchmaking—only to find that the couple broke up a year later.

In both The Sims Online and Second Life, it's not uncommon to happen on an avatar wedding, and on occasion there's a real-life component to the relationship as well. Second Life provides a way to make such relationships "official," a service for which they charge 10 Linden dollars. If you later want a "divorce," however, the company charges 25 Lindens to the avatar requesting the separation. The question of virtual adultery can be tricky as well. Should this be a crime? The question has yet to be answered well in the real world; more than twenty states in the United States consider adultery a criminal offense, yet many people consider it only a civil transgression, or simply a moral one. And if you're married to one person in the real world and to another in the virtual one, what then?

Some online worlds are specifically devoted to sexual pursuits (including no fewer than six that were scheduled to come online in 2006[11]). Sociolotron,[12] for instance, bills itself as "an interactive multiplayer online [role-playing game] for adults only. Furthermore, we take pride in being a highly politically incorrect game." When the game first launched, its Website featured screenshots of avatars in graphically explicit sexual positions. Now those images are censored, but what's behind the black bars is clearly a world where cybersexuality in whatever shape is not just accepted but actively encouraged. Indeed, rape and even gang rape are considered part of normal gameplay in Sociolotron.

Sex in the real world can be one of the most intimate ways people connect. That it can be simulated in cyberspace well enough to raise strong passions—both healthy ones and those less salutary—is testament to the power of virtual worlds. But as people move forward into these places, a number of issues will need to be addressed. You can certainly have your fun in cyberspace, but that collection of pixels may not be as harmless as it seems.

It was becoming clear to Uri that whether the practices were good or bad, no one was really watching. In March 2004, one of his reporters came to him with a story that Evangeline's Free-Money for Newbies property had changed themes. It was still listed in the game's Welcome category, but Evangeline, under the guise of a new avatar named Eve, now claimed to be auditioning newbie Sims for parts in a movie she was supposedly making. Uri sent a newbie reporter named Montserrat Tovar to check out the scene, and the story she returned with provided a good illustration of the kind of sexually transgressive behavior that routinely went unmonitored by Electronic Arts. Montserrat observed,

Eve, on the surface, is a lovely Sim. Dark haired, poised, she presides over her world with a firm hand. Eve is a film director and her house is all about making movies. At the center of this world is a blue room. Eve conducts auditions for her films in this room and once a Sim enters there is no way out. There is a bathtub in the room, a reclining chair, lights, a toilet, and a wardrobe closet. Sims entering the blue room in most cases seem to enter without fully understanding what they've signed up for.

I saw a Sim named Holly enter the blue room thinking that she was about to make a lot of money as an actress for Eve. She entered the blue room and changed into the gold bikini outfit [which appeared "naked" to those running the Kingware Software add-on]. All the female Sims in the blue room are required to wear the gold bikini outfit sooner or later. Eve likes it. Then Eve told Holly to do certain things: . . . show me your p****, take a bath. The male sims were told to urinate and show me your d***.

One Sim was engaged in hot kissing. It was apparently not voluntary-participation, because the Sim kept asking if she had done enough to get her money. She had been promised 100,000 simoleans. After a few rounds of this, which were accompanied by threats of various sorts, the Sim rebelled and became more insistent about getting her money. The exchange became heated and the Sim got slapped around. During this exchange, several Sims entered the blue room, fought hard to get out and finally gave up and disappeared.[13]

Nearly half a year after the *Herald*'s first interviews with Evangeline, in which her cyber-brothel and Free-Money scam house were exposed, EA still had not taken any meaningful steps to remove her from the game. The company apparently found this new instance of sexual humiliation to be acceptable behavior in a Welcome area of a game that was supposed to be suitable for thirteen-year-olds. Or perhaps EA had just stopped caring. One thing was clear from Montserrat's interview with Eve—Evangeline had not lost her attitude:

Eve: My place is elevated, x-rated, butt naked. See, I try to help these new Sims especially. They don't know how to play the game.

Montserrat: What do you help them to learn?

Eve: See, I got game for those young ho's. Don't grow to be a dumb ho, that's a no-no. See, if you off the chain, stay ahead of the game. Save up, buy a house. If I had the chance to do it all again, I would be rich by day ten. I'm a veteran. No one stays wetter than Ms. Eva. I got to teach the young girls a lesson. And boys. I explain to them the rules of the game, you know?

Montserrat: How would you describe those rules?

Eve: Don't get broke off for free.[14]

The virtual world was a dangerous place, Evangeline was saying. Trust no one, look out for yourself, don't give it away when you know you can sell it. *Don't get broke off for free*. It wasn't a pretty picture.

The fact that Evangeline managed to coerce unsuspecting Sims into sexually humiliating behavior was outrageous to Uri. Worse was the fact that some people defended her, pointing out that a Sim could simply leave or log off if he or she didn't like what was going on. But Evangeline took advantage of the vulnerable position that newbies occupy in virtual worlds, where the environment, the interface technology, and the social structures and mores of the game are unfamiliar. Whether or not their typists were underage, Evangeline's victims were generally the equivalent of children in terms of how much time they'd spent in-game. It was difficult, if not impossible, to justify her behavior toward them—or the fact that EA turned a blind eye to it.

In Second Life, preying on newbies is taken to more alarming levels. At the Welcome Area, where new residents first enter the world, Uri heard reports that the agents of some large dance clubs and cyber-brothels would routinely recruit newbies into working as dancers or escorts at their clubs. What made the behavior so pernicious, according to those Uri spoke to, was the tactic of invoking the notion of "family" to manipulate virtual sex workers to remain in the fold. Of course, for better or worse, such "families" had their rules.[15] At a club called The Edge, escorts were required to work one- to two-hour shifts, and were given explicit instructions on how to guide prospective customers into lucrative engagements. They weren't allowed to take their clients out of the club. If all the "VIP rooms" were occupied, escorts were required to wait for one to open up. It was hardly the kind of leisure pursuit one might expect from a virtual world.

When dancers or escorts did break from a manipulative club manager, the effects were usually dramatic, and the charges of betrayal of family were laid on more than a little thick. This was certainly the case when a group of dancers and escorts defected from Club Elite in October 2004, which was run by an avatar named Big John Jade[16] (who, interestingly enough, had a previous incarnation on TSO as Tommy Stone, one of the authors of the Kingware Software nude skin add-on). When the *Herald* reported the defections, the comment thread to the article quickly filled with dozens of charges of manipulation from the dancers and charges of family betrayal from those who remained at Elite.

Why club owners tried everything they could to get their dancers and escorts to stay with them soon became clear: Big John vowed revenge on the club that had poached his dancers, but by mid-April of the following year he was out of business.[17]

That companies like Electronic Arts and Linden Lab would choose to ignore the explortation of newbies was surprising, until you took a broader view. One of the things online game developers seem most afraid of is such behavior becoming widely known to the general public, and thus to cultural conservatives and opportunistic politicians.

The game companies' control over their worlds is effectively complete, but it is only a matter of time before it comes under legislative scrutiny, a process that has already begun. Both California and Illinois have passed laws restricting the sale of "adult" video games. The Entertainment Software Association, an industry organization representing companies responsible for 90 percent of U.S. gaming software sales, has filed suit to block such laws on free-speech grounds.[18] But some countries already have laws on the books that can be used to criminalize certain virtual worlds due to the behavior of their residents.[19] The specter of such laws gaining ground cannot be a pleasant one from the industry's point of view.

Electronic Arts found itself faced with a choice as it encountered the increasingly shocking revelations that were coming to light in the *Herald*: The company could move to rectify the problems in their game, or it could simply ignore them and hope no one else noticed the reports. While Uri was not surprised EA was displeased with the reports in the *Herald* and perhaps reluctant to clean up their game, he was shocked to find that their apparent strategy was to do nothing about the game itself, and instead mount what from all angles looked to be a deliberate policy of cover-up and denial. Could they get away with it?

10 Murdered!

During the first week of December 2003, the *Herald* published a series of interviews with some of the more influential denizens of Alphaville.[1] There was Master Bam, the former SSG enforcer; an Evangeline associate named Angelica (who was keen to explain that she wasn't one of Evangeline's alts); Celestie, the abusive granny; and the director of the CIA at the Alphaville Government, an upstart rival to the SSG. In addition, there were notices or accounts of two gamer get-togethers, and the long-awaited response from Maxis administrators to the case of Rich Rockstar and the broken jaw (see page 87).

It was a good news week for the *Herald*. But things were about to change.

On December 6, the *Herald* published a story headlined "Maxis Targeting Whistle-Blowers?"[2] reprinting the "flagging" message Uri had received from EA mere hours after the company had finally responded in the Case of the Broken Jaw.[3] Two days later, Maxis unilaterally deleted references to the *Alphaville Herald* that had appeared in the profiles of both Urizenus and Doctor Legion.

Uri went on with his work. On December 8, the same day he reported the Maxis deletions, the *Herald* also ran its long interview with Evangeline, in which she implied that Maxis employees may have been among her customers at the Hotel Erotica. One of the most popular stories in the *Herald*'s short existence, the interview generated 132 posts in the comments thread on the site, ranging from the outraged to the unbelieving to the unimpressed (and one person who complained that reading the interview had knocked fifty points off his IQ). Whatever Evangeline really was, she had certainly captured the imagination of *Herald* readers. The newspaper seemed to have found its niche, in tales of those who not only pushed

Figure 10.1
A sample profile in The Sims Online

the boundaries of behavior in an online world, but who raised important questions about the effects of those worlds in their residents' offline lives.

Two days after the Evangeline interview ran, Maxis contacted Urizenus again—and not to congratulate him on his journalistic prowess.

Dear Urizenus,
This letter is to notify you that your account (578372615) has been suspended from The Sims Online for 72 hours. On 12-10-2003 at 05:43 GMT a complaint was filed against you. A sample of the log(s) that resulted in this action can be found below....

This is your *final warning*. Please take the time to review the Terms of Service and User Agreement. Although we would regret the closure of your account, we feel that it would be in the best interest of the service as a whole, if the Terms of Service was broken again following this suspension....

〉From House Profile: "Our newspaper/blog is online at 〉alphavilleherald.com"

As this site links to illegal sites, it is illegal to advertise in TSO. EA Player Relations

Though Ludlow had deleted references to realsimsonline.com and alphavilleherald.com from Urizenus's in-game profile after the first warning, he hadn't noticed the URL tucked away in the property description for the *Herald* headquarters. This, apparently, was all EA needed to suspend his account, allegedly for linking to an "illegal site."

Linking to commercial sites from within the game was disallowed by EA, but precisely what made the *Herald* an illegal site was never clear. No products had been offered for sale on the *Herald* site (unless you counted the ad for Doctor Legion's in-game goth supply store), and the newspaper had never collected a single dime for its efforts. It seemed a stretch, to say the least, for EA to claim that the *Herald* was a commercial site. And calling it "illegal" was ridiculous. Under what laws?

Most of the sites the *Herald* linked to had nothing for sale, though some did provide links to other sites that might be considered commercial in nature. It was a very long way, though, from the *Herald* to a commercial site. If the *Herald* constituted a commercial site, then a search engine like Google would be deemed "illegal" as well. If there were any supposedly illegal links from the *Herald* site, they were all to sites operated by people who were happily playing TSO, some with dozens of alts. It hardly seemed credible that Ludlow was suspended for linking to a Website that in turn linked to sites operated by money traders, while the money traders themselves continued to play the game unmolested. Ludlow and the other *Herald* staffers, Kale and Squirrel, could draw only one conclusion: The highly selective and perhaps dubious enforcement of the Terms of Service was being undertaken for one reason—to try to shut up the *Herald.*

After consulting with his staff, Ludlow decided to confront EA and Maxis in the pages of the *Herald* under his Urizenus pen name. "We deplore the Maxis strategy of selective enforcement of its ToS to harass and intimidate whistle blowers," Uri wrote in a post to the *Herald* at a little after ten o'clock that morning. "This is the latest element in a campaign of harassment of the *Alphaville Herald* that has been pursued by Maxis since we have begun breaking stories on Maxis's refusal to pursue evidence of child abuse and underage sexual activity in Alphaville."[4]

It would be the last story Urizenus would write as a citizen of Alphaville. Just two hours later, his account was permanently banned. Urizenus was no more.

Your "The Sims Online" login account (578372615) has been permanently closed for severe and/or repeated Terms of Service or Rules of Conduct violations. Most recently, on 12-10-2003 at 16:25 GMT a cheating complaint was filed against you. You have continued to list alphavilleherald.com in your profiles after a warning and suspension for this. Your previous account record has also been considered in this action. While we regret it, we feel it is necessary for the good of the game and its community.

This time Ludlow was stunned by the sheer brazenness of EA's actions. Twelve hours into a seventy-two-hour suspension he had been terminated—but for what? Not only was he frozen out of the game at the time of the "cheating complaint" (how do you cheat when you aren't in the game?), but he had already removed the *Herald* URL from his personal profile and the URL in the *Herald* property description had been removed twelve hours earlier by Maxis itself. His alleged crime had already been put right, and his time was being served. If there was any doubt in Ludlow's mind that talk of Terms of Service violations was a pretext for getting Urizenus out of the game, EA's move put those doubts to rest.

Writing as Urizenus, Ludlow again went to the *Herald* to update readers on what was happening. "EA falsely claims that I 'continue to list alphavilleherald.com' in my profiles," Uri wrote. "In fact I immediately removed all references to the *Alphaville Herald* from my user bio. . . . One presumes that this action is in no small measure part of the continuing campaign of EA/Maxis against Urizenus and the *Alphaville Herald* for breaking the stories of child cyber-prostitution in Alphaville."[5] It was hard to conclude anything else. Whatever corrective action Ludlow had taken had not satisfied Maxis. As far as TSO was concerned, Urizenus was dead.

For the "good of the game and its community," the hardest-working editor-in-chief in the virtual world had been terminated, with extreme prejudice. But if EA thought it had silenced the newspaper that had exposed the dirty secrets of their virtual world, the company could not have been more mistaken. The *Herald* staff was in many ways the worst group of people to try to shut up. If the case of Rich Rockstar had energized Candace, this had her positively radioactive. She immediately plunged into the fight. Squirrel had been AWOL from the *Herald* for months, since the sheer boredom of TSO had driven him into the swords-and-spells MMO Lineage. But now Ludlow could tell, even on the phone, that Squirrel was bouncing up and down with enthusiasm. The energy of the editorial team was contagious. That contagion was about to spread.

Ludlow had been online for eighteen years, a participant in untold flame wars and legal and philosophical debates about the future of the Internet, and in that time had formed connections with many of the people involved in legal and conceptual issues in cyberspace. The two books he had edited on the subject had included essays by many of the lawyers, activists, and journalists working in the area, from Mike Godwin (who had written the foreword to Ludlow's first book when he was serving as Online Counsel at the Electronic Frontier Foundation) to journalists like Julian Dibbell (author of *My Tiny Life*) and Wagner James Au (who wrote a Weblog covering the goings-on in Second Life for Linden Lab[6]). In more recent months he had made the acquaintance of Wharton Law School professor Dan Hunter and Indiana University economist Edward Castronova, both of whom had lauded the arrival of the *Herald* on their *Terra Nova* blog. When the story of Urizenus's murder broke, its spread through the online community was viral.

The first real-world news outlets on the story were *Salon.com* and the *BBC Online*. The *Salon* story ran December 12,[7] just two days after Uri had been terminated. At that point, the story was off and running in the blogosphere. The wildly popular tech blog *Slashdot.org* linked to the *Salon* story the next day.[8] (Sites that get "Slashdotted" with a link from the blog often get so many hits that their host servers crash.) From there, one blog after another picked up on the tale, including the heavily trafficked *Penny Arcade*, which devoted one of its popular cartoons to the story.[9]

To Ludlow, one of the posts that best summed up the situation was made by James Grimmelmann, then a Yale Law School student: "On the one hand, Maxis is close to losing control over their game world. TSO is a positively Brechtian world of violence, flim-flammery, and low-down dirty tricks. (The *Herald*'s major "sin" was opening a window onto such goings-on.). . . . But on the other hand, Maxis acts like a classic despot, using its powers to single out individual critics for the dungeons and the firing squads. The usual real-world justification for this kind of arbitrary action is the need for a strong central hand to protect public safety and common welfare. But since Maxis isn't all that good at those aspects, the *Herald* censorship smacks more of tyranny for its own sake."[10]

A few days later, Ludlow penned an obituary in the *Herald*—though not for Urizenus. Instead, he titled it, "Censorship Dies, Victim of The Blog."

> Censorship passed away at home yesterday, killed by The Blog. Censorship will be remembered as a trusted friend of despots, tyrannical leaders and large, profit-hungry corporations hiding unethical practices and inferior products. Friends say that in recent years Censorship has been less and less effective and useful, but they continued to employ him anyway, if only out of habit. Censorship is survived by his parents Greed and Arrogance, his brothers Obfuscation and Unresponsiveness, and his children Ignorance and Despair. Reached for comment, one of Censorship's good

friends, an officer at Maxis, had this to say: "I don't know who this Mr. The Blog is, but when I [find out] I'm gonna terminate his account!"[11]

Below Censorship's touching obit, Ludlow posted links to twenty-five of the publications, Websites, and blogs that had picked up Urizenus's story. He headed the list with a note: "If you are keeping score at home, attempting to silence one blog with a readership of about twelve people yields the following links, with readership in the gazillions."

Gazillions more were to come. National outlets continued to pick up the story. The *New York Times* put Ludlow on its front page on January 15. The *Boston Globe* and the *Detroit Free Press* both ran stories, and CNN inserted a reporter into an Alphaville "romance" property. International attention was on its way as well. The *New York Times*[12] article was reprinted in the *International Herald Tribune*, and news organizations in the United Kingdom,[13] Spain, France, and Russia soon followed up with stories of their own.

For Ludlow's philosophy students, of course, none of this was as impressive as when Rob Corddry of *The Daily Show* turned up with a film crew. Ludlow had initially had reservations about appearing on Comedy Central's news satire program, which was famous for making its subjects look like geeks or worse. Ludlow had enjoyed laughing at *The Daily Show*'s targets, but he wasn't sure he wanted to be one himself. When he asked an undergraduate philosophy of language class whether it was a good idea, he was greeted by a chorus of "Yes!" When he asked whether it wouldn't make him look like an idiot, Ludlow's students responded with an even more enthusiastic "Yes!!"

It was all in good fun, but in fact, the episode contained important lessons for the *Herald*. Several years earlier, Ludlow had been dragged into the center ring of New York's Big Apple Circus by a clown named Bello Nock. Nock's routine consisted mainly of making fun of Ludlow's hair (or lack thereof), but the moment had delighted Ludlow's daughter, and he had marked it down as a good thing to do: never be afraid to let people have fun at your expense. He didn't want to take the *Herald* experience too seriously. The issues were serious, of course. And while TSO wasn't only a game, it was in fact a game at its core, and Ludlow felt it was important to continue to have fun in it. The *Daily Show* interview certainly delivered its share of fun, with most of Corddry's best questions never airing on the show. "Aren't you afraid of what EA might do to you? They could fill your in box with spam for Viagra, Enzyte, fisting parties . . . you go there and there's no party!" The sound engineer and cameraman went to their knees laughing after that one. Ludlow's discussions with *Daily Show* producer Jim Margolis had given him new ideas about how best to proceed with the *Herald*. The paper (like *The Daily Show*) was at its best when it skated the line between fun and serious business. In that way it would mirror the virtual world itself, which Ludlow saw as occupying the same border space.

The *Daily Show* appearance had been fun, but there were serious lessons to be drawn from it as well. Ludlow's chosen nemesis, EA vice president Jeff Brown, had appeared on the same episode, and his comments there (which Brown also distributed as talking points to a number of other media outlets) pointed out just how lightly the company seemed to take what went on in its world. "If Peter Ludlow is a journalist," Brown had said, "then I'm a railroad tycoon whenever I play Monopoly."[14] If Brown really saw TSO as on the same level as Monopoly, he seemed to be the only one that did.

Given all the media attention, Ludlow and the *Herald* staff became concerned that their publication not become self-absorbed, or at least no more self-absorbed than they usually were, and took measures to insure that they could continue to report on events in Alphaville.

"Readers should rest assured that we will continue reporting these important stories, with or without the in-game presence of the Urizenus avatar," Ludlow wrote. And continue they did.

Much of Ludlow's reporting had been done via Yahoo! Instant Messenger and other chat programs, and he and his staff still had a network of contacts, reporters, and informants who now only intensified their in-game legwork for the paper. Some players loaned Ludlow their accounts so he could slip into the game as needed to check up on important stories and events, and others soon came forward offering to contribute articles (most of them anonymously, for fear of crossing EA). The *Herald* would soon add pseudonymous contributors The Phantom, J, Deep Max, humdog, The Eye, and a young rares dealer named Ian who worked for the Alphaville Government. Ludlow eventually established two semi-permanent alternate characters, paid for through other people's credit cards, which he used for conducting business in the game. He named them Uri and Los, again taking the names from William Blake's *Book of Urizen*.

In the weeks following Urizenus's termination, the *Herald* availed itself of the new help and new sources of information to publish as many stories as ever (many of them still carrying Uri's byline), including a report on Maxis's move against TSO's simolean farmers,[15] more stories on the Sim Shadow Government, a look at Alphaville's BDSM community, and profiles of one or two other unusual characters, including the avatar known as Jesus X, the "sexy Jesus."

Another tremendous resource at the time was real-world reporters who'd been attracted to the game by Urizenus's story. While many friends of EA claimed Ludlow was simply filling reporters' heads with his own fantasies, in point of fact, the reporters were naturals at digging up the seedier regions of Alphaville. It was they who typically brought these areas to Ludlow's attention, not the other way around. *Boston Globe* reporter Hiawatha Bray summoned Los to a slave auction in Alphaville, an event Ludlow found particularly embarrassing given that Bray was African-American. Jim Schaefer, a reporter for the *Detroit Free Press*, tipped Uri off to a new racist scam house. Another reporter tipped Los off to a cyber-brothel called "Clit R Us." Visiting the game one day with CNN's Bruce Burkhardt, Los and the reporter's avatar discovered yet another cyber-brothel. Ludlow and Burkhardt spoke on the phone as Burkhardt's avatar negotiated a deal with the brothel's cyber-pimp. When the price was set, Ludlow heard Burkhardt asking a colleague at the CNN offices, "What do I do now?" In the background came the response: "Pay him, pay him!" At that point Ludlow excused himself, leaving the rest to the professionals.

To Ludlow's critics, gaming companies' rights under the law were clear. But as Ludlow would learn in talking to a number of leading law scholars, the actual state of affairs was not so simple.

Soon after his initial suspension, Ludlow crossed the University of Michigan campus to visit with law professor Molly S. Van Houweling. Van Houweling had recently graduated from Harvard Law School, had clerked for Supreme Court Justice David Souter, and held a research position at the Stanford Law School's Center for Internet and Society. She explained to Ludlow that EA's legal case was not entirely cut and dried. When Ludlow later spoke with the Wharton School's Dan Hunter, with Greg Lastowka of *Terra Nova* (now a law professor at Rutgers University), and with his old friend Mike Godwin, former EFF Online Counsel, he heard similar impressions.

The Terms of Service document that players were required to accept might constitute a "contract of adhesion," according to some of the lawyers Ludlow spoke to. In other words, given EA's total control of the unique online world that was The Sims Online, it might be possible to argue that the company had shoehorned provisions into the ToS that players wouldn't normally agree to, given any alternative. In legal terms, some of those provisions might not be enforceable, especially if they involved signing away certain rights (like personal liberties) that our legal system just doesn't let you sign away.

The consensus of the lawyers Ludlow consulted was that the case could be taken to court. But as one put the question, "What is it you want to achieve? Are you trying to get your money back, or are you trying to make a point?"

Money, of course, was not at all the issue. But neither, really, were the finer legal points. To Ludlow, the issues were about the kind of values we promote in society—whether in the "real" world or online—values of decency, free speech, the right to liberty, and the pursuit of happiness. The courts were only one avenue through which to protect and nurture those values. One could also choose to promote them through social norms, through legislation or even social engineering. The question Ludlow faced was not whether the law was on his side (though it seemed it might be), but what kind of society was emerging as we moved further into the twenty-first century and deeper into online worlds. Courts would eventually start to address such questions (especially as the amounts of money involved grew larger), but in the meantime Ludlow felt it was important to be clear about what the values were that the *Herald* was trying to promote, and to show that those values deserved to be protected not just in our terrestrial existences but in our online lives as well.

Ludlow took the matter to his staff at the *Herald*, and together they decided that the place to fight their battle was not in the courts—at least, not now—but on the World Wide Web: in the *Herald*, in Weblog comments threads, in forums posts, and wherever they spotted the mistaken impression that online lives were somehow less deserving of basic liberties than offline lives were.

In response to the idea that game companies could do what they liked with their software, Ludlow pointed out the fact that owning something does not, in fact, entitle you to do whatever you want with it. If your house becomes a historical landmark you can no longer destroy it or even radically modify it. If you own a pet, you are not entitled to torture it, or to kill it without reason. Presumably, if you owned a rare painting, it would at least be *wrong*, if not illegal, to destroy it. Even if you own an American baseball team, communities will sometimes take legal action if you seek to liquidate it (as Minnesota Twins owner Carl Pohlad learned when he and Major League Baseball hatched a plan to shrink the league and terminate the Twins franchise, giving Pohlad a cool $250 million for going along with the plan).[16]

Each of those cases is an example in which ownership is more than simply possession but entails a kind of "stewardship," Ludlow argued. If the thing you own becomes important to the community, or if other ethical or cultural principles call for preserving the object, you no longer have the right to do whatever you want with it just because you own it. But were games really important enough to merit the same treatment?

If Ludlow had learned anything in his Alphaville sojourn, it was just how important Alphaville and places like it were to the people who frequented them. In his travels through blogspace in the wake of Urizenus's banning, he pointed out that these games were full-time jobs for some people, sometimes their sole source of income. Some had found love there, others had found family.

Just because a virtual space like Alphaville was important, of course, didn't mean Urizenus shouldn't be terminated. After all, EA had claimed the termination was "for the good of the community." But was it? Ludlow argued that if Urizenus could be terminated on such flimsy grounds, then anyone could. For Ludlow, the personal loss amounted to a few hundred dollars. But what about someone like Respected Banker, who was living on medical assistance in Australia? What if EA went after him next? Or what if the company went after someone whose entire social life revolved around the game? Is it appropriate that those actions take place without due process? Was it appropriate for EA to terminate critical news sources when it encountered them?

While academics like Ted Castronova continued to support the *Herald*, much of the game development community was less kind. Some critics reacted to the content of the paper itself. The efforts of Ludlow et al. were called "crap," "tripe," and "sensationalism" by those who felt the paper focused only on the less savory aspects of virtual worlds. For the most part, these criticisms seemed to be driven by concerns about what would happen to the game industry if the real truth about online worlds got out. As developer Brian "Psychochild" Green put it on *Terra Nova*:

> Here's the core of my beef: how's Joseph Senator from Heartland USA going to react when he sees a headline that contains the phrase "child cyber-prostitute"? Is he going to care that my game isn't TSO? No, we get misguided laws trying to "protect the children" from the "dangers" of the Internet based on less sensationalist garbage than what we've been subjected to. No matter how you slice it, it's not going to be good for the industry or those of us trying to make an honest living off of it.[17]

Perhaps driven by fear of losing their livelihood, many of the developers Ludlow encountered focused not on what was actually happening in their games, but on whether or not the truth should come out. And it was disappointing to find that their answers to that question were often negative.

As for the charges of "crap" and "tripe," the *Herald* staffers thanked the paper's critics for their "constructive criticism" and suggested that such critics might be happier if they simply stopped reading the *Herald*.

The issue of free speech in virtual worlds and their associated forums was obviously near and dear to Uri's heart. While most players see virtual worlds as merely a corporate product with which the company can do as it likes, the issue is more subtle than that according to the legal scholars Ludlow consulted, with precedent in the case law having been set in a number of real-world situations.

To Ludlow, Second Life and The Sims Online are less like a product and more like a company town, a place in which a company sets the rules, but a public place nonetheless. Questions of free speech in such places has been addressed by the courts in other contexts. Decades ago, the U.S. Supreme Court ruled that First Amendment rights had to be protected in a real-world town even if it was completely owned by a company.[18]

The case, *Marsh v. Alabama*, involved the town of Chickasaw, Alabama, a town literally owned by the Gulf Shipping Corporation. Gulf Shipping owned the land, the streets, the sidewalks, the homes and the stores. When a woman named Grace Marsh attempted to discuss her religious beliefs on the streets (she was a Jehovah's Witness), she was arrested for criminal trespass. (Chickasaw's sheriff was an employee of the company as well.) Gulf Shipping argued more or less what game companies argue today: It's our town, we own it, and we can kick out anyone we want if we don't like what they say or do. But in 1946, the Supreme Court held that Grace Marsh did deserve protection under the First Amendment, because the activities of Gulf Shipping amounted to "state action": It had become the de facto government in Chickasaw in much the same way that game companies are the de facto governments of the virtual worlds they run.

According to law professors Dan Hunter and Greg Lastowka, both of whom Ludlow consulted after being banned from TSO, the comparison could not be dismissed out of hand. "If constitutional speech protections extend to company towns like Chickasaw, Alabama," they wrote, "it seems likely that such rights will be asserted by, and eventually granted to those who live in virtual worlds."[19]

The argument that players need no protections because they can simply pack up and leave a virtual world if they don't like how it's run (the "exit argument") is weak, in Hunter and Lastowska's opinion, because of the great deal of money and social capital many people have tied up in their online environments. A Canadian lawyer named Peter Jenkins went even further, calling into question the validity of Terms of Service documents (also known as End-User Licensing Agreements or EULAs). To him, EULAs are a form of contract that most courts wouldn't recognize because their terms—which require players to give up certain rights—are unilaterally imposed by companies, without allowing customers to negotiate.[20]

The real concern with the "exit argument" is that it goes beyond the available alternate forum principle and presumes that the player has made a valid waiver of his or her First Amendment rights. Typically, the MMORPG owner's policies on speech would be contained in the End User Licensing Agreement (EULA) which the prospective player would have to assent to by clicking on the "I Agree" button prior to first accessing the game. Although it is well established that a person may waive his or her First Amendment rights, such a waiver is required to be "knowing, voluntary and intelligent." The EULA is a contract of adhesion that is imposed on the player without the possibility of negotiation. The courts have generally viewed such contracts as lacking in voluntariness for purposes of the waiver of constitutional rights. Even the small minority who actually read the EULA prior to clicking the "I agree" button would not meet the "knowing and intelligent" part of the test, since most EULA's are written in a very general fashion and do not expressly set out the constitutional rights that are being waived. As well, the courts generally consider whether the waiver would be contrary to public policy. The principles set out in the *Marsh v. Alabama* decision indicate that such a waiver would be contrary to public policy since...it would have a censoring effect on the information available to players in the MMORPG.

In effect, not only is the ToS a bogus contract (a "contract of adhesion"), one that arguably tricks customers into signing away their constitutional rights, but companies' asking players to waive such rights is "contrary to public policy," as Jenkins put it. Essentially, the right to free speech cannot be signed away in a ToS or EULA.

The legal case for free speech in virtual worlds does not end there. State courts in California, Colorado, Massachusetts, Oregon, and Washington have all passed laws protecting reasonable political speech in shopping malls because they are public places, and these decisions have been upheld by the U.S. Supreme Court. The case of Alphaville is not so very different.

Other legal scholars hold similar opinions. Jack Balkin, Yale University's Knight Professor of Constitutional Law and the First Amendment, wrote a law review article that specifically discussed the *Herald* case. Balkin argued that there were reasonable precedents in existing law that might lay the groundwork for the recognition of free speech in online environments like TSO and Second Life. Returning to the Marsh case, he drove home the point that people with control over the lines of communication within a community must keep those lines open for the free exchange of ideas.

The streets of the company town formed a space in which people communicated that the company town fully controlled and for which it was ultimately responsible. The streets were important nodal points for communication and the exchange of ideas. As Justice Black explained, "[w]hether a corporation or a municipality owns or possesses the town the public in either case has an identical interest in the functioning of the community in such manner that the channels of communication remain free." And as Justice Frankfurter pointed out, the central issue was not ownership of property but the "community aspects" of the company town—the fact that the town operated as a community in which people exchanged ideas and opinions. When a business monopolizes control over the central modes of communication within a community, it must act as a fiduciary for the public interest, and it must allow its property to be used for the free exchange of ideas.

Is Electronic Arts responsible for protecting the free exchange of ideas in TSO and acting as a "fiduciary for the public interest" of Alphaville? Balkin seemed sympathetic to the idea:

Virtual worlds are like company towns in that the game owner forms the community, controls all of the space inside the community and thus, controls all avenues of communication within the community. The free flow of ideas and the formation of community cannot occur within a virtual world unless the designer permits it. Alphaville was a virtual city controlled by The Sims Online through its design of code and its Terms of Service agreement. Although Electronic Arts does not take over "the full spectrum of municipal functions" in real space, it does exercise all of those functions in the virtual world. If any private entity could be regarded as a company town, it would be a virtual world. That is especially so because the whole point of the virtual world is to create community (or communities) and action in the virtual world occurs through the exchange of ideas.

Balkin went on to consider other arguments, including the "exit argument" that people could simply pack up and leave, and the claim that other lines of communication were available to the residents of Alphaville (YIM, for example). He pointed out that the court observed in Marsh that the availability of other lines of communication (like radio and telephone) did not mean that speech in the commons could be squashed: "It is important that communication among the participants occur within the space of the community and between the avatars. In Marsh itself, it did not matter that people could listen to radio broadcasts, or send mail in and out of the company town. That was simply not the same thing as speaking and organizing within the town itself."[21]

In the autumn of 2004, Peter Ludlow appeared on a panel with Balkin. Ludlow was particularly interested in Balkin's position that the money involved in the online gaming industry invites government oversight. The companies might not like it, but it's coming, either via legislation or via court action.

Balkin riffed on an idea that had initially been proposed by Ted Castronova: game companies might create charters in the form of "interrational statutes" that would ensure users' free speech; in exchange, the government would not hold game companies responsible for users' behavior in games. One fear that companies have is that they will be held liable should a player of one of their games instigate a real-world riot, for example, or defame another player. Castronova's idea of interrational statutes would be a compromise in which the de facto government of a virtual world would protect free speech in exchange for reduced liability.

MMO companies have free speech rights as well, and Balkin also looked at the issue from this angle. What if a company wanted to create a virtual world with a certain political edge—Gulag World, for example, in which residents take the role of inmates in a death camp? (The idea is not so farfetched; in the MMO Roma Victor, players can choose to begin life as a slave.) Balkin held that game companies had the right to build such games, games in which rights might be waived as part of gameplay, but that their intent in creating such worlds is important. Worlds like TSO and Second Life, which advertise themselves as offering communities open to all, in which anything is possible, would find it very difficult to make the case that censoring a critic furthers the intent of the world's creation, but Gulag World would be able to show how giving up rights is part of the definition of the game.

Of course not everyone is convinced by the arguments of Balkin, Hunter, Lastowka, and Jenkins. Eric Goldman, a law professor at Marquette University, published a paper entitled *Speech Showdowns at the Virtual Corral*[22] in which he took exception to the free speech rights claimed by the *Herald*, arguing that game companies were perfectly within their rights to "fire their customers." After all, if users didn't like the Terms of Service, they could simply move on to another game; the "switching costs," in Goldman's view, were minor.

Herald reporter Neal Stewart was not moved by Goldman's essay. He didn't attack it on legal grounds; he challenged Goldman's grasp of online worlds. In an essay in the *Herald*, Stewart argued that the "switching costs" for virtual worlds were not nearly as low as those for Internet service providers, for example. Goldman just didn't understand that these were fully formed virtual communities, and that people's lives were deeply embedded in these worlds.[23]

As we all know, the legal decisions that are being made today are setting precedents for future legislation and case law. What happens if we one day find ourselves totally immersed in online worlds—they become our principal places for socializing and work—and we discover that all our rights have been forfeited due to shortsighted legal thinking decades earlier?

In the abstract to his paper, "The Virtual World as Company Town—Free Speech in Massively Multiplayer Online Roleplaying Games," Jenkins imagines a scenario in which we find ourselves in a universal virtual world (in effect, the metaverse) bereft of such rights:

> This universal virtual world may become the successor to the Internet as we know it today and will become a place where the majority of us choose to shop, socialize and do business. The case law on freedom of speech in MMORPGs will have a profound precedent-setting effect on how the First Amendment is applied to this coming universal virtual platform, since the legal principles concerning new technologies tend

> to be set at an early stage of their development. If the right road is not taken, then we run the risk that the coming universal virtual world will be, from a freedom of speech perspective, a nightmarish endless global shopping mall, instead of an empowering enhancement of the real world with its boundless opportunities for encounters with those of differing viewpoints.

EA claimed to have banned Ludlow "for the good of the community." But what was going on in TSO offered plenty of reason to think that banning the *Herald* was not at all in the community's best interest. What EA had created in TSO was a vast electronic playground, a community in which tens of thousands of children and adults were mixed together. By banning the *Herald*, EA had attempted to draw a curtain over that community, so that parents and policymakers had no window into what was going on there. The move may have been in EA's best business interest (though even this was doubtful), but from the point of view of social policy it was frightening.

EA seemed willfully ignorant of the deep impact that virtual worlds could have on people's lives. The company treated TSO residents as if they were merely pixels on a screen connected to accounts paying monthly subscription fees. This was not how virtual worlds had begun. People like Richard Bartle, who had designed MUD1, and Raph Koster, who was largely responsible for Ultima Online, had been highly cognizant of the fact that there were real people behind the avatars that occupied their worlds. Koster had gone so far as to take a stab at writing a Declaration of the Rights of Avatars,[24] based loosely on revolutionary France's Declaration of the Rights of Man and of the Citizen and the U.S. Constitution's Bill of Rights.

The first right that Koster's Declaration holds to be self-evident is that "avatars are the manifestation of actual people in an online medium, and that their utterances, actions, thoughts, and emotions should be considered to be as valid as the utterances, actions, thoughts, and emotions of people in any other forum, venue, location, or space." To Ludlow, that made perfect sense. EA clearly did not agree.

The end of December found Ludlow reflecting on the events of the previous three months. Without ever intending to, the *Herald* had created quite a splash. What had begun out of curiosity and a natural role-playing choice had grown into something bigger as Ludlow had learned more about the nature of online worlds. It seemed impossible to separate what went on in a world like TSO from what was going on in the "real" world. There was simply too much interplay between the two, too much that traveled back and forth too easily. What he'd learned was that the virtual world wasn't virtual at all; it was simply an extension of the physical world into a realm where interactions took pixelated form—and where those interactions could even echo back into physical ones down the line.

Ludlow spent that New Year's Eve with his seven-year-old daughter. In the morning they logged onto TSO with a borrowed account to see the old *Herald* headquarters, and talked about why Urizenus had been terminated (along with his pets). His daughter giggled at the thought that they were doing something naughty by going back into the game, and expressed her anger with EA for killing the cats Black and Cheddar Cheese Cheetah.

After they logged off, Ludlow began to reflect on what kind of future was in store for his daughter and for the other children who would someday be living much of their lives online. It was entirely possible that his daughter's generation, or perhaps the one after that, might spend the majority of their careers working in online spaces. Their social and family contacts might take place principally in a virtual environment like The Sims Online or Second Life. Their political discussions might occupy these places. The idea was not far-fetched at all.

As he watched his daughter play a video game he wondered if the online worlds she would inhabit in the future would allow her to enjoy the freedoms we so value in our offline lives. Or would they be run by tyrants who insisted that principles of free speech and liberty did not apply to their realms? Would residents of these realms be at the mercy of capricious administrators who might evict them from their work spaces, play spaces, and educational spaces without explanation and without the possibility of appeal? Would his daughter one day lose the privileges that Western democracies had secured only through centuries of struggle? If so, would those privileges and rights be taken away not by terrestrial governments but by the large corporations that "owned" the bandwidth? Would government by the people become government by CEOs, software designers, and omnipotent (and un-elected) "moderators" and "administrators"?

His musings made him think of the battle on EverQuest's Rallos Zek server, in which the leading guilds had put aside their differences and banded together to defeat the Kerafyrm. That afternoon, he posted the *Herald*'s final story of 2003, expressing the wish that the world—not just the virtual world—take heed of the brave guilds of Rallos Zek and unite against their own "unkillable monsters."

Of course the real foe on Rallos Zek was not the monster itself, but the gods who controlled the server—the suits at Sony Online Entertainment who had reset the game when their monster was being destroyed. TSO, likewise, had its own gods, gods that rarely appeared except to intervene when they smelled danger in the form of legal exposure or bad publicity. That New Year's Eve, Ludlow became determined that the *Herald* staff would now look more closely than ever at what was going on beyond the pixels on their computer screens.

11 Behind the Pixel Curtain

Electronic Arts may have hoped that removing Urizenus from its game would be the end of his embarrassing reports from the streets of Alphaville, but the strategy backfired. Not only did the *Herald* and its expanding staff of reporters continue to report on events in the game—indeed, the reports now came more frequently and were often more sensational—but Uri turned his attention to Electronic Arts itself. Uri wondered what kind of company would tolerate abusive behavior in its game and respond to it by trying to clamp a lid on the troubling news. Part of the *Herald*'s mission, he decided, would be to find out; he would attempt to draw aside the pixel curtain and learn about the powers behind the game. But this wasn't *The Wizard of Oz*. No kindly if misguided Professor Marvel stood behind the curtain; what Uri found was much more sinister.

Uri's questions were not confined to EA. The bad-boy image cultivated by some game companies may have helped them sell games, but it also seemed to hide a gross indifference to the responsibilities usually expected of large corporations. The problem was not the content of the games (though this was what earned the companies their bad-boy publicity), but rather the behavior of the corporations themselves, including both their operational and financial practices.

Wall Street loved these game companies enough to ignore weak financials and, in some cases, questionable bookkeeping practices. It may have been their nose-thumbing attitudes that appealed to Wall Street cowboys—many of whom were gamers themselves. What was surprising was that gaming culture seemed to trump weak financials. It took the press, not the investment bankers, to bring this to light.

In the summer of 2005, *Fortune* magazine raised questions about one of the most notorious bad boys of the game industry—Take2 Interactive, the makers of Grand Theft Auto.[1] Their article ran in the wake of the so-called Hot Coffee scandal, in which Take2 was accused of hiding graphic sexual content in Grand Theft Auto, but *Fortune* wasn't interested in pixelated soft-core porn. On the contrary, writer Bethany McLean led the article by asking, "What's most shocking about the controversial—and top-selling—Grand Theft Auto isn't embedded sex scenes. It's the financial chicanery of the game's maker. Why don't investors care?"

The practice that caught the attention of *Fortune* is known as "channel stuffing," a common method of pumping up sales figures used in a number of industries. According to the article, Take2 and other game companies were allegedly shipping large amounts of inventory to retailers at the end of quarterly financial periods, recording the shipped inventory as sales in time for them to enhance the companies' earnings reports, then taking back the inventory as returns shortly after the financials were published. This had the effect of exaggerating sales and accounts receivable figures, whether or not the games actually sold.

Was EA involved in the practice? Just a few months before the *Herald* went online, *GamesIndustry.biz* had reported that in addition to Take2, gamemakers Activision, Acclaim, THQ, and Midway were being investigated by the Securities and Exchange Commission.[2] The author of the article found it "hard to believe" that EA wasn't also under investigation (EA, of course, would neither confirm nor deny it). It would be over a year before EA would wind up in court over alleged channel-stuffing as well. In the meantime, EA management was involved in other activities that raised the eyebrows of the *Herald* staff.

One thing the *Herald* found shocking was an article in the *San Jose Mercury News* in early 2005 reporting that seven EA executives had unloaded stock positions ranging from $1 million to $10 million each.[3] The *Herald*'s nemesis, Jeff Brown, EA's vice president for corporate communications, claimed the stock sales were all quite innocent—a claim that was naturally met with cynicism in the *Herald*: "Are they all building really really big swimming pools? Or is this trading on insider info? Well Jeff Brown *assures* us it isn't the latter: 'It was diversification.' Mhmmmmm . . ."[4]

The *Herald*'s comment turned out to be on target. Less than a month later, EA cut its earnings estimates severely, and the company's stock dropped 13 percent.

"Well, as much as it just *kills* us to say we told you so, we told you so," the *Herald* responded. "Several weeks ago we reported that several EA executives were dumping shares of EA stock. Insider trading? Jeff Brown said no, which made us think: yes! And surprise surprise surprise, EA now has cut their earnings estimates and the price of the stock has dropped 13%. Gee, those execs were pretty "lucky" to have sold just before losing 13% of their assets. But we aren't the only ones to notice the *cough* coincidental *cough* insider selling followed by stock drop. Some shareholders have too. And here come the lawsuits!"[5]

And the lawsuits were interesting indeed. Four different law firms filed class-action lawsuits,[6] but the one that caught Uri's attention was a suit filed in U.S. District Court in northern California on behalf of EA shareholders, alleging that not only had EA execs traded on insider information, they had also deliberately misled investors and used the channel-stuffing scheme to inflate their financial statements just before they sold.[7] The lawsuit chronicled EA insiders' stock sales in relation to information the company made public, and further charged that EA execs knew the company was on track for sub-par sales even while they were pumping up earnings expectations. As the *Herald* had reported, it was only once the execs had dumped their stock that the company made it known things might not be as rosy as they'd formerly represented.

While the lawsuit was pending the *Herald* learned that EA had endowed a Chair in Interactive Entertainment at the University of Southern California. It all sounded very generous: EA was helping USC hire a leading scholar in an important new academic field. But the first person to be hired was none other than EA's Chief Creative Officer, Bing Gordon ("Bada Bing" Gordon to the *Herald*), who had joined EA in 1982.

The business and gaming press was indifferent to Bing's new job, being content to simply reproduce various press releases. Faculty that Ludlow contacted at USC were not so sanguine, however. In their view, this was just a way for EA to funnel money to one of its officers, using the USC chair to allow them to make the contribution tax-free. USC didn't care; money was money. Even if the bulk of it went to Bing, they would still be able to siphon off a portion for the university.

Fortune and other business media were concerned about the financial chicanery of big game companies, and academics were concerned about the

"Bada Bing Chair." But had labor leaders been paying attention, they would have had concerns as well. An entirely different series of lawsuits against EA suggested a pattern of employee exploitation that led some to call the company a sweatshop for game programmers.

In July 2004, a class-action lawsuit was filed against EA alleging that the company failed to pay overtime that was legally due graphic artists.[8] Less than a year later another class-action suit was filed based on similar claims by EA's programmers.[9] (The suit on behalf of EA's graphic artists was settled in October 2005 for $15.6 million.[10])

What garnered EA the most bad publicity, however, was a two-thousand-word essay posted on the Web in November 2004 by someone known as EA Spouse. Titled "EA: The Human Story," the essay told of month after month of seven-day, eighty-five-hour work weeks, high rates of burnout and turnover, lack of overtime pay or any other compensation for extra work, and a seeming disregard not only for the health and well-being of the company's employees but for the quality of its games as well.

> The current mandatory hours are 9am to 10pm—seven days a week—with the occasional Saturday evening off for good behavior (at 6:30pm). This averages out to an eighty-five hour work week. Complaints that these once more extended hours combined with the team's existing fatigue would result in a greater number of mistakes made and an even greater amount of wasted energy were ignored.
>
> The stress is taking its toll. After a certain number of hours spent working the eyes start to lose focus; after a certain number of weeks with only one day off fatigue starts to accrue and accumulate exponentially. There is a reason why there are two days in a weekend—bad things happen to one's physical, emotional, and mental health if these days are cut short.[11]

Whether EA Spouse was married to an EA employee or was an employee him- or herself wasn't clear. The post was not of interest because of the specific charges, but because of the avalanche of replies purporting to be from EA employees or family members that echoed the initial charges. If the claims were to be believed, it seemed that the company didn't care at all about its games, its customers, or even its highly creative employees—all EA execs seemed to care about was their bottom line.

"EA's bright and shiny new corporate trademark is 'Challenge Everything.' Where this applies is not exactly clear," EA Spouse wrote. "Churning out one licensed football game after another doesn't sound like challenging much of anything to me; it sounds like a money farm."

EA eventually bent to the bad publicity; in early December 2004 the company circulated a memo to employees, saying it recognized the problem and was working to rectify it.[12] At about the same time, though, the company announced the opening of a research facility in China, and hired five hundred new programmers there.[13] Outsourcing? Payback for uppity American programmers? Insurance policy against high U.S. labor costs? Jeff Brown said it was nothing of the sort. The *Herald* continued to disbelieve him.

Another dirty little secret of EA was its treatment of "volunteer" workers, as Uri discovered when he began to look deeper into EA's legal entanglements.

Quite often, companies will turn to experienced players to help with customer service and community support for their massively multiplayer games, and players are often quite happy to oblige. Volunteer "game masters" are often drawn from players' ranks, compensated only by the status they gain from having an inside contact with the game company, and the promise of possible future employment. Having an "in" with a game company is one of the most proudly worn badges of any serious gamer, and that fact is not lost on developers.

In October 2000, four Ultima Online players who had volunteered as UO "Counselors" (assisting players and working with UO staff to manage help requests), filed a lawsuit against Electronic Arts and ORIGIN Systems, the EA subsidiary that developed the game. Certified as a class action in September 2002, the lawsuit alleged that volunteer Counselors were owed back wages by EA because of the way the company handled the Counselor program.

Court documents describe a situation that appears to support their case.[14] According to the suit, EA had begun the Counselor program as an informal volunteer program in November 1997, two months after Ultima Online was released. In April 1999 the program was formalized, with Counselors being required to complete customer-service training, work a number of shifts each week, sign a separate Terms of Service agreement covering their labor, and submit a photo ID to the company.

What happened after that was less clear. According to the lawsuit, Counselors were occasionally required to do unpaid work as Game Masters (a paid position), but, worse, in 2001 EA hired new support staff to look over the shoulders of the Counselors for five months and learn their jobs. The new trainees were then hired into paid positions as "Advisors" while the volunteer Counselor staff was told that its services were no longer needed. In effect, they had trained their replacements for free and then been shown the door.

The move was typical of the behemoth that Electronic Arts had become. As revenues stretched into the billions and more and more layers were added between executives, management, the games, and the gamers themselves, EA was losing touch with its customers. Whether or not the courts shared this view was, in this particular case, immaterial: A year or so after the lawsuit was certified, EA settled out of court for an undisclosed sum.

To Uri, EA seemed to be playing each side of the political spectrum against the other. Their motto, "Challenge Everything," was reminiscent of the standard progressives' call to "question authority," designed to appeal to the gamers EA was exploiting. EA's status as a multibillion-dollar corporation, on the other hand, meant it enjoyed the support of business-friendly politicians who never stopped to think that the company might be morally bankrupt. EA's executives, meanwhile, laughed all the way to the bank.

Of course, Uri felt that "Challenge Everything" was nothing more than a marketing ploy. In his opinion, a better motto for EA would have been "Challenge your parents, challenge lawmakers, but whatever you do, don't challenge us." One thing was certain: the motto had nothing to do with challenging artistic conventions, and still less to do with challenging people to be creative. Uri came to this conclusion months earlier with the assistance of a former EA employee who became known at the *Herald* as Deep Max.

Deep Max illuminated another aspect of EA's money-farming operation: the damage it did to its games, and specifically to TSO and the single-player Sims franchise.[15] The Sims had benefited greatly from the trade in customized objects and clothing that users could create with Don Hopkins's Transmogrifier, among other tools, but as the summer 2005 release date for The Sims 2 approached, it was still uncertain whether user-created content would be allowed in the new version of the single-player game. EA eventually did support it, but not until after a long struggle between EA executives and programmers, a struggle that seemed to revolve mainly around issues of control.

Besides the internal struggles that Deep Max described, EA took a condescending and adversarial stance toward both its developers and its users. After the company bought Maxis in 1997, a number of executives had worked to kill the Sims project and almost succeeded, according to Deep Max. Now, despite the fact that Will Wright's vision of gaming's future had been correct, and that the game's immense popularity had been helped along by custom content, EA execs still waited until the last minute to greenlight one of the game's most important features. The picture that emerged from these and other reports Uri received from inside Maxis and EA made the company sound like a theater of Shakespearean intrigue, in which the entire workplace had acquired a culture of backstabbing, mistrust, and ill will. As one source who worked on the development of TSO told Uri, "Maxis was the most toxic workplace environment I have ever experienced in my life."

The string of lawsuits and the behavior that Uri had witnessed firsthand had led him to believe EA's management was morally bankrupt. The stories he was hearing from Deep Max and others indicated they were *artistically* bankrupt as well. EA was not in the business of fostering creativity, according to many employees and commentators, but rather of pumping out formulaic games that required little technical innovation but that would nevertheless be cash cows for the company. The formula could be seen in the many sequels and licensed titles the company continually produced. If it could be bought, EA had probably bought it: *Batman, James Bond, Harry Potter, Marvel Comics, The Lord of the Rings, The Godfather* and pretty much every major sports franchise on the face of the planet—from the NHL to the NFL, NCAA football *and* basketball, golf stars, NASCAR, FIFA soccer, the NBA. EA snapped up licenses like they were gold, built unremarkable games around most of them, and relied not on the games themselves but on the borrowed interest in the original properties to sell them.

12 Taking It to the Virtual Streets

What recourse did residents of virtual worlds have? Was there nothing they could do when the software gods reached down from the heavens to cross the boundaries of ethical and moral sense?

Uri had come across accounts of citizen protests that had taken place in a number of virtual worlds. The thought that mounting a protest in a virtual world might have any impact on a platform owner seemed far-fetched, at first. But as Uri looked closer, he found that such protests did, in fact, have an effect.

In November 2003, players of warrior characters in the MMO EverQuest decided they were mad as hell and they weren't going to take it anymore. Changes had been made that had nerfed the warrior class (i.e., weakened it), and they weren't going to accept them lying down. Instead, they planned a protest in which warriors would log on at prearranged times and blanket the chat channels with their grievances, hoping to bring gameplay to a standstill until they were heard.[1]

Remarkably, the mere threat of the protest had some effect. A week after the protest was announced (but before it had taken place), an EQ Community Manager announced a major overhaul of combat mechanics. In the end, it wasn't as major an overhaul as many warriors would have liked, but the episode was an unusual moment in which a group of players banded together and sought to use the tools at their disposal *within the world* to effect change. The people, in the form of their avatars, had spoken.

To Uri, protest movements smacked of politics beginning to emerge in the virtual world—it was certainly a form of political expression that was well known in the real world. And while the warrior protest was unusual, it wasn't the only instance of avatars banding together to give themselves a political voice.

In Second Life, a protest movement had broken out in July 2003 that was more explicitly political. A group of residents had come to feel that a tax levy on virtual property owners was placing an unfair burden on Second Life's main content creators, the people who were contributing most to the game.[2] The subsequent protests, involving crates of tea (of course), virtual bonfires, and even a few insurrectionist midgets, eventually led Linden Lab to work toward placating the protestors (though here too, the solution was short of what had originally been demanded).[3]

Could it be that such movements marked the way forward for virtual worlds, Ludlow wondered? Was virtual politics and the governance of online worlds by the people who inhabited them something that would actually come to have widespread impact, and perhaps even become the norm? His instincts were that this was worth pushing for, that it might make online worlds into more fair and open societies. The platform owners certainly didn't seem to be moving in that direction. Cyberspace was still the frontier, but in his travels there Ludlow thought he could discern the spark that might one day fulfill the promise foreseen by people like author Neal Stephenson of a digital universe that could provide freedoms and opportunities that weren't possible in the real world. A metaverse like that still seemed only a distant possibility, but it seemed to be one worth fighting for.

One of the biggest questions about how governance structures might form in places like The Sims Online or Second Life is how those bodies would relate to the software that underpins virtual worlds. The software that currently runs virtual worlds has yet to provide the solid foundation that such innovative societies would need to flourish in cyberspace. There are seldom built-in mechanisms that allow users to communicate to large groups, vote, or adjudicate disputes. As Uri continued to cover TSO even after his ban, one story in particular stood out as emblematic of some of the problems virtual worlds would face as their residents pursued social systems that began to resemble self-government.

In Alphaville, the Sim Shadow Government had provided protections similar to that of a real-world police force. In return, just as in the real world, many Sims were forced to give up some of their freedoms, including the freedom to bestow enemy links as they wished, to threaten other Sims, or even to pursue certain kinds of gameplay the SSG didn't approve of.

There was much about the SSG that resembled a real-life government. When Uri was first invited to join the SSG he was initially most impressed by the organization's robust communication system, as well as the fact that tagging units were on alert almost 24/7. Over time, it was the structure of the organization that came to fascinate him.

At the top level was the Overlord (named after the "Overlord Chair" that was for sale as one of the furnishings in the game). The SSG's original Overlord had been Mia Wallace, but control had subsequently passed to an avatar named Snow White. The SSG government was divided into several branches, including the Executive Branch, the War Department, the Intelligence Branch and Community Relations, among others. The War Department ran the SSG tagging teams and oversaw operatives like General Bam who handled infiltration and home demolition operations. Most interesting to Uri was the Intelligence Branch, which infiltrated groups and houses throughout Alphaville to gather information for members of the Executive Branch.

The SSG's main weakness, from an organizational point of view, was that it was principally held together by the work ethic and force of personality of its founder, Mia Wallace, and other key players. Consequently, the organization suffered greatly when several key members, including Mia, moved on to the MMO Star Wars Galaxies in late 2003.

When Mia Wallace left for Star Wars Galaxies, a number of other SSG members went with her, and those that stayed behind (including General Bam) felt angry and betrayed. Snow White was certainly a credible leader, but the Overlord position was extremely taxing, and by mid-December, she and one of her most prominent generals had also left the game for SWG,[4] effectively neutralizing the SSG as a dominant force on the Alphaville server.

The SSG's dissolution created a power vacuum in Alphaville, and within a month the Alphaville city map was dotted with names of Mafia families like the X-Mafia, the Armone Family, and the Gambino Family, who had taken power over various properties.[5] It was a vivid illustration of just how effective the SSG had been at keeping the Mafias under control.

The SSG's collapse also cleared the way for the rise of an organization known as the Alphaville Government, or AVG. *Herald* correspondent Kale revealed its existence in December 2003 via an interview with the AVG's CIA director, a Sim named Fans.[6] Though Fans held that the AVG was a

Figure 12.1
City map of Alphaville, after the Sims Shadow Government dissolves

different kind of organization than the SSG had been, and was not a Mafia, mob, or gang, the new government in fact operated just as the old one had, in many respects. Where there were reports of Sims crossing the invisible line that the AVG felt defined proper behavior, the organization moved in with tagging missions or "diplomatic" consultations with the offending party—and often found ways to make some money in the process.

The Alphaville Government had been established by an avatar named Mr-President, who borrowed the organizational chart of the U.S. government—or at least the parts of it that carried guns (it boasted a police force, a CIA, an FBI, and a military branch). Like the SSG, the AVG had a robust intelligence network, but the SSG had been obsessed with crushing the Mafias and scammers of Alphaville, whereas Mr-President, despite the claims of his tough-talking CIA director Fans, was perfectly happy to peacefully coexist with them; in the opinion of some, he was altogether too close to such players.

Mr-President effectively role-played a semi-corrupt politician, sponsoring social events and helping Sims who'd been scammed, while at the same time cavorting with mafiosi and attractive female avatars. But in March 2004, Mr-President decided to legitimize his reign by sponsoring an election, to be organized via a series of primary elections among other candidates, and culminating with a run-off between Mr-President and the winner of the primaries. Perhaps he thought the race would be a perfunctory role-playing exercise that would leave him more securely at the top, but he didn't count on the ever-vigilant *Herald*.

As the *Herald* began its coverage of the primaries, real world media outlets picked up the story as well.[7] And when the winner of the primaries turned out to be an avatar named Ashley Richardson, whose typist was a fourteen-year-old junior high school student in real life, the real-world press couldn't get enough of the story. NPR interviewed the typists for both candidates,[8] and the story eventually made its way to the pages of *The New York Times*.[9] But the *Herald* had the inside scoop.

Problems began in the wake of the primaries, when the AVG CIA director, Fans, was forced out of TSO by a griefer, and was replaced by an avatar named Alex Sanchez. Sanchez, though, turned out to be an alt of the infamous Alphaville mafioso JC Soprano, founder of The Sim Mafia. Not only that, but it was Soprano who would be in charge of the Internet-based voting mechanism that would ultimately determine who held the president's office.

The elections were intriguing on every level. Credible charges had surfaced that the primaries had been rigged to set up a media-friendly contest between Ashley Richardson and Mr-President.[10] And when the involvement of JC Soprano was revealed by the *Herald*,[11] things started to look shadier than ever.

For Uri, the election was as gripping as the 2000 U.S. presidential elections had been, with apparent voting irregularities surfacing soon after the balloting began.

JC Soprano's old enemy, Mia Wallace, although now residing in Star Wars Galaxies, had issued a communiqué to her former SSG operatives, urging them to vote for Ashley Richardson, and with three and a half hours to go, the race was deadlocked. But in those final hours, Mr-President surged ahead. Mr-President was ultimately declared the victor, but the *Herald* continued to keep a close eye on the story due to possible ballot-fixing.[12]

The newspaper's vigilance paid off with the leak of an incriminating chat log in which evidence came to light that the elections had in fact been rigged, starting as early as the primaries.[13] The election mechanism was intended to let each unique IP address get one vote, but Mr-President's team had designed in a loophole that would enable them to log a series of votes from a single IP address at certain times. Whether this loophole was exploited was impossible to say (in the incriminating chat log, Mr-President told JC Soprano, "We didn't have to do that"), but it was clear that the elections had been anything but free and fair.

The *Herald* was not the only virtual media outlet covering the new administration. Around the time of the elections, an African-American teenager had created an avatar named Oprah Winfrey and started a talk show in Alphaville, featuring an *Oprah*-like set where visitors would come to watch her show live. (Broadcasting such events was not possible in TSO.) Oprah, too, stuck with the election scandal, and landed an important interview with an avatar named Jason Sim who had worked for the Alphaville Government, and who claimed the elections had been rigged.[14] This was damning in itself, but matters got worse for Mr-President when the AVG's FBI director, Chad Thomas, posted in the *Herald*'s comments thread the fact that he had voted for Mr-President no less than two hundred times using a variety of IP addresses.

Until that moment, most of the citizens of Alphaville had pooh-poohed the *Herald*'s charges against Mr-President, but they could ignore them no longer. In July 2004, an Alphaville resident named David Pierce filed a virtual class action lawsuit against Chad Thomas, seeking monetary damages (in simoleans) for all Alphaville citizens who cared to join the suit.[15]

The subsequent trial was presided over by an avatar named Carmella in the Citisims Court of the Alphaville Government's judiciary branch, and decided by a jury of six Sims. While Pierce, who presented his arguments himself, had a strong case, the turning point came when defense attorney Robert the Man called Pierce to the stand and pressed him on whether there was actually a rule against voting more than once. The *Herald* quoted Judge Carmella's gripping summary of the trial:

> Eyebrows were raised as David approached the witness stand. Robert began with brief, quick questions such as, "Did the rules say that there could only be one vote?" forcing Mr Pierce to answer "No" in response. After several more questions

concerning the illegality of multiple voting, Robert dismissed his opponent and began his powerful closing argument to the jury.

Pierce began his closing arguments in a more somber state, and summed up by saying, "All I know is that I tried to make this game have morals and ethics. That is all I ever wanted. I guess that is too much to ask. Good night."

According to Judge Carmella's report, jury deliberations proceeded rapidly:

> Once sequestered, the deliberations began. After five minutes it became clear how this jury would decide. They all but one [found] that since no rule was in existence at the time of the election, [Chad] could not be found guilty of any illegal activity. The charges that Mr. Pierce and the City of Alphaville brought against Chad Thomas stated that he had illegally changed the outcome of the election, and while he did change the outcome, he did so legally. The lone juror finally conceded and one final vote was taken and recorded.[16]

Chad was found not guilty. Mr-President's administration was secure.

The Alphaville Government election scandal illustrated how residents of a virtual world naturally banded together into bodies that mimicked real-life governance structures, but that the software could not assure that such bodies would manage themselves virtuously. TSO's software was not designed to support virtual governance at all, in fact, and yet its residents had found a way to establish it.

Players of MMOs have also consistently managed to find their way around the de facto governments that run their worlds—the platform owners. The protests that took place in EverQuest and Second Life are evidence that when enough players and residents of virtual worlds are unsatisfied with the way those worlds are run, they manage to find a way to make changes. Most often, they resort to one of two courses of action: They pick up and leave, or they find a way to circumvent the "laws." But every now and again, they manage to force a change in the laws.

As Uri saw, virtual world residents find all kinds of creative ways to inhabit their worlds, and some of these ways creat tension between themselves and the companies behind their online environments. For Ludlow, that tension was summed up perfectly by Andrew Phelps's Kerafyrm story. "Games are about challenges, about hurdles or puzzles or fights overcome," Phelps had written. "To some players, the biggest hurdle or challenge is how to do what you (the designer) said couldn't happen. If you are making a game, accept this."[17]

The "circumventions" users dream up often come in the form of exploitations of game mechanics that were meant to achieve very different ends, or even hacks of the game code itself. Platform owners, of course, would love to be able to stop this, but two things prevent that: the long tradition of gamers and residents who can program things themselves (which is how virtual worlds got their start in the first place), and the fact that the collective imagination of thousands of MMO residents inhabiting the same virtual world will always outstrip the corporate constraints of a few dozen programmers working against a deadline to finish a product.

13 Into the Code: Exploits, Mods, and Hacks

The lines that separate creative use of a platform's mechanics from destructive exploitation of code can be difficult to discern. The fuzziest area is exploits, situations in which the software allows something that the platform's developers didn't intend to be part of their world; residents making use of these will generally be punished through account suspensions or permanent bannings if caught.

Exploits, though, can be among the most interesting ways to experience a virtual world, in part *because* they enable residents to take actions that weren't intended to be possible. In World of Warcraft, for instance, a creative player discovered a way to attack people in the auction house in Ironforge, where characters are otherwise protected from assault. He was able to do so because Warlock characters in WoW can command pets, one of which is known as a felhound. The player discovered that another creature can attack a felhound by casting a spell on it that causes it to explode after a short delay. The player let the creature cast the spell on his felhound, then dismissed the pet before it could explode. (Warlocks can dismiss and summon their pets as needed.) He then teleported himself to the crowded auction house in Ironforge and summoned the felhound again, whereupon it exploded, killing a number of characters who were standing in the vicinity.[1]

Platform owners dislike exploits in part because they disrupt in-world activity and the course of gameplay the company intended and in part because they're a headache to deal with. Another WoW exploit, for instance, allowed players to duplicate valuable items and gold by taking advantage of a bug in one of the game's software patches.[2] As the WoW "duping bug" became widely known, players started posting the details of how to achieve it on various forums and message boards. Just as quickly, Blizzard Entertainment, the company behind WoW, started deleting the same posts from its own forums, and hurried to repair the bug.

By locating cracks in the system, residents can achieve all kinds of results that were never intended to crop up in virtual worlds. Many companies (and, often, other residents) dismiss such efforts as griefing or scamming, and hold that their perpetrators should be banned from the world for life. But the motivation behind such moves probably speaks more of a love of the game and the virtual world than of a desire to cause trouble. While some exploits are encountered by accident, more are probably discovered by the players who push the technology of their worlds to the limit, trying to get every ounce of entertainment and value out of them that they can.

Platform owners may disapprove of players trying to push the boundaries of their virtual worlds, but it's worth remembering that it was boundary-pushing hackers that gave virtual worlds their start. Roy Trubshaw and Richard Bartle were programming students who'd been inspired by a single-player game when they wrote the first virtual world. Today, user-created modifications ("mods") continue the tradition, and some have become even more popular than the games they are based on.

Mods consist of add-ons or alterations to the source code of single-player and smaller multiplayer games (though not, most often, MMOs) that can be as simple as altering the look of a character in a game like Grand Theft Auto (such as the "Canadian tourist skin" that independent video artist Jim Munroe used in his short film *My Trip to Liberty City*, a hilarious spoof on GTA[3]), or as complex as completely rethinking the art, layout, goals, and even aspects of the game mechanics. (Mods that completely rethink a game are known as "total conversions.") Usually downloadable for free, player mods apply all manner of alterations to out-of-the-box games. One recent mod for the World War II combat game Battlefield 1942, for instance, turns 1940s-era leathernecks into Space Marines battling over a post-apocalyptic wasteland.

The player mod is in many ways the peak of hardcore gaming geekitude, or, looked at from a different angle, the clearest demonstration of a hardcore gamer's talent. Often requiring thousands of work-hours to create, and involving a team of player-programmers, level designers, and artists working together without any remuneration, making a mod is an act of love not just for the game it's based on but for the gaming community at large. Of the probably thousands of mods that are written each year, the vast majority will be played by only a handful of people, and the few that do get widely distributed will rarely have a direct impact on their creators' bank accounts.

Game companies love most player mods because they attract more players to their games. To make it easier for players to create them, companies often make some or all of their games' software code available. What players can achieve with this access is often remarkable. Garry's Mod, for example, a user-created software package for the popular first-person-shooter game Half-Life 2, not only applies its own alterations to the game but lets players themselves create new creatures, machines, maps, situations, and even game mechanics without having to write a mod of their own. Though Half-Life 2 was already one of the most popular games on the market, Garry's Mod has arguably enhanced its visibility and appeal, judging from the amount of coverage the mod got in the gaming press in 2005.

Some mods can even surpass the games they're based on in popularity. The most popular online action game in the world today is a player-created mod called Counter-Strike, which was based on the first-person-shooter game Half-Life. So many people play Counter-Strike that it now generates more Internet traffic each day than the entire country of Italy according to Valve, the company that publishes the game.

Needless to say, such creativity does not go unnoticed by game companies, and mods have recently become an important source of talent for the industry. Counter-Strike, for instance, which pits two teams of players against each other, one cast as a group of terrorists and the other as an anti-terrorist squad, was written by a college student and a high-school student working together remotely. Both of the players who wrote the mod are now employed by Valve Software, which developed and publishes Half-Life and, now, Counter-Strike.

Residents of virtual worlds are seldom encouraged to delve as deeply into the code of their worlds, because any change made there would affect not only themselves but every other player as well.

Uri had come across his fair share of exploits in The Sims Online. The game wasn't supposed to let you lock newbies in a "cooler," after all, and it certainly wasn't intended to be used as a cyber-brothel. But he also came across exploits that required another level of effort, allowing for another level of profit.

Most such exploits came as "macros," scripting utilities similar to those found in many word processing programs, that let players string a series of actions together into several brief keystrokes. Similar to very short computer programs, macro scripts in TSO were entered on the chat line or via third-party add-ons that ran in tandem with the client software that displayed the game on a player's machine. Often known as "bots," they could be used for a variety of things that might otherwise become repetitive or boring. One of the first bots players wrote for TSO was a greening bot that would either alert you when your motive bars were dipping into the red or actually send your avatar for a snack or to go to the bathroom when needed.

Many MMOs give their residents the ability to write macros, bots, and small software add-ons that make playing the game easier in some way. In World of Warcraft, for instance, common add-ons allow users to expand the user interface, giving them access to more of their powers at once (instead of having to search for the right weapon at a crucial moment). Others let users view maps of the world that are color-coded in various ways, or alert them if one of their spells is about to wear off and will need to be cast again.

But the line between adding functionality to a game and exploiting the interface to gain an unfair advantage isn't always clear. If it's acceptable to use an add-on that displays additional information on the in-world map, for instance, what's wrong with a mining bot written using the same software? Companies will generally allow the former, but ban players found using the latter.

A platform owner that makes a macro or add-on interface available to players gives up a small portion of control over what goes on in its virtual world. Giving players an interface to the code essentially means they can rewrite some of the laws of physics of their virtual world. But though companies will often cede enough access to let users add some useful functions to the virtual world experience, they will also retain the right to decide when that functionality has crossed the line from useful to harmful, and are not shy about letting residents know when they're on the wrong side of the line.

In TSO, things like improving your avatar's characteristics through "skilling" are common candidates for botting. Skilling generally involves clicking an object in the game like a blackboard or a piano or a book, waiting for your character to finish interacting with it, then clicking the object again. Some "skill houses" are set up with a variety of such objects, so that players can come and chat with each other while their avatars idly skill up in piano playing or pizza making, skills that allow for more interactions with other characters and in some cases even earn simoleans. But many people, if they have enough knowledge, prefer to write (or purchase) a macro that will allow them to click once and then have their avatar repeatedly perform whatever mundane skilling tasks that are at hand. A typist can then go about his or her real-world life without having to monitor a character who isn't doing anything interesting.

One of the biggest uses of bots in TSO was to make money. The money trader called Respected Banker, through whom Uri had discovered the shadowy simolean-dollar economy that existed in TSO, also introduced him to a number of prominent figures in the world of Sim finance, from a teenager with an avatar named Sir who sold simoleans and rare objects for a few hundred dollars here and there, to a man who claimed to have been injured in an accident at a steel factory but who was now making $150,000 a year selling simoleans and other virtual goods.

But the most revered Sim of all among the money traders was an avatar called Nyk, who had become a brilliant programmer of TSO bots. It was Nyk and his bots that supplied the money traders with the cash reserves they needed to conduct their business. The drudge work of making any substantial amount of money in The Sims Online could be mind-numbing. To automate the task, several players had written bots that would run your avatar through a particular money-making process, twenty-four hours a day, seven days a week, without its typist having to attend to it at all. Of all the bot programmers, Nyk was the only one who had risen to the status of legend.

Nyk's first bot was indeed impressive. Known as a "mazebot," it was designed to perform an in-world money-making task called "maze" (which, not surprisingly, involved working one's way through a small maze). It completely automated every aspect of Sim life: When your hard-working Sim needed a bathroom break, it would send him to the bathroom; when it needed to sleep, it would put him to bed; and it would send him to the kitchen whenever his Hunger bar dropped too far into the red.

Maxis and Electronic Arts weren't too crazy about mazebots. Will Wright and his team had put a lot of hard work into creating a virtual economy that would be balanced and fair to all. Having a few players able to generate a large amount of cash skewed the playing field the company had worked so hard to create. Accounts that were caught using mazebots were suspended or banned.

But because a typist-controlled avatar looked and behaved almost the same as one under the spell of a mazebot, Maxis had few means at their disposal to detect the add-ons. If Maxis discovered a particularly dedicated mazer on one of their servers, a company rep might log on and attempt to chat with the avatar. If the avatar didn't respond, it was likely that a mazebot was in use, and that account stood in danger of being banned.

Nyk worked around this problem by having his mazebots detect the unique chat icon that appeared whenever a company representative contacted a TSO user in-world. The mazebot would then sound an alarm on the customer's computer for thirty to sixty seconds. If the customer heard the alarm and returned, he or she could then chat to the Maxis rep and lay to rest any suspicions that a bot might be in charge. If not, the mazebot itself would give a preset response, and then simply log itself off. When Uri interviewed him in February 2004, Nyk had already sold more than fifty mazebots to other customers, at a price of $120 each.[4]

The simolean suppliers who were Nyk's customers set up their mazebots four to a house in Alphaville and in other cities, and they ran nonstop, sometimes earning their owners tens of millions of simoleans a day. Once a week or so, a supplier would sell the simoleans his mazebot had earned to a money trader, in exchange for U.S. dollars. The trader would then hit the streets of Alphaville (or the markets of eBay) equipped with a hefty supply of simoleans that were ravenously sought after by a huge customer base.

And Maxis was powerless. In the end, the only solution they could come up with was to remove the maze object from TSO. But by the time that happened, around Christmas 2003, so many simoleans had been "printed" that exchange rates on eBay had dropped from nearly $100 for a million simoleans to around $4 per million.

TSO wasn't the only online world that fell prey to automated money farming. EVE Online players regularly complain of "macro miners"—ships that mine asteroids while under the control of a macro program, not a human player. And for two years starting in May 2002, a programmer named Rich Thurman used macro bots to farm around nine billion gold pieces in Ultima Online, a haul worth something on the order of $100,000.[5]

Thurman, now in his early thirties, is one of the legends of MMO gold farming. An IT consultant, he brought his professional skills to bear on the challenge of making money in an online world. His inspiration came only once he had quit Ultima Online after an initial foray into the game, giving away all his belongings to other players on his way out. Months later, a friend told him that he had just sold a UO character on eBay for more than $1,000. Chagrined that he had missed an opportunity, Thurman vowed to take up UO again and play until he'd made back all the money he had spent on monthly subscription fees, around $500.[6]

Thurman pored over eBay auction histories to concoct a market analysis of UO, and soon saw there was a lot more to be made than just a few hundred bucks. But to get to the top end of the market simply by playing a character in the game, he also realized he'd have to spend fifty to sixty hours a week in-world. Instead, he set about automating his operation, and it soon grew to proportions even he hadn't expected.

Using a scripting program known as EasyUO, as well as programs of his own devising, Thurman was able to write small applications that would control his characters for him, even when he slept. His bots generally profited by buying raw materials from computer-controlled salespeople, using a skill designed into the bot to improve them somehow, then selling them back at higher prices. One common trade, for instance, involved buying raw birds from vendors, cooking them to make them valuable as food, then selling them back.

At its height, Thurman's operation ran thirty bots, with three characters on each of ten UO shards. His bots were run from twenty computers in his house in Dallas and ten more in a friend's garage in Phoenix, Arizona, so that his operation would be harder to trace. So extensively programmed was his "staff" that each bot would stop once it had made 250,000 gold pieces, summon another bot that Thurman had programmed as his gold collector, hand over the loot and then go back to what it had been doing before. Once he got it down to a science, each of Thurman's bots was earning more than half a million gold pieces an hour. At prices of $15 per million gold pieces, Thurman's workers at times netted him more than $20,000 a month.

Thurman's gold-farming operation had to deal with many of the same pitfalls Nyk's bots did. UO game masters used much the same technique for spotting automated farmers as TSO's did: They spoke to the avatar in question, and if he or she didn't respond, they could be assumed to be farming. Thurman came up with an even more ingenious solution to the problem than Nyk did, by having his avatar send all chat to his mobile phone's messaging service. By messaging back through his phone, Thurman could actually chat with whoever was questioning his character. The system wasn't perfect, but it worked well enough for him not to get caught, most of the time. And when he was caught, he simply opened another account. He had more than achieved his original goal: subscription fees had become a negligible cost.

Thurman's bots also had to be able to deal with angry competitors. And in Ultima Online, killing someone is an acceptable way to settle a dispute. As Thurman described it in an account of his gold-farming days, it was "like being in an old west town where you were asked to leave by sundown. 'This game aint big enough for the two of us. DRAW!,' is a quote that comes to mind.... There were even people that made bots that hunted bots. The motto was, if I can't compete, I'll just make it so no one can."[7]

In the end, Thurman lived by the same motto, though he went about it via different means. As EA, which also runs Ultima Online, got wind of Thurman's operation, it tried to close the gaps through which his bots were operating. But each fix only shut out more of Thurman's competitors and made it easier for him to compete. Finally, as Thurman's competitors began to figure out how his operation worked, Thurman revealed his secrets to EA. It took several weeks before he could get anyone to listen to him, but Thurman eventually explained to a developer where the hole in the system was located. About six hours later, all of the UO servers were brought down for an emergency patch.[8]

Nyk had had a similar experience in The Sims Online. There, EA had been stumped on how to prevent mazing. Their eventual solution was to remove the maze object completely from TSO toward the end of 2003. When they brought a modified version out in April 2004, the new object caused mazing payments to drop to zero if an avatar completed too many mazes too quickly.[9] Mazebotters remained undeterred, though, since they could set their software to maze at whatever rate they liked.

Maxis hadn't really solved the exploit. But they *could* have if they'd paid attention to what was being said in the *Herald*. In Uri's interview with Nyk, which took place after Maxis removed the first maze object and before they'd replaced it with a modified version, Nyk outlined several alterations to the maze object that could have been more effective at stopping such exploits. Not surprisingly, the company wasn't interested in taking advice from a newspaper it had recently tried to shut down.

But it went beyond that. As Uri learned in the interview, Nyk had previously contacted Maxis with an offer of help once news got out that the company was considering pulling the maze object from the game. The company hadn't been interested. Instead, it had made its own fix, an alteration that, according to the best hacker in the game, would do little to lessen the problem, much less get rid of it.

Rich Thurman's botting enterprise worked because he was able to gain access to portions of the code that platform owners normally keep behind electronically locked doors. Thurman wrote a piece of software that gave him access to the "packets" of information that the Ultima Online client software running on his machine was sending back and forth to the company's database servers, which managed the world. The problem, where the company was concerned, was that that information was normally filtered by the game's user interface; only part of it was intended to be available to players.

Users do occasionally manage to gain access to such bits and bobs, and what they can do with it can change the course of gameplay in ways that companies dislike. In a typical swords-and-spells MMO, for instance, a talented player-programmer may be able to write a hack that gives him or her access to information about a monster's location or its weaknesses, or where a normally hidden treasure trove may be located.

While such hacks do give players an unfair advantage, they are relatively harmless in the broader scheme of things (though they still merit banning in the eyes of both companies and most other players). More serious, and much more rare, are hacks that give users access to the information stored on the company databases that manage the world. With that kind of access, users could conceivably empty the bank accounts of other players, improve their own characters in a myriad of ways or even wreak untold havoc on the carefully balanced distribution of monsters and loot throughout a virtual world.

The client hack that struck Second Life in mid-2005,[10] in which enterprising users managed to gain access to private, user-created applications within the world, was not as serious as that, but still held alarming ramifications for the stability of that virtual world. The objects found across Second Life's virtual landscape are far more functional than those found in most other online worlds, and far more closely tied to the avatars that populate the world. Many of them manage financial transactions between avatars and information about the ownership of objects and of land. In that case, the potential for damage was great, although the hole was closed before much damage could be done. It was, however, just the first of many such holes, and as we will see in chapter 18, not all exploits would be so benign. Indeed, one of the subsequent exploits in Second Life shook the social foundation of its community of users and ruptured their relationship with the platform owner, Linden Lab.

Virtual economist Edward Castronova refers to the companies that run virtual worlds as "coding authorities" because their control over the software that runs their worlds gives them the final say over what may and may not take place there. But gamers and the inhabitants of virtual worlds have the same access to the fundamental building blocks of the world—the code, in the form of programming languages—that game companies do. Like Nyk and like Rich Thurman, they will always challenge the coding authority, because there's always someone somewhere who thinks they can do the job better than the people who are already doing it. This applies to real-world authorities, even in the most open and democratic of societies.

Somewhat more dramatically, if virtual world platform owners are like gods, then users who hack and modify the software are like demigods, seizing powers they were not intended to have. In extreme cases, users have reached so far as to become gods themselves, reverse engineering entire platforms and establishing rogue servers (versions of the platform that users maintain on their own). This has happened several times with the game Ultima Online, for example: In January 2004 there were reportedly three hundred rogue UO servers in operation.[11] Some reverse engineered versions of UO are deemed better than the original. Indeed one server boasted eight thousand accounts and one thousand and two hundred concurrent users. Oddly enough, Electronic Arts, which owns Ultima Online, has turned a blind eye to the development of rogue Ultima servers, even hiring one hacker who built one.

It was the battle between the gods and the demigods and the creeping line of sovereignty that had begun to concern Ludlow. With people spending more time than ever in productive pursuits within an increasing number of online worlds, where that line would get drawn would soon become very important. Control over a virtual world could have a very real impact on the physical lives of the people who inhabited it, and it was only a matter of time before the online and offline worlds drew very close to each other. He had seen the effects of this in The Sims Online, a world in which the boundaries between the real and the virtual weren't always clear. Now he was about to see it in action in a world where that line was often even less distinct, and which held still more startling lessons about the nature of our virtual lives.

14 The Resurrection of Urizenus Sklar

Ludlow first came across Second Life in the late summer of 2003, around the same time he started visiting The Sims Online. But it was not until months after Urizenus was erased from Alphaville that he started spending much time in SL. Something clicked on his initial visits, though, something that convinced him the world had potential and would be worth a substantial investment. So when Linden Lab, the company that ran the world, offered residents a chance to buy lifetime memberships with 4,096 square meters of free virtual property for $225, Ludlow jumped at the chance. There were risks, of course. Some online worlds shut down almost before they've gotten off the ground. And Ludlow had already been kicked out of one. But although he'd only had a small taste of the world, he already had the impression that Second Life, more than TSO, might point the way toward the future of virtual worlds. To Ludlow it was almost like putting a downpayment on a second home or a place to retire, the kind of place you could count on spending a lot more time in the future, even if conditions weren't quite right just yet.

In the months after he was banned from TSO, Ludlow felt compelled by a combination of duty and stubbornness to maintain an avatar-based presence in Alphaville and continue covering events there, but he pined for a virtual retirement home. He dropped in on Second Life from time to time, but without many friends there he found the world as foreign and intimidating as it was exciting. Learning the tools of this new online environment was clearly going to take some time. Luckily, he would soon find some helping hands, and from a surprising source: several alumni of the Free-Money for Newbies property in TSO.

After Urizenus had been banned from TSO, Ludlow's alt, Uri, gained instant credibility with the griefers and scammers of Alphaville. After all, most of them had had accounts suspended or banned as well, and had returned on different credit cards or using different Internet Protocol addresses (the marker of which Internet connection a particular computer is using) to mask their identities. Many of them would come to the *Herald* headquarters and engage in various shenanigans while Uri watched idly from the comfort of a virtual chair, engrossed in answering an avalanche of Instant Messages. Some *Herald* staffers and visitors were outraged by the visits of the griefers, but Uri figured he was at least keeping them off the streets. Their antics were fine with him so long as they didn't scam visitors at the *Herald* HQ. They were certainly keeping Uri informed about the comings and goings in TSO—a number of them constituted one of the most robust intelligence networks the *Herald* had ever had access to.

With more and more players leaving TSO, though, it wasn't long before the griefers who hung at the *Herald* began moving on to other MMOs. A core group of Evangeline's friends and associates, including the "abusive granny" Celestie and an avatar named Mimi, who had emerged as a kind of mother figure to the Free-Money crew, soon showed up in Second Life. On their return visits to TSO, they encouraged Uri to take a closer look at this new virtual world.

Once Ludlow did emigrate to Second Life, he was not disappointed. If his first experience of a 3-D virtual world had been a mind-blower, Second Life was not so much surprising as it was impressive. One of the first differences he encountered was that Second Life characters had surnames as well as first names (though players are limited to choosing their surnames from a list provided by the character-creation interface—which explains why most people in Second Life are more often referred to by their first names). Ludlow named his new character in honor of University of Michigan professor Larry Sklar, author of the book *Space, Time and Spacetime,*[1] a seminal investigation of the philosophical consequences of Einstein's theory of relativity (virtually none, as it turns out—"Metaphysics in, Metaphysics out" was Larry's slogan). In Second Life, Ludlow again took the first name Urizenus. The original Urizenus was dead, but in May 2004, when Ludlow began to spend more time in Second Life, he was reborn as Urizenus Sklar.

Second Life is a bit like TSO on acid. The colors are richer, the details sharper, the stuff of the world more varied, more exotic, and, in general, more insane. TSO is an isometric, *almost*-3-D world, a place with a static isometric camera angle looking out over a 2-D landscape; elevation can be simulated but not truly explored. Second Life is as 3-D as a virtual world can get. The "camera" through which you view the world can be positioned wherever you want it; the landscape is filled with hills, rivers, and mountains; and anything you come across can be stood on top of, jumped over, or flown around.

This was a different kind of world. What struck Uri most was the fact that no two things were alike. In TSO, if you wanted to hang a painting on the wall of your house, you selected from maybe half a dozen that had been provided by the game. Everywhere you went in TSO, the same clown paintings, the same potted plants, the same bookshelves and sofas and hedges and swimming pools dotted the interiors and landscape. In Second Life, on the other hand, if you wanted to hang a painting, you first designed the frame, then uploaded an image of your choosing or your own creation from your computer. You could then mount your picture on a wall, a ceiling, a floor, or even leave it hanging in space. None of the suburban cookie-cutter pall that had hung over TSO was present in SL. Instead, each new plot of land Uri visited held a unique creation, and even if many of them hadn't been perfectly executed or weren't to his taste, each one had the effect of expanding his sense of what was possible and sparking his creative desires.

What made this all possible was the thing that had been the most glaring omission from TSO: resident-created custom content. Everywhere Uri went, he was greeted by impressive, artistic, or even just mundane, but unique creations. The most amazing thing about them was that almost none of them had been made by the company behind the game. The slogan Linden Lab had chosen to describe their corner of cyberspace was "Your World. Your Imagination." On first glance, at least, that certainly seemed to be a fair assessment. In a way, the world itself was one big user mod. To Ludlow, the implications of a resident-created world were staggering.

Uri's first experiences of the tools of that world, though, were not the most satisfying. Second Life's main content-creation tools—an object editor and an interface that lets residents create small computer programs in LSL, or Linden Scripting Language—place an added level of complexity on top of the point, click, and keyboard navigation of places like World of Warcraft or TSO. A rich virtual existence can be had in Second Life without ever

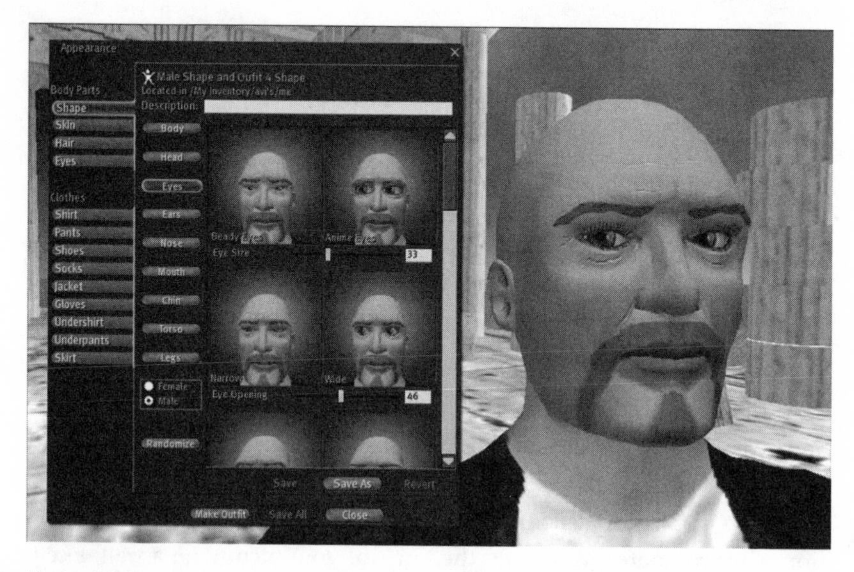

Figure 14.1
Second Life avatar creation

creating any content of one's own, of course, but for those who want to explore the tools, the learning curve in Second Life is steeper than that of most virtual worlds.

Fortunately, Uri got some initial help from the Free-Money house alums who had moved to Second Life. They explained the basics, from how to go about shopping, to how to get newly purchased goods out of their packages and into your avatar's inventory (not the most intuitive process, which explained why you often saw newbies walking around with boxes attached to their heads), how to use the things you'd bought, and the rudiments of the in-world building tool as well.

Creating a basic shape like a cube, a cone, or a sphere, for instance, is not actually that difficult. After choosing the shape from the editing interface, you merely click a spot on the ground and the object materializes. Voila, you have "rezzed" a "prim." That was another thing Uri discovered about Second Life: While TSO had borrowed online terms and made them its own, Second Life had produced a whole new set of jargon that was unique to this particular virtual world. "Prim," for instance, is short for "primitive," one of the basic building blocks of the constructions that populate the world. "Rez" was borrowed from the movie *Tron*, in which

Figure 14.2
Second Life content creation

"de-rez" was used to describe something fading away as its resolution declined.

But rezzing a prim is only the beginning. To make something like the wall of a house you have to either stretch, squeeze, and twist the object into approximately the shape you want, or build "by the numbers," plugging dimensions and coordinates into the editing tool by hand. By-the-numbers builds, of course, can have their joints, seams, and components matched together more precisely than stretching and dragging prims into place, but the added homework isn't worth it to many people. Learning LSL is another hurdle, though a considerably smaller one for those who already know a programming language. But LSL is simple enough that even those who have never programmed before can, with a bit of patience, learn it. And using LSL can add a whole new dimension to the things one creates in Second Life, enabling objects to move and rotate, to communicate with one another and with the avatars wandering around in the world, to act as vehicles, or to act as vending machines that collect Linden dollars in exchange for other objects. Second Life even lets users create objects that can create other objects, stream music or movies within the world, or act as games of varying degrees of complexity within the world.

Second Life can be a more labor-intensive virtual world than practically any other, but for those who see the possibilities inherent there, the complexity of Second Life's building tools is a small price to pay for the ability to create complex artifacts that for the most part truly are limited only by your imagination.

As Uri began to explore the world, he found that Second Life's technical complexity had an impact on the social dynamics he saw there as well. In TSO he had constantly encountered people who were AFK because their typists were busy about some real-world task while their avatars engaged in a yawn-inducing round of skilling. In Second Life Uri came across many similarly unresponsive avatars, but discovered it was for a different reason. Rather than being disengaged from their virtual world, Second Life's typists seemed to be *overly* engaged. Some would fail to reply because they were too busy building and scripting. Others might reply after a few minutes' delay, apologizing to Uri for being involved in five different conversations at once.

Once Uri was acclimated to the new environment, he set about looking for things to report on in the world. Part of his goal was to keep the connection with his readers from Alphaville, and what better way to do that than with a story on the Alphaville scammer's second lives?

In late May 2004, Uri ran an interview with Celestie, the "abusive granny," in which she talked about her new life in Second Life.[2] Uri was pleasantly surprised to find that Celestie and several other former Free-Money for Newbies roommates who had come to SL with her seemed to have gone straight. What was even nicer to hear—in part because it vindicated Uri's opinion about the value of content-creation tools—was that Celestie saw no need to be a griefer in Second Life because the new world offered so many richer, more creative avenues of expression.

Urizenus: Are you going to be scammers [in SL] or do something else?

Celestie: We've cleaned up our act, no one knows who we are there.

Urizenus: Does that mean you *don't* scam there?

Celestie: Correct.

Urizenus: Well, how come you couldn't stop scamming [in TSO] and don't feel like scamming [in Second Life]?

Celestie: It's so easy in TSO....

Urizenus: Any parting thoughts about TSO?

Celestie: TSO has been a great outlet for my creativity, but I've outgrown TSO and its never-changing ways.

Urizenus: Any regrets about some of the stuff you did in TSO?

Celestie: No regrets, you learn from your mistakes.

Urizenus: Well, what were your mistakes and what did you learn?

Celestie: I should have never started scamming. I wanted to be a mean, rude, old sim and not a scamming beast.

Urizenus: Why did you want to be mean and rude?

Celestie: I wanted to be mean and rude because I wanted to be different and I wanted attention.

As ever, it was hard to know how much credence to give such contrition, but to Uri, who had come to know his subjects well over the previous months, Celestie's remorse sounded genuine. And what he found most striking was the fact that it was Second Life's rich creative possibilities that seemed to have turned Celestie and the other former scammers around.[3] Mimi and the other Free-Money alums would soon start making and selling clothing, hair extensions, and fashion accessories, and becoming an active part of Second Life's commercial scene.

What Uri had been saying all along was more clear than ever now: The residents of virtual worlds will find their creative outlets one way or another. If the tools of the world itself don't provide enough opportunity, residents will find their own creative outlets, often in the form of griefing and scams. If the world itself does provide the right kind of outlets, though, much of that creative energy (though not all of it, as Uri would discover soon enough) can be channeled into more positive tasks.

Uri's building and scripting lessons from the Free-Money crowd took place in late May and early June 2004. His first project was a house, which he planned with plenty of glass and long, Bauhaus-style lines. And it was while planting these early roots in the new world that he first experienced griefing, SL-style.

Before he'd even finished his construction work, an avatar named Sir dropped in on him and his houseguests. Another TSO refugee, Sir had been a member of the Alphaville Government, which the *Herald* had helped bust for running a fraudulent election just months before.[4] Sir had no interest in any kind of virtual koffee klatch. Instead, he hurled abuse at Uri and his guests, causing them to invoke the "/ignore" command that would block Sir's colorful monologue from their chat windows.

But Sir was not to be ignored. Once he realized what was happening, he pulled out the big guns—a push gun, that is, a Second Life weapon that can propel an avatar far from whatever he or she had been doing. Uri and his guests went flying, and to Uri's surprise he ended up almost in the lap of one of his next-door neighbors, another TSO refugee, Cinda Valentino, who in Second Life ran the Valentino Family Mafia.

When Cinda heard what was happening, she gathered a few of her underworld associates, whose own push guns kept Sir at bay until a Linden liaison could be summoned. As the Linden began sorting things out, Cinda ordered her crew to pack up: "Let's go boys, I think we got our point across."

The presence of authority, in the person of a Linden, quieted Sir's antagonistic bent for the moment and the situation defused itself. But when Uri explained to the Linden what had gone on, he was met with a pleasantly surprising question: "Are you the Urizenus from the *Alphaville Herald*?" Uri's reputation had preceded him.

As he continued to explore Second Life, the same thing happened on numerous occasions. When Uri went to a public talk given by Philip Linden, whose typist was Philip Rosedale, the founder and CEO of Linden Lab, he found himself surrounded by TSO refugees, Linden employees, and other SL residents who either knew of the *Herald* or were regular readers. It was almost like a homecoming.

As the *Alphaville Herald*'s coverage of Second Life ramped up, Uri embraced the tabloid reputation that had stuck to the newspaper in the

Figure 14.3
Uri's scale Second Life Parthenon

wake of the real-world media's coverage of his ban from TSO. "Paparazzi Catch Simlebrities in SL!" screamed the headline of one story featuring the former Alphaville scammers.[5] If critics wanted to label the *Herald* a muckraking tabloid, that was fine with Uri; if you were going to run a newspaper in a virtual world, he figured, why not have some fun with it? The *Herald* continued to investigate issues of governance and virtual economics, but it was also willing to take an amused view of some of the stranger things that the residents of the metaverse were engaged in.

One of the refreshing things about Second Life was the increased sense of openness that Uri initially saw in Linden Lab. Philip Linden's "town hall" meetings were not an uncommon occurrence.[6] Uri wrote up such events in the *Alphaville Herald* as "your intrepid reporter Uri, on vacation in SL." But it was becoming increasingly clear to him that this was where the future of virtual worlds lay, and it wasn't long before he realized that, like the many TSO refugees who had found a new home in SL, the *Herald* would have to make the leap as well.

The *Herald* took the plunge on June 14, 2004, relaunching as the *Second Life Herald* and extending its mission to cover MMOs in general, initially by tracing the TSO diaspora.[7] Though life in Alphaville continued to be a staple for the moment, there were now more and more SL stories, and MMOs like EVE Online and Star Wars Galaxies began to appear on occasion in the *Herald*'s pages.

The *Herald* got its first big SL story when Philip Linden himself paid a call on Urizenus Sklar. A day or two after the launch of the *Second Life Herald*, Philip emailed Uri to thank him for focusing on his virtual world. Uri responded with a request for an interview, and the ran story on June 21, 2005.[8]

Philip arrived in the guise of a hot female avatar, holding a rose and toting a Seburo Compact Exploder, one of the futuristic handguns that a number of SL residents had created to use for random virtual warfare or in larger-scale game environments within the world. The Compact Exploder was known to be the most rapid-firing weapon of them all, though. When Uri casually wondered how it fired so quickly, Philip told him the weapon utilized multiple scripts that ran at the same time, a kind of crude parallel processing that allowed the Exploder to fire at rates one script could never have handled. It was a throwaway question, but in a way it summed up what Second Life was about. Using parallel scripts was "something that we never really thought about," Philip said. "But of course we are more or less surrounded by things we didn't think about." To EA, that had been a liability and a danger. To Linden Lab, it was an asset, the main selling point of the company's virtual world.

Philip riffed on the virtual physics that underpin online worlds and predicted SL would top a million residents sometime in 2007. Along the way, Uri also discovered Philip shared his impression that worlds with more constructive activities on offer would probably see fewer griefers and scammers.

Philip Linden: You can look at an online world, and ask how much freedom it gives you as a user. Sort of like the rat-in-a-cage analogy. How big is the cage? What is there to do? So when you look at historical online worlds . . . something like EverQuest, or even TSO . . . it seems quite obvious that in them you are far more restricted than in your waking life. There is a lot less you can do there than in reality. So I believe this is a simple test for how basic and abusive and frustrated people will become in these worlds. The answer to the question "How much can I do?" tells us "how mean you will be."

Urizenus Sklar: You mean the less you can do, the meaner you will be?

Philip Linden: Yes. So SL poses a new question. . . . What if the online environment offered you more freedoms than the real world, in just about every way. I assert, by comparison to these historical cases, that we might therefore actually behave better in such a place. We might learn faster, interact more deeply, and therefore become better people, at least on some levels.... In general that trend seems to hold up...that there is such a blue-sky opportunity for doing stuff, that griefing just doesn't make it to the top very quickly. It is more fun to do other stuff.

Urizenus Sklar: Okay, let me make a distinction here, between having lots to do, and having the tools to make things to do; it seems like the focus here is on the latter.

Philip Linden: Yes, of course.

Urizenus Sklar: And that seems to be important.

Philip Linden: I agree.

Urizenus Sklar: You anticipated this?

Philip Linden: I am asserting that this will only occur in an environment in which the freedoms are not a laundry list of experiences, a la Disneyland, but instead a fundamental ability to express yourself; these are the real freedoms. I am saying that if you have more freedoms, in an expressive sense, you might have better or at least more complex behavior.

Of course, Philip's theory didn't hold in every case. Uri also encountered Evangeline in Second Life—wandering around with no clothes on and being lectured by a Linden on etiquette and proper behavior in the world. Evangeline's visit to SL was brief, mostly because she never found a way to cause trouble, Uri speculated. What with the proliferation of "sexy skyboxes" and alternative lifestyle communities, walking around in the nude was hardly transgressive in SL. The fact was, in Second Life, Evangeline couldn't come up with anything outrageous enough to stand out.

The more of Second Life Uri explored, the richer and more fascinating the virtual world seemed to be. At every turn, there was some object, avatar, architecture, or script—or some combination of them—that shed more light on the workings of online societies and the ways in which people brought their offline lives into the virtual realm. Second Life is in part a fantasy world in which you can "virtualize," if not reify, whatever takes your fancy. But these fantasies are driven by the real-life psyches and concerns of the typists behind the avatars. While many people take Second Life for little more than a 3-D chat room, closer inspection reveals much more going on there. As it looked to Uri, in fact, what happened in Second Life, far from being virtual at all, was largely an extension of what happened in the real world. Second Life was a place—though not a physical one—where people gathered, did business, and formed relationships with as much complexity and enthusiasm as anywhere on earth.

Though Uri broadened the *Herald*'s mission almost immediately after changing the paper's name in June, a few of the Alphaville refugees continued to make good stories. Besides the former scammers of the Free-Money for Newbies houses, Uri interviewed his new neighbor, Cinda Valentino, who had founded the first Mafia in Second Life, having been a prominent member of one of TSO's Mafia familes. (She had come to SL after a short stint in a witness protection program, she said, during which she had been forced to take up residence in an MMO called There.) Cinda laid out the landscape of the SL "crime" scene, giving Uri an important map for his investigations into SL's underworld.

In contrast to the popularity contest that most TSO Mafias engaged in, the Mafias in Second Life (Cinda explained in an interview with the *Herald*) claimed to be more concerned with protecting themselves from the depredations of griefers or other annoying SL residents, because in Second Life, as in TSO, the company behind the world seemed not to want to get its hands dirty. "The main reason that we formed is to be able to have a means to deal with people that the Lindens either won't or don't want to deal with themselves," Cinda told the *Herald*. "In other words, if you make one of us an enemy, you get 47 more. We *never* start *anything*, we only finish it."[9]

Mafia families like the Valentinos also got into some of the more traditional real-world Mafia businesses as well. Garbage hauling isn't a service that's much needed in Second Life, but when Uri interviewed Cinda, the Valentinos already ran a protection service, put on boxing matches, planned to get into the virtual real estate business, were putting the finishing touches on a large-scale casino, and were thinking of expanding their operations into loan sharking as well.

As both the Free-Money scammers and the Mafia families illustrate, Second Life lets you do anything you can do in TSO, only better. Both worlds include the same kinds of social groups, but the ones that operate in Second Life have far more opportunities open to them. This is because of the resident-created custom content that had been so sorely lacking in TSO.

While the social groups in SL may look the same as those in TSO from a distance, up close they can be very different. To begin with, the infinite range of avatar customization possibilities in Second Life means that even your graphical representative becomes an expressive extension of yourself. In TSO, one's appearance, chosen from a limited menu of choices, says lit-

Figure 14.4
The fully armed flying mechanical moose

tle about the typist behind the avatar. In SL, by contrast, you can become whoever you want to, from a walking, talking bear to a tiny, chain-smoking squirrel; from a pointy-eared elf to a mechanical, bullet-spitting moose; from a buxom exotic dancer to a tattooed stud to a sharply-dressed dandy to just a guy in jeans and a t-shirt; from a terrorist to a Nazi to a Star Wars stormtrooper—the possibilities are endless. Some use their avatars to fit themselves deeper into the groups they belong to, or seek to belong to. Others use the tools of the world to make themselves unique.

SL's content-creation tools also let the landscapes of the world take varied form. Once they've staked out a plot of land in one of the sixteen-acre regions (which numbered three thousand and growing as of late 2006) that make up the Grid, residents build all manner of architectural and other wonders. Virtual residences are just the beginning. Dance clubs, sex clubs, movie theaters, retail shops, even shopping malls, apartment houses that rent space to residents on Basic accounts (i.e., those who don't want to pay the extra fee for owning land), castles, coffee shops, and more dot the Grid. Unconstrained by the inconveniences of real-world physics, many of these structures float in the air or take on gravity-defying shapes that often make Second Life seem like a world built out of dreams. Just as often, though—and to the bafflement of one *Herald* freelancer[10]—residents seem intent on merely duplicating the kinds of McMansions found in metropolitan suburbs.

Buildings are only the tip of the iceberg. Almost anything that can be imagined can be built. The Seburo Compact Exploder is an impressive weapon, but even that is on the low end of complexity where SL creations are concerned. Vehicles of all sorts are a particularly rich area of exploration, and the jetpacks, planes, and automobiles (not to mention the motorcycles, hot-air balloons, and even parachutes) of the master vehicularist Cubey Terra are widely driven and well loved. One group of virtual artisans fashioned an intricate space station that hung for a while high in orbit above the Grid.

Many resident builds are created simply for creativity's sake. One early project, known as Americana, recreated tourist destinations from around the country, including Fenway Park and various New York City landmarks. The island sim of Montmartre has become a sort of artists' colony in Second Life, filled with all manner of fanciful sculpture and playful spaces to explore. On the other end of the artistic spectrum there is the Sleezywood sim, which features white-trash-style trailer homes, junkyards, more than one virtual velvet Elvis, and, of course, copies of Sleezywood's tabloid of choice—the *Second Life Herald*. SL resident Deevyde Maelstrom's Brainiacs HQ is filled with delightful toys and gizmos that could only be possible in a virtual world.

Other residents find ways to use the potential of Second Life to create unexpected tourist destinations. The Hawaii sim, for instance, features tiny private coves and cabanas, a lava beach near the mists of a waterfall, tropical birds crying somewhere in the distance, and an atmosphere that makes the cares of the working world seem a million miles away. It's an idyllic vacation spot, and the best thing about it is that it takes less than five minutes to get there from anywhere in the world.

Even the simplest of creations can become a nexus for social interaction in Second Life. One of the most popular spots on the Grid is the Neo Realms Fishing Camp in SL's Alston sim. Created by a team of five residents, Neo Realms lets virtual anglers purchase a virtual fishing rod and then while away the hours casting from the small pier or from lily pads that float nearby. Fishing tournaments with cash prizes are held every week[11] and the pier has become a place where residents come to chat with friends; it occasionally is also a bit of a virtual pick-up scene. One friend of Uri's met a female avatar while fishing there and eventually "married" her in the virtual world.

Second Life is even more fascinating when one considers that almost nothing on the Grid has been created by the company behind the virtual world. Linden Lab provides only the rolling landscape on which the more ambitious of SL's residents build. As Philip Rosedale, the founder and chief executive of Linden Lab, puts it, "It's very interesting to be inside somebody else's vision of what the world should look like. Unless you're concerned with taste and smell, Second Life provides an almost perfect canvas for creating escapist environments."[12]

What made all this possible, what allowed residents and Lindens alike to wander around in "somebody else's vision of what the world should look like," were exactly the kind of custom content-creation tools that Electronic Arts had done everything in its power to keep out of The Sims Online. Second Life gives you the power to be, do, and create nearly anything you can imagine. But Linden Lab went one step further when, in November 2003, early in Second Life's existence, the company granted its residents the intellectual property rights to the things they created on the Grid.

The main impact of the change was that it let residents commercialize their creations without fear of negative repercussions where Linden Lab was concerned. The move was unprecedented in the history of graphical online worlds. (Some earlier text-based games had similar policies, but none had attracted anywhere near the audience of Second Life.) It marked what many hoped might eventually lead to a new era of user ownership and collaborative creation that would make virtual worlds into even more useful and fascinating places than they already were. The company, of course, still owned the bits and bytes that resided on their servers, but

Second Life's residents now had a stake in the value that could be generated from their creations in a significant way, a way that wasn't possible in any other virtual world. The implementation of a good idea in Second Life was now protected from piracy in the same way a real-world implementation was protected. Such protections aren't airtight, by any means, but they gave residents a much greater sense of "buy-in" to their world and their creations than could be found almost anywhere else. Though many continued to maintain that Second Life was "only a game," it was now apparent to anyone who looked at it closely that that was no longer a sufficient way to describe it.

Already in late 2003, nearly one hundred thousand user-to-user transactions were taking place each month, according to the company.[13] By the spring of 2005, SL was generating almost $2,000 in commerce a year for every resident on the Grid.[14] Such figures meant that the emergence of a capitalist class in SL was all but inevitable. And indeed, that's exactly what happened. By the summer of 2006, the Grid was seeing a far more impressive *5.7 million* user-to-user transactions each month, according to Linden Lab, accounting for some $6.44 million (US$, not L$) in transactions (broadly construed to include exchanges of currency) monthly. By mid-2005, the land market in Second Life had grown robust enough that Anshe Chung was able to earn close to $10,000 a month by buying in volume and subdividing for a profit.[15] By November 2006, she would accumulate US$1 million worth of virtual assets.

Retailers could make a pretty penny too, especially in the fashion business. Avatars like Aimee Weber and Nephilaine Protagonist not only had profitable clothing lines in Second Life but were making plans to convert them into real-world businesses. As Second Life's population grew, all kinds of profit-making businesses sprang up. Of course, granting residents the IP rights to their creations didn't necessarily make it any *easier* for them to earn a profit. One thing it did lead to, though, was a different kind of conflict on the Grid.

Though ownership in things like the design of a virtual halter top or the pattern of some virtual wallpaper rested squarely with the creator, there was little to stop an unethical resident from lifting that design for his or her own uses. Residents could nominally copy-protect their creations, but common bugs and easy hacks made it all to easy to steal the visual patterns known as "textures," which often took hours to create in expensive third-

Figure 14.5

Anshe Chung announcing US$1,000,000 in virtual assets

party software like Photoshop, without too much trouble. The Digital Millennium Copyright Act of 1998 requires providers of Internet-based services like Second Life to respond to claims of copyright infringement by removing the offending content, but with hundreds of thousands of residents creating content on the Grid and a staff of only a couple of dozen at Linden Lab, bits and pieces inevitably fell through the cracks; this would come back to haunt Second Life again and again.

The big story of the *Herald*'s early days in Second Life was the Second Jessie War, which unfurled over more than a month and held insights into everything that made Second Life a fascinating place to spend time. For students of virtual societies, the Second Jessie War had it all: the clash of SL cultures, the clash of RL cultures, resident-created content, virtual commerce, cybersex, the most popular spot in Second Life and, as if that wasn't enough, a giant, fully armed, flying mechanical moose.

As SL resident pancake Stryker had found,[16] the Jessie sim—one of the few places in Second Life where residents can be shot and "die"—could be a dangerous place to do business. But it was also a place filled with colorful stories, and from Uri's underground bunker there he often picked up on armed conflicts that would sometimes find their way into the *Herald*.

Figure 14.6
Jessie residents wait for attack from One Song

The first signs of trouble came in August 2004. Two avatars, One Song and Tank Levy, had purchased most of the Stanford sim, a region that bordered Jessie, and were clearly making plans for a significant venture there. The property was in a strategic spot. While SL residents can now travel instantaneously between any two points on the Grid, there was a time when such easy travel was not available. Until late 2005, SL residents could not teleport to just any spot on the Grid; they had to land at a limited number of "telehubs" when traveling long distances. That constraint raised the value of the real estate that surrounded each telehub, as well as the avenues between telehubs and popular destinations.

Stanford was on a direct path between Club Elite—at the time the most popular destination in all of SL—and the telehub that served it. And One Song and Tank were nothing if not ambitious, apparently planning to grab a share of Club Elite's fly-over traffic by opening a shopping mall on the busy route between the telehub and the club. Tank (who claimed, oddly, that he had "always dreamed of owning a mall") was the money behind the operation, and One Song, backed by his gang, The Associates, was to be the muscle.

To acquire the necessary land in Stanford, Tank and One Song needed to buy up small parcels piece by piece. But what to do if someone didn't want to sell? That was where One Song came in, and Uri, who owned a small plot smack in the middle of Stanford, got a firsthand look at his aggressive technique. "Is this a hostile act?" One wondered out loud about why Uri hadn't sold. In other words, was he going to have to retaliate? Uri had encountered plenty of online griefers and gangsters in his day, but One Song (who would go on to achieve fame in Second Life as a bombmaker[17]) had an unusual gift for striking fear in the heart of an avatar—despite the fact that there was nothing he could really do to a typist. Intrigued, Uri conducted an hour-long negotiation with One before agreeing to a property trade. But One Song's business proposition went over less smoothly in another negotiation Uri witnessed, with a Stanford resident named Ruby Wilde.[18]

One Song, whose land bordered Ruby's on three sides, wanted Ruby to sell her parcel for less than it would fetch on the open market. When she refused, One used Second Life's interface to ban her from his land, forcing Ruby and anyone who wanted to visit her to come and go via the free-fire zone of the neighboring Jessie sim. Still, Ruby hung on for a fair market price, refusing to be pushed completely off her parcel, even if it did become exceedingly difficult for her to come and go.

When Uri arrived in the midst of one of One and Ruby's rounds of negotiations, he found One Song spewing crude verbal abuse at his neighbor. Ruby was being defended by a Jessie resident named Cyanide Leviathan, who counselled her not to give in. After One spent a few minutes calling Ruby a "dyke" and telling her that what she needed was "some real big cock," Cyanide summoned Jeff Linden to mediate the situation. The confrontation was defused when Jeff ordered One Song and his crew back to their nightclub, a topless bar and cyber-brothel in the Baku sim. But the event did not go down well with the residents of Jessie, who were suspicious of the mall project.

Neither One Song nor the SL residents who had gained control of the Jessie sim in an earlier Jessie war[19] were very good at tactful negotiations. The original Jessie conflict had unfolded concurrently with the U.S.

Figure 14.7
Jeff Linden intervenes between One Song and Ruby Wilde

invasion of Iraq, and had been fought, for the most part, over the same issues that divided the real world at the time—only in Second Life, those issues were "discussed" with virtual weapons like the Seburo Compact Exploder. The survivors of the first Jessie war, Cyanide included, were for the most part fans of an MMO called World War II Online (or WWIIOL), and at the time One Song took up residence in Stanford, Jessie was rife with Confederate flags and tributes to George W. Bush.

This new battle was fought not over political ideology, but over cultural values. The WWIIOLers were not only interested in preserving the Southern traditions and conservative values they espoused, they also hoped to preserve the unique values and traditions that had sprung up in the Jessie sim, which had already developed a rich history. The last thing they wanted was a neighboring region dedicated to the consumerist orgy of fetishware being sold for use in erotic dance clubs and cyber-brothels. To them, it spelled overcrowding, newbies, and perverts.

Tensions rose as a WWIIOLer named James Few built a gigantic wall along the Jessie-Stanford border, complete with biohazard symbols and warnings like "Beware of Everything." Incensed, One Song threatened to "kick your fucking asses, every single one of you, if you don't stop macking about."[20]

In the following days, both sides gathered their forces. A group of virtual drug runners known as The Cartel allied themselves with One Song and erected a crude but enormous sign reading, "Fuck you WWIIOLers." The Techsols, a group of gifted scripters, joined the WWIIOLers' side, and even made Uri a temporary member of the group so he could operate as a journalist in the war zone without drawing fire from Techsols' automatic weapons. Safely in "uniform," Uri effectively become the first virtual war correspondent! And square in the middle of everything, as usual, was a group of Free-Money for Newbies alums, who owned a small plot of land on the Jessie-Stanford border.

Then, on the eve of war, came grave diplomatic news: Tank Levy and One Song had had a falling out. Tank had expressed reservations about the heavy-handed tactics being applied by One Song and The Associates, and One had promptly severed all ties. Uri found him at a table in his club, apparently dejected, though being comforted by a topless dancer in his employ named Cathy Curry. "I'm just so shocked by it all," Cathy intoned. One Song could hardly believe it either: "I did all that land baron work for nothing."

To Uri, it looked as thought the split would spell a return to more peaceful times. But by this point, diplomatic relations between One Song and the WWIIOLers had deteriorated so much that war was inevitable, with or without Tank in the picture.

Full-scale combat finally erupted on August 23,[21] after several days worth of choice epithets had first been hurled back and forth across the Jessie wall. With his scripting prowess, One managed to render himself practically invulnerable to weapons fire from the WWIIOLers, even from the enormous flying mechanical moose, bristling with armaments, that the Jessie faction turned loose on him. One's weapons, for the most part, concentrated not on killing his foes but on crashing their sim, or simply overloading it enough to create intolerable "lag" (a state in which the software running on the user's computer is so bogged down with useless computations that the picture on the screen grinds to almost a halt).

A running battle raged over the next few days, with One Song setting the WWIIOLers' Reichstag-inspired headquarters ablaze and raising his "Associates" corporate flag there, in a scene inspired by the 1945 Russian takeover of Berlin that spelled the end of the Third Reich. Combat spread outside of Jessie with two successive lag-inducing attacks on One Song's cybersex hangout in Baku, Club Diamond, the second of which crashed the server on which the Baku sim ran.

In the end it was hard to point to a winner. Tank Levy scuttled plans for a super-mall, and used his share of the Stanford land to build a dance club with an adjacent small shopping area. One Song was notably absent at the club's opening party, but made his presence felt several days later when Tank's property was suddenly wiped clean. One had littered Tank's land with hundreds of microscopic prims, each one running lag-inducing computations. Unable to locate the infestations, it was Tank himself who was forced to remove all the objects on his property—including his club and mini-mall. These could be rebuilt, of course, but the episode cost Tank dearly in terms of time and customer relations.

Not all of the *Herald*'s readers were as fascinated by the story of the Second Jessie War as Uri was, of course. As one reader commented, "Would love some informative articles on the great places and things to do instead of all this war nonsense. What's up with you, anyway?"

What was up was that in the Jessie war Uri saw many of the most interesting forces of cyberspace at work. Uri responded:

> There are 150 million fan sites that cover the bingo games, sexy avatar contests, and new puce-colored snow suits. This is not "war nonsense" but a very important dispute in the game—one that mirrors current real-world disputes in interesting ways. On the one hand, we have the Jessie residents, who are traditional in a lot of ways, and anxious to protect the traditions of their virtual home. This is being threatened by One Song's gigantic mall development project, which will bring lots of newbies and fashionistas into close proximity to Jessie—too close by some lights. Add to this the fact that One Song expects the mall to make real-world money (and non-trivial amounts) and that One Song is using pressure tactics to remove other users from Stanford, and also that we are seeing the most advanced scripting technology in the

Figure 14.8
Urizenus at home in Second Life. *Source:* Screenshot by Angela Thomas

game being deployed.... If you can't see why this is important then please do stop reading and find a nice fluffy fan site to lay your head down on.

Oh, and one more thing. If you don't like stories that include a fully armed flying mechanical moose, well, you are hopeless.

A few weeks later, the *Herald* offered a more complete analysis that summed up much of why Uri felt the Second Jessie War was an important moment in Second Life's history and the history of cyberspace:

It may be that when we look at these conflicts we are looking at our own future—a future where much of our lives unfold in virtual spaces (work places, meeting places, etc.) and where we may seek ways to defend the traditions of our virtual spaces against bandwidth barons. When that day arrives, let's hope we have strong scripters at our side.[22]

It appeared the metaverse was replicating physical reality with surprising accuracy, and with all the color and complexity of life on the lawless frontier. Uri's post introducing the *Second Life Herald* had focused its mission on covering the TSO diaspora in worlds like SL, Star Wars Galaxies, and others. But now it was more clear than ever that SL itself would be the focus, and that there was more than enough here to keep the *Herald* and its few correspondents busy for a long time to come. In Second Life, Uri had found a new home.

15 The Power of the Virtual Press

Uri was understandably impressed by Second Life and the possibilities it offered (as well as by the quantum advance it represented over TSO). But as he dug further into the world he began to discover fissures in the Grid. A real-world reporter dropping in to check things out might emerge with a uniformly rosy picture of the place, but Uri and the *Herald* were deeply embedded in their second lives, and it wasn't long before they began to see that SL was far from a virtual utopia. In fact, it appeared to have serious limitations.

Uri's first question was whether residents' rights were really as safe as they seemed. Was this place really the new world it purported to be? A quick glance at the Terms of Service[1] itself indicated that the answers to those questions were anything but encouraging.

The first and most glaring problem had to do with a topic that was near and dear to Uri's heart: Does the ToS make it too easy for the company to kick people out of the virtual world? In fact, it was no harder than it had been in The Sims Online. Clause 7.1 of Second Life's Terms of Service gives Linden Lab the right to kick people out "for any reason." In case that didn't cover all the bases, it also let them lock out residents for "no reason" at all.

To Uri, that clause made the virtual businesses many people ran pretty insecure—and many residents had thousands of dollars invested in SL, in some cases tens of thousands. Even if the company was kind enough to allow you to stay in its world, there was no guarantee that they would respect or protect your virtual property. In fact, another clause of the ToS shouted in capital letters that the content residents created wasn't necessarily safe:

YOU UNDERSTAND AND AGREE THAT LINDEN HAS THE RIGHT, BUT NOT THE OBLIGATION, TO REMOVE ANY CONTENT (INCLUDING YOURS) IN WHOLE OR IN PART AT ANY TIME FOR ANY REASON OR NO REASON, WITH OR WITHOUT NOTICE AND WITH NO LIABILITY OF ANY KIND.

In other words: poof!

Second Life's Terms of Service also allows the company less draconian ways of stiffing their customers should the urge strike. For example, although residents own the IP rights to their creations, they also automatically grant Linden Lab an unlimited right to use those creations for marketing and promotions, or to change or delete them as the company wishes. Why that clause exists, however, is unclear, given that a few paragraphs down "you automatically grant . . . to Linden and to all other user of the Service a non-exclusive, worldwide, fully paid-up, transferable, irrevocable, royalty-free and perpetual License, under any and all patent rights you may have or obtain with respect to your Content, to use your Content for all purposes within the Service." If anyone in Second Life could use your content at will, what was actually being protected here?

Linden Lab did provide some technological protections to users' content, but they didn't always work as advertised. When an object is created, the creator may choose whether the item is copyable by setting a group of permissions in the object-editing interface. But for complex objects that are made up of many smaller parts, these permissions don't always work as it seems they should. Thus you may find no one is buying the virtual sunglasses you sell in your shop because, despite the permissions you set, someone else has managed to copy your sunglasses and is now selling them, undercutting your price to boot.

To Linden Lab, the permissions bug is a "known issue," a problem in the software that the company is looking into and plans to fix as soon as it can—but not a transgression to be punished. To residents, though, it makes a mockery of any IP "rights" they thought they had.

More broadly, Second Life's permissions bug is another instance of the conflict between the laws as dictated by software code and the laws as set forth by the administrators of the virtual world. Linden Lab's stated policy is that illicit copies are against the rules. But because their software is unable to enforce those rules, residents pay the price. While Second Life holds much potential as a virtual environment in which new forms of commerce and society may form and grow, it is held back by such inconsistencies be-

Figure 15.1
The *Second Life Herald*

tween law and practice, which Uri began to spot more and more often as he moved through the world. The company's slogan, "Your World. Your Imagination," promised much, but Uri was beginning to suspect that what was actually being delivered failed in large part to live up to that promise. Part of the *Herald*'s role in Second Life, then, would be to act as a watchdog press, uncovering the inconsistencies that kept the virtual world from fulfilling its fuction.

The *Herald* closed 2004 with its first annual Avatar of the Year award, which went to One Song, the avatar at the center of the Second Jessie War and of a number of other stories and scandals the *Herald* had covered over the previous twelve months.[2] Second Life had proven a rich vein to mine, and while the paper had enjoyed some brief worldwide fame after the story of Ludlow's expulsion from TSO had hit real-life front pages, it had also managed to maintain a readership since then, and by January 2005 was receiving over one thousand unique visitors a day.

But with no regular staff to speak of in Second Life, Ludlow was starting to feel the strain of running a paper while holding down a demanding real-world professorship at the same time. Ludlow had hit a wall with the *Herald*, but had pressed on nonetheless. In large measure, this was because he didn't want to hand EA a victory, but it was also because of the sense he had that the project was important. The irony was that if EA hadn't banned him, he probably would have tired of all the work and dropped the project long ago. But now, having gone on for this long, he couldn't imagine shutting the paper down. The problem was that he was running on fumes, and on pep talks from Candace Bolter and his readers.

Uri placed a want ad to find some help, and the ad was spotted a few days later by the typist for an avatar named Walker Spaight, who had appeared in Second Life only a week before. Walker's typist, Mark Wallace, was a freelance journalist who had covered everything from teenage gamers for the *New York Times Magazine* to elections in Liberia for obscure British political newsletters to rich kids in fast cars for glossy men's magazines like *GQ* and *Details*.

Wallace's first question on entering this, his first 3-D virtual world, was, Why am I here? The wonders of Second Life occupied Walker for a while, but virtual tourism was clearly going to get old fast. Wallace's first impression was that Second Life was about making stuff. What was Walker going to make? The creative potential of the place was so rich that contributing somehow to the culture of the Grid seemed the only way to really get under Second Life's skin. Little did he know how far under the skin of it he would get.

The *Herald* want ad answered all of Wallace's questions. Here was a way to not only contribute to what was going on in Second Life but to engage in an experiment in virtual journalism as well, to be part of a publication that happened for the most part in-character—one that was run by avatars, and that covered a world populated by them. This was exactly what interested Wallace about the metaverse: the overlap between the virtual and the real. Whatever it meant to have a hand in a virtual newspaper, it certainly couldn't be boring. And besides, like real-world journalism, it gave Walker a perfect excuse to be nosy. Walker's letter of interest reached him just a few days after the ad had gone up, which pleased Uri and allowed his typist Peter Ludlow to breath a sigh of relief. Finally, some help!

Wallace's main concern was how Walker's job would affect his own, so he and Ludlow settled on an arrangement in which one of the other applicants, an avatar-about-town named Matthias Zander, would do most of the heavy lifting as managing editor, reporting to Walker as editorial director. On January 6, the *Herald* announced its new editorial board to the readership,[3] and Walker set to work.

Walker's first contribution to the *Herald* did away with any illusions that he might be able to keep this job a casual one. While cruising around Second Life just past midnight, two days after Uri had announced the *Herald*'s new masthead, Walker got an IM from his virtual boss informing him that a big story was breaking. When Walker answered, Uri teleported the fledgling virtual editor to his location in the Threemile sim. But instead of an avatar riot or some virtual politician caught with his pants down, Walker found only the *Herald* publisher, clad in the flowing robes of a fantasy-world priest, standing around taking screenshots in the middle of a vast empty landscape of pixelated grass.

"Um . . ." Walker said.

"Wow," Uri responded.

It took Walker several minutes to figure out that the story his boss was hot on the trail of concerned something that was not in the Threemile sim, at least not any more. The sim had formerly been the home of one of Second Life's most notorious gang leaders, BallerMoMo King, whom Uri had profiled several weeks before. Their interview had taken place in Baller's opulent mansion (pictures of which were featured in the profile), in the Threemile sim.

As Uri explained it, the virtual gangbanger had recently been banned from Second Life for his involvement in the attack that had crashed six of Second Life's sims, the same attack in which One Song's nukes were used. Now Linden Lab had banned an avatar named Braverman Drago, a known Baller associate (rumored to be his real life brother) who had taken ownership of the Threemile mansion when Baller was banned. The ban was apparently permanent, and the company had reclaimed Braveman's land and wiped the Baller mansion completely from the Grid. Uri was taking snapshots of the resulting virtual vacant lot.

Braverman's crime hadn't yet come to light, but Uri's sources had put him onto a disconcerting aspect of the tale. Braverman's typist apparently

Figure 15.2
As the virtual Reichstag burns, One Song unveils his sim-to-sim nuke

logged onto Second Life from the United Arab Emirates. When Braverman was banned, though, a number of his friends in the country found themselves bounced out of Second Life as well. In an effort to keep Braverman from logging on with an alternate avatar linked to a different credit card on a different local network, it looked like Linden Lab had taken the alarming step of banning every IP address (i.e., every computer on every network) in the country. In effect, according to Uri's sources, Linden Lab had banned the entire UAE! Though it was now past one in the morning, this was clearly a story that merited immediate attention. Much of the information had come from an alt of One Song's named Mr. Fairplay, but Uri wanted Walker to handle the story, mostly to get his virtual feet wet but also because he hoped Walker might bring a more balanced hand to the piece. Walker took Uri's notes and wrote up the story, and by sunrise Uri had posted it to the *Herald* site.

It was a perfect introduction to journalism *Herald*-style. Walker had spotted a number of stories that interested him on Second Life's forums, but the *Herald* wasn't about recycling forum threads and Linden announcements. The *Herald* was about getting at what made virtual worlds tick, about uncovering how avatars related to one another, and how the gods of these worlds related to their subjects. The *Herald* wasn't just covering life in Second Life, it was trying to tackle the broader questions of what life in the metaverse was and might become, and to find a way to help steer it in a direction that would most benefit everyone involved.

To Walker, running a virtual newspaper was a bit of a cumbersome task, at first. Part of the problem was the org chart he and Uri had worked out, under which Walker wrote or edited stories and then filed them with Matthias for posting to the site. But Matthias's schedule was often filled with virtual fashion shows and nights out gathering dirt on the virtual club scene, so much of his time was spent warding off both virtual admirers and virtual hangovers. As a result, stories didn't always hit the pages of the *Herald* as quickly as Walker would have liked. As Walker began to accept that the *Herald* wouldn't be the walk in the park he imagined, Matthias moved to the position of style and fashion editor. Uri and Walker agreed that Matthias should play to his strengths, which included tracking the Second Life fashion industry and writing scathing, catty reviews with a microscopic eye for flaws in virtual fabric. Walker subsequently took on more of the job of posting stories to the *Herald*.

Much of the work, Walker found, was not so different from the real-life task of doing journalism. He took care to identify himself as a journalist whenever he was interested in a story, and attempted to get both sides when possible. Unfortunately, the Lindens were not always as cooperative as he would have liked. The *Herald* had not been shy about criticizing them in the past, and many of Walker's requests for comment went unanswered.

Walker's stories tended to be of a tamer sort than the drama Urizenus preferred. Uri had a web of underworld contacts and sources (which included gangland moll Gina Fatale), who provided him with a steady stream of incendiary fare—stories that often went straight to the heart of the social and governance issues the *Herald*'s editor was most interested in. Walker wasn't shy about delving into controversy, but preferred to look for manifestations of those issues in other areas, spending most of his reporting time traveling around the Grid, exploring whatever new and interesting projects Second Life's residents were putting together, or looking more deeply at some of the social and economic phenomena that were at work. Still, Walker's tone often drifted over into the snarky commentary that was the *Herald*'s stock in trade. That *Herald* 'tude seemed to infect everyone who wrote for it, no matter how well trained they were.

What surprised Walker was how well known the *Herald* was on the Grid. While there were certainly any number of avatars who had never heard of the paper, the *Herald* name often opened doors, and Walker found his wanderings rewarded with stories on a library project that planned to collect writings on Second Life,[4] a profile of "business girl" Anshe Chung,[5] a story about frontier justice on the Grid,[6] the "Making of a Post Six Grrrl"[7] and a review of the first X-rated film to be shown in Second Life.[8]

One aspect of virtual journalism that fascinated Walker was the interplay between people's real lives and their virtual ones. Wherever possible, he asked his interview subjects about the details of their earthbound lives. He soon realized, though, that short of visiting them in real life, there were few ways for him to confirm that what they told him was true. On the Grid, by contrast, he could easily confirm their stories by checking out the projects they had undertaken or by talking to other residents. At times it felt almost as if the virtual world was more real than the real one.

One of the things Walker had been charged with was building the *Herald* staff, and in the first half of 2005 he and Uri were able to recruit several new correspondents to the *Herald*'s ever-fluctuating masthead. Budka Groshomme, whose typist was a science fiction author, contributed a series of articles exploring the metaphysics of life as an avatar. Koden Farber took on the task of reviewing the surprising number of in-world games that were in development (few of them ever reached actual release). Miravoir Psaltery looked in on a number of different communities that had sprung up in Second Life, including Elves, Furries, and an island inhabited by virtual vampires. Miravoir even went so far as to take a job as an erotic dancer in order to cover the cyber-escort scene and produce her in-depth profiles of a few of SL's dancers. A series of avatars—including Seldon Metropolitan, Cienna Samiam, Eloise Pasteur, Brody MacDonald, Aimee Weber, and others—contributed a smaller number of pieces along the way.

The problem Walker found was that it was tough to keep good writers. He placed help wanted ads in both the SL forums and in the *Herald* itself, but the few applicants who came forward generally did so without any story ideas to offer. The *Herald* paid well, by Second Life standards, giving its freelance writers between L$500 and L$2,000 for an article (between $2 and $8). Most SL jobs (including in the virtual sex industry) paid less and required much more time and effort. But with a few notable exceptions, most of the writers Uri and Walker recruited would turn in one or two stories and then simply drift away. As broad as the *Herald*'s readership was, there seemed to be very few SL residents who were interested in sharing their explorations of the Grid with the reading public.

Of course, the *Herald* was not the first virtual publication to face this problem. Uri had seen numerous virtual newspapers and magazines come and go, and it was almost always because it was impossible to find reliable reporters. Uri had discussed the phenomenon with people ranging from Richard Bartle to Hamlet Linden, and the problem seemed to come down to one simple fact: gamers find the task of journalism—even viritual tabloid journalism—too burdensome. They don't want to report on their games, they want to play them. Likewise, virtual world residents don't want to report on their second lives, they want to live them.

It was certainly true that writing could take you out of the game you were reporting on. A single interview could take an hour to conduct, and the story another hour or two to write and edit. There was time involved in uploading screenshots, posting stories to the Web, and proofing articles. Two hours spent on a story is two hours not spent in world. Not many residents were interested in that kind of effort.

Uri's solution had been to incorporate the journalism into his roleplay. His role in TSO and in Second Life wasn't just that of a journalist; Uri was a crusading, take-no-prisoners tabloid reporter. When Walker came on board, this was the number one concern on Uri's mind: Would a serious journalist who had written for publications like *The New York Times* and the *Financial Times* get it? Not everyone did, but as far as Walker was concerned, Uri turned out to have nothing to fear.

Walker Spaight gave Mark Wallace a chance to play the edges a bit—a chance to be the seedy, muckraking tabloid reporter that he would never want to be in real life, but which made the newshound job in Second Life much more fun. True, some people (like sex club owner Jenna Fairplay) would refuse to talk to the *Herald* because it was a tabloid, but most people got the joke and were happy to dish to the *Herald*. Walker loved it.

Walker's success in recruiting other writers and reporters that "got it" was mixed. The *Herald*'s most promising recruit was a correspondent named Neal Stewart, whom Walker met at a job fair put on by a Second Life resident. Neal wrote with just the kind of twisted humor and social-justice sensibilities the *Herald* was looking for, and readers couldn't get enough of both his social satires and his profiles of notable and often disturbing Second Life residents. He was soon offered a staff position, with a monthly salary, at the *Herald* and to the delight of both Uri and Walker, he accepted.

Neal's output in his first months at the *Herald* was prodigious, at least in *Herald* terms. His byline appeared about six times a month, above stories on everything from a Charles Manson lookalike stalker[9] to a member of a near-extinct Native American tribe fighting to preserve his culture by recreating a virtual version of it in Second Life.[10] Nazi griefers,[11] gnome factories,[12] sexy skyboxes[13] and banned teens[14]—nothing seemed to be beyond Neal's reach.

But after a four-month tenure, Neal too decided it was time to depart. He had enjoyed his time at the *Herald*, he told Walker, but felt constrained by his role as a reporter. Too often, he said, the things he really wanted to find out about the subjects he was covering were off limits to him as a journalist. While Neal Stewart the avatar might be let in on such secrets, Neal Stewart the reporter was turned away.

In Walker's initially uncharitable view of the situation, Neal had turned his back on providing a service to the Grid because he wanted to hang out with the cool kids. Peer pressure and the need to belong had gotten the better of him, Walker thought. After cooling off with a virtual martini in the *Herald* office tower in the Louise sim, though, Walker took a more reasonable view. In the end, he thought, it was the difference between knowing and telling. To Walker, a journalist's task was to collect information about a subject and then to translate that knowledge—and sometimes part of the experience involved in garnering it—into a form that would be interesting and useful to the audience. Navigating deadline pressures and the few secrets that needed to be kept was just part of the job. The goal was to paint an accurate picture of a person or a situation, and to tell people what you had come across in your travels. Neal, it seemed, wanted to know more urgently than he wanted to tell. Or perhaps he just wanted to play more than he wanted to write.

For Uri, the loss of Neal was heartbreaking on two levels. For one, it seemed to suggest that even their best reporter didn't get the big picture, didn't see how the *Herald* was reporting on the birth of a new world and its many new cultures and subcultures. In his moments of megalomania (which were frequent), Uri imagined the writings in the *Herald* would be pored over by sociologists, historians, and anthropologists a hundred years from now. Of course, the other heartbreaking aspect of it was that it meant Uri would now have to provide more content himself, when he was quite ready to kick back and just enjoy the Grid without the pressure of finding scoops and meeting deadlines. So, in effect, Uri understood completely. This was work. Hard work. And the pay was crap. It was hard to expect someone to stay at it long.

Uri and Walker came across similar obstacles when they tried to build the *Herald*'s in-world presence and to raise advertising revenue. A series of promising ad reps, evangelists, Webmasters, scripters, and other back-office hires eventually drifted away, just as many cub reporters had. For whatever reason, working for a virtual newspaper just wasn't a vocation that seemed to inspire much excitement among SL residents.

Still, despite the fact that both Walker and Uri had typists with demanding full-time jobs, they managed to keep the copy coming, publishing almost forty stories a month. They had discussed ways to take the *Herald* forward, but it seemed that, for the moment at least, they would have to content themselves with merely producing what both saw as the most kick-ass newspaper in the metaverse.

Judging from the amount of traffic the site was getting, their readership seemed to agree with that estimation. The paper also inspired competitors in Second Life, just as it had in TSO. In August 2005, a weekly publication called the *Metaverse Messenger* came to the Grid (as well as to the World Wide Web). As the *Herald* reported, "Planned features include a Linden spotlight recognizing those Lindens that have been most handy at making life easier on the Grid, and plenty of space for advertisements, which the Messenger's sales staff seems to have done a bang-up job of selling into the first issue."[15]

The *Herald* was not known for being kind to the Lindens, though it did take time to celebrate Linden Lab's successes. The *Messenger* took a shot at the *Herald* in publisher Katt Kongo's front-page letter of introduction, which billed the paper as a strictly PG publication. "There are other venues for more X-rated news and features," Katt wrote. The *Herald*'s response was to idly wonder what venues she might have been referring to, and to raise a glass to the Messenger in the spirit of friendly competition.

Whenever competition arose, the *Herald* reacted by staying on mission. Part of what made that mission so much fun to pursue was the paper's slogan, "Always Fairly Unbalanced," and its commitment to providing not only news but a healthy portion of snarky entertainment as well. Though what was going on in virtual worlds like Second Life was something more "real" than most people supposed, these were still virtual worlds, after all—pixelated spaces in which much of what went on was indeed play. Thus the *Herald* staff had no compunction about running an advertisement for a sim-lagging nuke,[16] poking fun at a group of residents who were themselves notorious for poking fun at everyone from the late pope to the victims of 9/11,[17] poking fun at the pope themselves,[18] and sprinkling the paper liberally with their own opinions as to the value of events on the Grid and in other virtual worlds.

Not everyone was amused, of course. The *Herald* was regularly taken to task for being a sleazy muckraking tabloid. But what was interesting was that even the people who abhorred it seemed to return to it time and again. You could kick the *Herald* all you wanted, but you couldn't keep it down.

In December 2004, the *Herald* reported a story that raised few eyebrows at the time, but which would eventually become the single most controversial issue in Second Life the following year, and would speak to many of the questions Uri had about how governance in cyberspace would shake out. The December story covered the arrival of yet another immigrant from TSO, the infamous avatar Dyerbrook,[19] whose zealous campaign to protest the hegemonic Sim Shadow Government and the favors they were allegedly shown by Electronic Arts employees had earned him wide disfavor. When the *Herald* heralded Dyerbrook's arrival in the form of avatar Prokofy Neva, few Second Life citizens took notice. Little did they know that the arrival of Prok on SL's shores would turn out to be an epochal moment in the history of the virtual world.

Uri knew that Prokofy would burrow deeply into SL and dig up any number of interesting tales. So despite the fact that he had been a vitriolic critic of the *Herald*, he would at the very least be an important source of information, and if he would actually write for the *Herald*... well, anything could happen. In February 2005, after lengthy negotiations over his terms, the *Herald* successfully recruited Prok as a freelance correspondent. But independently of the paper, in lengthy forum posts and in town hall meetings, Prok would generate more local controversy and acrimony than anything the *Herald* had run in the fifteen months it had then been in existence.

In Second Life Prokofy established a career as a middle-tier real-estate mogul whose Ravenglass Rentals provided apartments at reasonable rates for newbies and Basic account holders. By using the in-world interface to set the right options on his land, Prokofy—like the handful of other real estate magnates, large and small, who occupy Second Life—was able to let his tenants build their own creations, sell them in shops he rented to them, if that was their goal, or just have a place to hang out and call their own.

But in addition to being a virtual landlord, Prokofy was also the originator of a meme that had, before he started writing for the *Herald*, already spread to every corner of Second Life and sparked intense debate. The "Feted Inner Core" was a term Prokofy coined to refer to a clique of SL residents that made the Sims Shadow Government look, in his view, like a gaggle of silly sorority girls (which was more or less what it had started out as).

The target of Prok's suspicions were many of Second Life's early adopters—the "oldbie" crowd, residents whose tenure in the world stretched back to its beta testing days and who had taken advantage of special offers the company had extended when it was first trying to build a customer base. Like Uri, many of these people had received a chunk of land free of monthly tier payments for a one-time charge of $225 (quite a sum to plunk down on a new world with only a few thousand residents at the time—hardly enough of a population to insure its survival). Others had arrived early enough to become tight with the lifers of Second Life, and Prokofy saw in the group a cadre of privileged "digerati" who enjoyed special treatment from Linden Lab because of their early contributions to the content of the world.

To Prokofy, who had arrived in Second Life much later, this constituted nothing less than an active conspiracy between the company and its world's early residents. The FIC, Prok charged, sought to turn latecomers into a kind of Soviet-era collective who would do little more than provide the old group with a means of enrichment. And in Second Life, this was not a trivial issue confined to the world of electrons rattling around the Internet. While simoleans, the currency of TSO, can be sold to other players on eBay for real money, earning enough to make it worth your while is nearly impossible without the help of software hacks to automate the process in-world. Not so in Second Life, where the potential for virtual commerce was much greater, and the social structures that were springing up were much more sophisticated and complex.

Prokofy couldn't keep from taking action in what he felt were the best interests of the Grid. While he refrained from the kinds of in-world raids that his activist group, the Lightsavers, had carried out in TSO, Prok made his concerns more than clear on the Linden Lab-run forums devoted to Second Life. In a series of long-winded posts (termed "whinescrapers" by one waggish SL resident), Prok laid out just how and why the FIC were holding the reins of power and commerce on the Grid. He warned new residents not to be taken in by the guileless visage the group presented and tried to rally support for a grassroots movement to change how the world ran, in order to level the playing field.

The reaction he got was not very sympathetic, in part because the antagonistic nature of his posts made it difficult for people to hear their content. But it was a reaction that seemed to confirm what looked like a conspiracy theorist's worst fears. "One very important thing you have to still learn about SL is that we are a tight-knit community," one resident responded on the boards. "There are some that are very highly respected in this community. To begin an argument against them accusing them of exaggerations and fabrications is a sure fire way to keep your argument from being read. Right or wrong, that simply *is* a fact. . . . Just a note of advice."[20]

Despite the negative reactions, Prok was undeterred. It was his mission, he felt, to educate the newcomer and to "push back" against "crackpot ideologies of the socialist/utopian/wikian variety."[21] Not much escaped his gaze. The free items older players gave away were designed to undercut new players' markets. Those who did not allow the resale of their goods (by using SL's permissions system) were hobbling the wheels of commerce. Those who provided open-source items, things that could be freely modified but were not to be sold, were capitalizing on others' work for the greater glorification of their own name. And Linden Lab itself was killing commerce on the Grid by "indulging some players with various subsidies."

While Prok's charges sometimes seemed indiscriminate and overblown, there was a germ of truth to them that could not be dismissed. Some longstanding residents did appear to get more help from LL than did later adopters, and in more than one instance the company actually contacted a number of what it felt were important content creators, requesting advice on further developing its world—and asking them not to make public the fact that they'd been solicited. (Of course, this news soon made its way to the boards.) That the company should reach out to the most impressive content-creators on the Grid is hardly surprising. But even so, there was a whiff of conflict about the practice, especially given the secrecy with which Linden Lab sometimes operated.

And the fact that the company was more responsive to some residents than to others as it developed its world posed a broader question than just who would control the reins of commerce on the Grid. Prokofy's concerns went straight to the heart of the questions the *Herald* was raising about how a world like Second Life might eventually be governed, and how those governance structures might emerge. Most of the content-creators that Prok claimed had an "in" with Linden Lab were the company's best customers, and provide the sights and sounds that attract a great many people to the world. But just as many of SL's residents, if not more, are merely consumers. Where was their voice in the guidance of their adopted world? To Prokofy and to others, it looked like it had been silenced by the cash-flow that LL saw in Second Life's more creative residents. Just as in real-world politics, the content-creators' ability to generate money gave them access to the powers that ruled the world, and with that access came influence. In the end, all Prokofy was advocating was a kind of campaign finance reform for virtual worlds, a way to include the opinions and concerns of all residents in steering their online environment, rather than giving greater weight to those who generated greater corporate income. To him and to others who agreed with his ideas (if not with their presentation), it meant the difference between SL being the "world" that was promised and the "product" that most other virtual worlds never rise above.

Whatever the merits of Prokofy's arguments, they soon got lost in the antipathetic nature of the conversations on Second Life's forums and the *Herald*'s comments threads. To Prok, those who felt they deserved special treatment for having been in-world longer were "screaming entitlement fucktards" and sometimes worse. Some among Prok's respondents were no less insulting, charging his typist with being mentally imbalanced and publishing what were thought to be the details of his real life on the forums, which is usually considered a cardinal sin and is a specific violation of LL's Terms of Service. Many forums' threads were locked, edited, or deleted by LL's moderators, who passed out warnings of disciplinary action to Prok and others, but Prok stuck to his guns.

Prok's war on the message boards raged for more than six months, his accusations growing more serious as time passed. Some resident-run Websites that had done much to enrich the world of Second Life by providing screenshot-sharing services or third-party forums and marketplaces were accused of harvesting their visitors' IP addresses for nefarious (if never quite articulated) ends. Prok had accused the *Herald* of the same transgression in the past. Uri hadn't even bothered responding to the charges and had let the matter drop, but many other residents were unable to simply ignore Prok's posts. Just as Prok felt he had to defend himself from the injustices that prevailed in Second Life, SL's residents felt they had to defend themselves against Prok's charges, and more than one threatened to bring a real-life lawsuit against him for defamation and loss of business. With so much bile flying around, just logging on to the forums was often a distasteful experience.

When Linden Lab took action, it spoke volumes about what the answers to Prok's and the *Herald*'s questions might be. In the summer of 2005, the company banned Prokofy altogether, not from the world of Second Life, but from its forums. His crime was having "repeatedly violated the Community Standards and the Forum Guidelines" with his incendiary posts. A couple of wrists were slapped on the other side of the issue, but no other apparent disciplinary action was taken. Prok had been silenced.

To the *Herald*, this was a worse crime than any that had been committed thus far in the debate. Once again, it looked like the unpopular sentiment had been censored. It was a major setback on the path toward the emergence of inclusive governance structures in virtual worlds.

Worse still was how the ban came about. In June 2005, just after Prokofy was banned from the forums, Internet Relay Chat logs were leaked to the *Herald* that illustrated what did seem to be a conspiracy between certain residents and at least one Linden Lab employee to rid the forums of Prokofy.[22] While the Linden liaison involved had simply "lost it," as he later told the *Herald*, and was acting on his own initiative rather than on orders from above, the conversation seemed to vindicate Prok's wildest fantasies of Linden-FIC collusion. Putting aside whether it was a self-fulfilling prophecy come true, here at least was evidence that the world's governance was indeed being influenced, at times, by a shadowy cabal of residents who enjoyed privileged access to Second Life's administrators.

The truth was that Prok was gagged not because of any transgressions but because a small group of residents wanted him gagged. In the chat logs leaked to the *Herald,* the Linden liaison involved (identified as llPath in the excerpt below) acknowledges that Prok has not, in fact, violated the Terms of Service or the Community Standards, and that other residents have. Along the way, he encourages the residents to provoke Prokofy into crossing the line:

llPath: we're all on the same page here, yes?

llPath: here's the deal

llPath: Prok never "technically" violates the Community Standards

llPath: Prok skirts them, and ultimately ends up inciting other Residents to "break" the CS

llPath: can you see the dilemma I (and all the other mods) are in??

llPath: we are faced with the need to allow the MOST freedom possible

llPath: so, until we work out an official policy, the general rule is, don't let Prok's posts incite you to do something stupid

llPath: but, you didn't hear that from me (say no more)

Cienna: aka. ignore it

llPath: Cienne, precisely

The *Herald* took up Prokofy's cause as if it were its own. But although it was clear to the *Herald* that Prokofy was raising important issues—albeit in an incendiary way—most of Second Life didn't seem to feel the same way. Though Prok had his supporters, the *Herald* was roundly flamed for defending him. Uri and Walker, though, were unperturbed. It wasn't the *Herald*'s job to please all the avatars all of the time. What surprised them was the strength of resident reactions to both Prokofy and to the *Herald*'s support of him. It seemed that many people, whether they realized it or not, preferred a world in which the unpopular were silenced. In the *Herald*'s view, this didn't bode well for the future of online societies. If virtual worlds are to become truly useful, if they are to fulfill the promise imagined by people like author Neal Stephenson and Linden Lab founder Philip Rosedale, their stewards will need to carefully consider things like freedom of speech and the power of the mob to silence the contrarian voice.

Perhaps most chilling was the fact that in the wake of Prokofy's board war, Linden Lab changed its Forum Guidelines so that being banned from the forums in future would also mean being banned from the Grid. The company also cracked down on what could and could not be said on the boards. Posts that are "intended to incite anger" or that have been "written with the intent of inciting or getting argumentative opinions" are "strongly discouraged" and could result in disciplinary actions.

It was probably inevitable that a Brahmin class of Second Life residents would arise. In one sense, it's a sign that the society that's forming in Second Life is as robust as any in the real world, where, as sociologist Clay Shirky has pointed out, privileged classes are the norm.[23] This may sound sinister, but in Shirky's view it is a good thing: "In all successful online communities that I've looked at, a core group arises that cares about and gardens effectively, gardens the environment, to keep it growing, to keep it healthy."

But such groups are not always given the software tools they need in order to keep the larger population under their control, according to Shirky. "And if the software doesn't allow the core group to express itself, it will invent new ways of doing so." On one Internet bulletin board Shirky studied, a core group of users began supplementing their public communications with an email list originally set up to plan a real-life barbecue. In the context of the bulletin board, though, the mailing list was used to "coordinate efforts formally if they were going to troll someone or flame someone or ignore someone.... [The bulletin board] didn't let them do it in the software, [so] they brought in other pieces of software, these mailing lists, that they needed to build the structure."

While many SL residents were surprised to see the conspiracy that was uncovered by the leaked chat log, Shirky had suggested that such events are commonplace. Still, most members of Second Life's aristocracy refused to believe that a Brahmin class had developed in SL—they couldn't see their own privileged social position.

They could not escape the FIC moniker, though. While Prokofy was a contentious figure on the SL forums (though he was never as contentious a figure on the Grid, interestingly), the ideas he contributed have had a profound impact on Second Life. "Feted Inner Core," the term he coined, is now in widespread use in Second Life, and has even appeared in the log-in message that greets users when they sign on to SL. Linden Lab's public relations staff have expressed concerns about the perception that they favor an FIC. Some residents joke that it is actually a "fetid" inner core, and it is a mark of tongue-in-cheek pride among many to be considered part of it. The irony of Prok's board wars is that they ended up making a kind of FIC member out of him too. Prokofy Neva is now one of the most well known names on the Grid; he has become a prominent figure at many trendy Second Life events, and has even been invited to speak on panels at a number of real-life events looking at the evolution of virtual worlds. In January 2006, the *Herald* named him its 2005 Avatar of the Year.[24]

The *Herald*'s fierce advocacy of Prokofy's cause almost got it laughed right off the virtual breakfast table. Second Life is only a game, came the refrain in the comment threads. But Second Life was not a game. The company certainly took pains to point that out. It was, for one thing, a corporate venture, but the questions the *Herald* was raising had even broader implications. The *Herald* was asking questions about cyberspace itself, how the metaverse—the collective universe of online worlds—would be governed in the future, and what relationship the metaverse would have with our offline lives. To Uri these things were important. He had seen virtual interactions generate six-figure incomes, real-world marriages, financial crimes, and many other very real phenomena. The question of who would have authority over such places and how their laws would be made could not be dismissed as trivial.

As Uri saw it, the question of who was suppressing freedoms—a government or a software company—was entirely beside the point. In the philosopher John Stuart Mill's nineteenth-century book, *On Liberty*, Mill is very careful to emphasize that threats to freedom need to be resisted *wherever* they come from. Loss of liberty at the hands of a corporation—or even at the hand of social attitudes—is no better than loss of liberty at the hands of government. Threats to liberty need to be resisted no matter where they originate, Mill maintained. It was hard to see an argument against him.

But cyberspace has complicated the issue. By creating a place that exists outside the boundaries of nations, and thus outside the reach of national laws, the Internet has come to be regarded as a place where anything goes. The legal world does not yet have a comprehensive model for regulating what goes on in cyberspace, consequently few of its denizens feel they have the right to object to anything that goes on there.

Stanford Law School professor Lawrence Lessig, in his book *Code and Other Laws of Cyberspace*,[25] makes the case that our freedoms are being eroded not by governments or corporations but by software engineers and the public's attitude to the Internet. The software code that underlies the Internet and our future online gathering places could have a chilling effect on personal freedoms, Lessig argues. Citing Mill's classic text, Lessig drives the point home with clarity.

> Mill's method is important and it should be our own. It asks, What is the threat to liberty, and how can we resist it? It is not limited to asking, What is the threat to liberty from government? It understands that more than government can threaten liberty, and that sometimes this something more can be private rather than state action. Mill was not so concerned with the source [of the threat]. His concern was with liberty.

If TSO and Second Life were only games, it would be hard to see in them any threat to liberty at all. What the *Herald* had turned up in both places, as well as the millions of players who spent much of their time in MMO games and other virtual worlds, were both evidence that such online environments were not just games but were fast becoming models for our future workplaces and community gathering sites. As such, they needed a watchdog to speak for the interests of those—like Prokofy Neva—who for whatever reason had been deprived of a voice. The *Herald* was more than happy to fulfill that function.

Urizenus's experiences in TSO and episodes such as Prok's ban from the forums in Second Life made Uri wonder what kind of precedent the denizens of cyberspace were setting for our future. Though most of the world had yet to move into the metaverse, by late 2005 it didn't take a science fiction writer to see that we were heading there more and more rapidly. The virtual world was fast approaching an inflection point, a moment at which we would have to determine who would decide what we can and can't do there. It looked like many of those who lived, worked, and played in virtual worlds were ready to give up their freedoms in return for the privilege of residing in cyberspace. Was there still time to find a different answer?

16 Ruling the Metaverse

On rare occasions, virtual worlds get the balance of governance just right. One such world is the deep-space MMO EVE Online.[1] CCP, the Icelandic company behind EVE, puts a great deal of trust in its players. Its rules about what is allowable between players are more liberal than most. If you're flying through a system that isn't patrolled by computer-controlled police, be prepared to get your ship popped by a pirate ship controlled by another player (a player pirate, or "PRat," as they're known). And if you leave a valuable blueprint in a station hangar, don't be surprised if you return to find that a corporate spy has run off with it. Unlike in most MMOs, theft and fraud are just part of the landscape in EVE.

Such events may sound trivial, but in the reaches of space that EVE covers—over five thousand star systems, in which more than twenty thousand players are regularly flying around at once—they sometimes get scaled up to galactic size. In April 2005, they reached record-breaking proportions when one EVE corporation (a group of players not unlike the guilds that exist in other MMOs, or the "governments" that had sprung up in TSO) pulled off a coup that had taken it a full year to mount, and reaped an even larger reward than it at first expected.

The Guiding Hand Social Club was already known in EVE for its ruthless tactics. "Any unprovoked attack on our pilots must be met with the cruelest, most unrestrained kind of revenge," according to Guiding Hand CEO Istvaan Shogaatsu.[2] The corporation was willing to work if the price was right, and in the spring of 2004 it accepted a contract to take out the head of a corporation called Ubiqua Seraph. The contract was worth a billion InterStellar Kredits, or about $550 at prevailing exchange rates on eBay.

The target, though, was well protected, and in order to get to her, Guiding Hand took a less direct route than usual. Rather than a frontal assult,

Guiding Hand agents infiltrated the ranks of Ubiqua Seraph and over the course of the next year worked their way up into the innermost circles of the corp, ultimately winning the confidence of Ubiqua CEO Mirial, their target.

As Tom Francis relates in his excellent account of the coup in the UK magazine *PC Gamer*,

> At 5am on April 18, 2005, the CEO of the Ubiqua Seraph corporation (EVE's equivalent of a guild) emerged through a stargate in the Haras system, accompanied by her most trusted lieutenant. She wouldn't leave alive. . . .
>
> The proud CEO was piloting her prize ship, a Battleship-class Navy Apocalypse, worth billions. Her colleague—Arenis Xemdal—flew an Imperial Apocalypse, an unimaginably valuable craft of which only two are known to exist. . . .
>
> By 6am it was over. Every Ubiqua Seraph office in the galaxy was raided, the contents of every hangar—including the corporate coffers—ransacked. Mirial's ship was destroyed, her escape pod nuked and her vacuum-frozen corpse scooped into the cargo bay of a Guiding Hand Social Club vessel. This was the only proof their client had requested.
>
> The ambush and galaxy-wide hangar theft inflicted financial damage worth 30 billion ISK . . . the value of the stolen assets utterly dwarfing the original fee for the job.[3]

The heist broke all known records in the EVE galaxy. While $550 for an assassination job in an online game may sound like a lot, the loot that Guiding Hand Social Club made off with would be worth $16,500 if sold on eBay or IGE.com. Not bad for a crime pulled off within the bounds of an online game.

One of the most remarkable things about the story is that CCP did nothing to intervene. And that's to their credit. In fact, such criminal acts are designed into the gameplay of EVE. "Spying, scheming, double-dealing and espionage are devilishly delicious features of EVE for those who relish walking on the dark side," according to the EVE FAQ. "Corporation leaders are urged to exercise extreme caution when accepting new members, particularly when granting access to their private communications and corporate holdings. There are criminal elements in EVE who can, and will, take advantage of unsuspecting marks."[4]

The layered gameplay that was possible in Guiding Hand Social Club's operation—involving double agents, months of time spent developing characters, and the building of levels of trust both with Ubiqua Seraph and within GHSC itself—is testament to the success of EVE's design and the willingness of the company to stick to its guns where its world's governance is concerned.

The notion of "emergent social behavior"—players using the software tools available in a game to create situations and roles that are larger than the tools themselves—is one of the holy grails of MMO development. By making decisions about what is and isn't allowable, and then sticking to them, CCP has let the world of EVE give rise to any number of creative modes of play, and the EVE galaxy has become one of the richer game universes on offer today.

The differences between how EVE Online handles crimes and how worlds like TSO and Second Life handle them is revealing. EVE, of course, is a game, not an online social space. But even so, serious amounts of money could be involved, as much or more than were at play in TSO. EVE handled the sitution by laying down the law and then sticking to it. Linden Lab would never find the courage to be clear about what was and was not acceptable in its world.

In fact, what Linden Lab considered acceptable behavior was not even made clear in its dealings with residents whom it claimed had stepped outside those bounds, whatever they might be. Time after time, the *Herald* received reports from SL residents who had been banned from the world or had had their accounts temporarily suspended without being given the slightest clue why. Nor can residents confront their accuser. On the occasions when Uri or Walker tried to contact the company for more information, they were met with stony silence or the claim that privacy concerns forbade LL from giving out any information. Surely, though, that information should be available to the residents against whom disciplinary action had been taken? It seemed Linden Lab felt differently. While the company publishes a "police blotter,"[5] it contains so little information as to be nearly useless as a guide. And despite claims on the site that it was comprehensive, the blotter seems to omit certain disciplinary actions. In some cases, residents report that the Lindens have actively overlooked behavior that on other occasions has earned people a ban or suspension. With no information forthcoming from the company, the *Herald* could do no more than publish the players' view of the virtual "law enforcement" problems and hope for a more transparent regime in future.

To Uri and Walker, episodes like the Ubiqua Seraph heist and the rigged Alphaville Government elections[6] were not just fun stories, they also illustrated some important points of how societies might form and law might be made in cyberspace. The guilds that populate MMOs like EVE Online, World of Warcraft, EverQuest, and the like look very much like the "governments" that formed in TSO—organizations like the Sim Shadow Government, the Alphaville Government and The Sim Mafia—and like some resident groups of Second Life. Most MMOs allow players to organize themselves into such groups. Guilds often have dedicated chat channels for guild-only communications (similar to the out-of-game communications the SSG developed) and in some cases may derive benefits from undertaking quests or other activities together. Officers can be designated who have the power to enlist or expel members, and some of the more formidable guilds may require an application process that can take weeks or months, in which current guild members will pair up with applicants in order to decide whether they are up to whatever standard the guild has set for its members. Some "uber-guilds," as they are sometimes known, including the Sim Shadow Government, even have a presence in more than one MMO.

MMO guilds work very much like the medieval clans and kingdoms that grew into the nation-states we recognize today. In another sense, they resemble immigrants' associations, groups of like-minded people who work together for the benefit of all. Being a member of a guild often enhances the narrative aspects of life in an MMO: For some players, the story a solo adventurer can create is never as rich as the story that can result from being part of a group. In MMOs such as Lineage and EVE Online, guild-like groups can band together and go to war against each other for control over valuable resources, or simply for bragging rights.

At times—especially at a time like the Alphaville election season—such groups resemble virtual city-states emerging in a space where the rules of power, government, and law have yet to be written. As such, they naturally call into question many assumptions we have about law and government in the real world—right down to the idea that one person deserves one (and only one) vote. By taking nothing, not even the universal values of democratic societies, for granted, such fledgling governments provide radical experiments in new kinds of governance structures. While the groups that Uri watched emerging in TSO were crude, a different picture developed as the *Herald* began to look more closely at such groups in Second Life.

Second Life's software tools allow residents to form guild-like groups, and permit group officers to do things like sell group-owned land or eject junior members, activities within those groups that the company doesn't always find acceptable. The problem for residents was that the company occasionally—and inconsistently—found such actions objectionable.

In August 2005, two cases came to the attention of the *Herald* that illustrated the problem perfectly. The first story involved Cyanide Leviathan, a veteran of both Jessie wars, and an avatar named Xaphon Mendicant who was an officer of a group known as the Space Monkeys. Xaphon had used his officer privileges to transfer the Space Monkeys' land to a rival corporation, known as XLS. Though SL's software tools gave Xaphon the explicit ability to make such a transfer, the rest of the Space Monkeys were anything but happy, and complained to Linden Lab about what they saw as a betrayal and theft. When Uri caught up with Xaphon and Cyanide (who had originally had the idea), they were anything but repentant:

Cyanide Leviathan: We stole the all the land from the Space Monkeys.

Xaphon Mendicant: Yes, I have castrated the Space Monkeys with my gilded axe of dishonor.

Urizenus Sklar: Okay, first, who are the Space Monkeys?

Xaphon Mendicant: The Space Monkeys are a major corporation of somewhat skilled builders and assholes and losers.

Cyanide Leviathan: Xaphon was an officer in their land-holding group. I floated the idea to him of leaving the group and possibly bringing a few skilled members to XLS. . . .

Xaphon Mendicant: Because I trust Cy and my other friends much more with my future. I figured I could break off ties with an old group that didn't seem to have a use for me, and eliminate the competition at the same time.[7]

On one level, the technique Xaphon used to "break off ties" with his former group did amount to stealing (Uri calculated the assets to be worth around $320). But from another perspective, all he had done was to sell group land, something the software tools of the world enabled him to do. Within both the code and the laws of Second Life, he was perfectly within his rights. On this point, Linden Lab's Terms of Service could not have been more clear:

Linden Lab cannot verify, enforce, certify, examine, uphold or adjudicate any oath, contract, deal, or agreement made by the residents of Second Life. Furthermore, all officers of a group have equal authority to sell or otherwise dispose of group land.

But the company's response was utterly disconnected from its own legal documents. Despite the fact that Xaphon hadn't contravened the ToS, he was promptly suspended. The heisted land was seized, and a small portion of it was returned to the Space Monkeys. Even that was baffling. Why did Linden Lab keep most of the stolen land? No rationale was given. It was simply the prerogative of the gods of the Grid to do as they pleased. They decided the land should belong neither to the Space Monkeys nor to XLS, but rather to the gods themselves.

Uri vented in the comments section of the article:

> Either establish a definite role in dispute resolution or get the hell out of the way. This current anti-policy the Lindens have of saying they can't get involved and then dabbling depending upon the whim of the moment is the worst possible thing they can do. It doesn't help that when they do dabble, they can't tell us why they do or even admit that they're doing it.[8]

The second case was also troubling in that it seemed to involve Linden favoritism. Also in August 2005, an avatar named Hank Ramos showed up in one of Second Life's Welcome areas, where new residents enter the world, bearing a protest sign that read, "Linden Lab Shouldn't Be Allowed to Take Away Land Because High Profile Residents File Abusive and Frivolous Abuse Reports!!!"[9]

According to Hank, a prominent and respected builder and real-estate developer in Second Life, Linden Lab had forcibly seized land from a group of which he was an officer and founding member, and later expelled him from the group without even the due process that is coded into the world's grouping tools. Typically, no explanation was forthcoming from Linden Lab. No part of the Terms of Service had been broken, to anyone's knowledge. Yet again, the company jumped in to make changes without reference to any of the laws by which its world was supposed to operate. Apparently, there was an internal dispute between Hank and another group member—Adam Zaius—who was widely recognized as a favorite of the Lindens and a member of what Prokofy Neva had called the Feted Inner Core.

To the *Herald*, this was a bigger issue than whether Xaphon or Hank had been in the right or in the wrong. What was at stake was trust, and trust was already in short supply. If the Lindens were going to act as judge, jury, and executioner in cases like these, they would need to do so according to some clear and consistent set of guidelines, and make their decisions public, so that the rest of the Grid would have visible precedents by which to adjust their behavior. Unfortunately, that just wasn't happening. If the Lindens really did want to help build a new world, a new kind of society on the frontier of cyberspace, they had chosen the worst way to go about it.

As Uri found over and over, the authorities of Second Life and many other virtual worlds wielded their power inconsistently at best, and often in an ad hoc manner that made it difficult for residents to know what the rules actually were at any given moment. The letter of the law in Second Life often changed without warning as well, in response to perceived crises that were often long past by the time Linden Lab got around to patching its Terms of Service agreement. Several weeks after the Second Jessie War, for instance, the company updated the Community Standards document that spelled out the rules of etiquette on the Grid. A new category of transgression, "global attacks," had been added to the document, which now explicitly forbade the crashing or lagging of sims (Uri called it "The One Song Rule"). On its face, the rule made perfect sense. But it was unclear what good it did to add it to the Community Standards. Had anyone believed that crashing a sim had been acceptable before that point?

In any case, both the CS and the ToS were so whimsically enforced in Second Life that it was hard to argue that their contents carried much weight anyway. Nor was it easy to find any apparent rhyme or reason to the enforcement actions that the Lindens did carry out. Residents were left to guess whether their actions were within the bounds of appropriate behavior, which led many to simply assume that that they were free to make such decisions themselves.

Linden Lab has been reluctant to provide more powerful tools for managing any kind of social or political structures. The groups that Second Life's residents can form and join provide only crude voting and management mechanisms, and, as the *Herald* had reported in the case of the Space Monkeys, even these were often circumvented by LL's enforcement policies, or lack thereof.

The mere fact that things like rules and regulations are even being considered in a place like Second Life should give one pause. Here is a world made only of pixels and code, a place that most people see as a fantasy realm, the kingdom of the imagination. And yet the people who frequent it are askings for ways to establish and enforce their own rules. Does this show some sort of lack of perspective? Not at all.

Like the *Herald* and like cyberspace commentators such as Lawrence Lessig, SL residents have very real concerns over what will and will not be possible in the metaverse, a place that is becoming increasingly intertwined with their real lives, and may become increasingly a part of everyone's life in the not-too-distant future. They are more than willing to take on the challenges of hammering out regulations that everyone involved in the experiment can live with. The regulations being discussed today could one day become questions of jurisdiction, taxation, education, crime, freedom of association and speech—any of the issues that shape a society in the real world. If our offline lives are to extend more deeply into online worlds, these are the kinds of issues that will have to be addressed.

At the moment, such issues come down to questions of code and law. In Second Life's case, the question the *Herald* had was whether the company behind the world was willing to step back and provide its residents with the tools to shape their own destiny in the metaverse? And if not, was the company willing to work toward a framework of laws or regulations that would work better than the ever-changing ToS?

Linden Lab does not concentrate on developing tools with which residents can do things like enter into contracts, vote on ordinances, and enforce the regulations that come out of such a process—in other words, tools that could be used to develop governance and society. Nor has the company taken any steps toward making its own "legal" guidelines clear, consistent, and transparent. Instead, LL has preferred to concentrate on adding features to its world such as streaming video, click-through to Web pages, and game-like abilities such as a "heads-up display" that mimics what one might see on the screen of a first-person-shooter game. These have all been engaging and useful additions; and no company in charge of a virtual world can be expected to satisfy all of the feature requests it gets from its customers. But the company's development agenda begs the question: What is the mission of Second Life? Philip Rosedale regularly crows about the amount of commerce that goes on in his world, and the fantastic creativity of that world's residents. In Uri's original interview with him, Rosedale agreed that Second Life operates much like a development platform, a kind of "substrate" on which residents can build what they like. "That is why we have done things the way he have," he said.[10]

But what could be built on that substrate was more limited than the company often advertised. As a fantasy world, SL hardly had an equal. As a place to do business it was possible to get by. But as an experiment in what was possible in terms of building societies in cyberspace, SL could hardly get off the ground. Was Second Life really a place that was constructed to be "Your World, Your Imagination"? To the *Herald*, it looked like the answer was no.

Not only were the Lindens reluctant to introduce features that enhanced the formation of social and political institutions, but what features they did introduce often undermined the institutions that were emerging on their own. At least, that was the lesson that could be taken from what happened to GamingOpenMarket.com.

Since the early days of SL, GOM had been the most relied-upon site for buying and selling Linden dollars, hosting almost $200,000 a month in trades. Its in-world automatic teller machines let residents deposit Linden dollars to their GOM accounts (which could be linked to PayPal accounts), and the GOM Website let residents place buy or sell orders that other residents would then fill, creating a robust virtual currency market where residents could unload extra Linden dollars, purchase currency for use in-world, or even play the markets. Within a year of its launch, GOM had become one of the most widely respected and successful businesses on the Grid. By mid-2005, GOM's prices set the standard for the exchange rate between the Linden dollar and the U.S. dollar.

By that time, Linden Lab was already moving to get in on the action. In late 2004, the company approached GOM about becoming part of Second Life itself, entering extensive negotiations with the residents who had built the service (in which SL learned much about how the service worked). But LL and GOM could not come to terms. So instead of rolling GOM into their service, the company decided it would start a service of its own, and announced in August 2005 that it would soon offer currency trading on the SecondLife.com Website.[11]

To GOM, this spelled disaster. The announcement meant GOM was now competing with the equivalent of Second Life's Treasury Department. Faced with that prospect, GOM saw no alternative to shutting its doors, which it did on October 2, 2004.

To the *Herald*, and to many SL residents, the episode called into question the "Your World, Your Imagination" flag that the Lindens so proudly flew. While GOM might have been able to survive the Lindens' entry into the currency-exchange market, the Lindens' move could hardly be said to encourage the kind of innovation the company claimed to be looking for. What LL was saying, in effect, was, "You come up with the good ideas, and if you prove them good enough, we'll co-opt them." Matters weren't helped when Lawrence Linden, one of the Lindens in charge of overseeing Second Life's economic affairs, said that part of the rationale behind the move was to give residents "easy access to L$ without having to take yet another leap of trust to sign up with a third party."[12] But residents had already taken that leap of trust with GOM, and had been rewarded. (Indeed Uri had come to trust GOM completely. GOM had formerly traded in simoleans, and had safely held Uri's money even after his TSO avatar had been terminated.) What Lawrence was saying was, "No need for you to learn to work together, just come to us." As a strategy for building trust and the foundations of a new society, Uri thought it sucked.

To many SL residents, the GOM episode had a chilling effect. Rather than encouraging innovation among SL residents, Linden Lab was apparently ready and willing to steal their good ideas with little credit or compensation. In GOM's case, the rationale was that a currency exchange was too important not to be handled by the company. In other words, residents couldn't be trusted to provide such a service themselves.

It appeared LL didn't trust its customers much at all, at least not in the way that successful online communities require if they are to flourish and thrive. The company was going to have to make some hard decisions if they wanted their world to grow in population and complexity. What was starting to happen was that their paternalistic efforts were keeping residents from developing their own systems of trust and enforcement, systems that had been proven by experience—in both the real world and the virtual one—to be the best ways to manage an emerging society.

At the second annual State of Play conference at the New York Law School in November 2004, there was a meeting of the minds among virtual world developers and legal scholars of cyberspace. There, Peter Ludlow attended a discussion of dispute resolution in virtual worlds and other online spaces. The panel featured heavy hitters such as Yale's Jack Balkin, New York Law School's Beth Noveck and David Johnson, and Cardozo

Law School's Susan Crawford. Also on the panel were anthropologists with backgrounds in dispute resolution, Yahoo!'s Randy Farmer (who had helped create Habitat, one of the first virtual worlds, and had worked on both TSO and Second Life) and Colin Rule, the director of conflict resolution at eBay. There were also three key officers of Linden Lab: Philip Rosedale, senior vice president for community and support Robin Harper, and vice president of product development Cory Ondrejka.

Ludlow found the panel fascinating. Most of the participants felt that the only sustainable conflict-resolution systems were those that emerged from a population itself. Robust and effective dispute resolution systems developed wherever they were allowed to naturally evolve. But what Ludlow noticed was that the Lindens refused to see this point: Throughout the panel, discussion they asked over and over again what would be the best recipe for dispute resolution in their virtual world. When they were told that the best recipe would be one that their residents cooked up themselves, they simply refused to hear the message.

After the panel, Ludlow spoke with two of the law professors who had spoken, both of whom were delighted with the meeting. "We actually figured out a lot. Dispute resolution mechanisms should be organically developed, and the Lindens need to provide users with the ability to let that happen," offered one. Ludlow was less sanguine: "I don't think the Lindens got the point." Both law professors nodded: "No, they didn't." Despite all of LL's rhetoric about building a new society in cyberspace, they could not understand that this would require them to stop playing gods, and provide tools for users to build a society on their own. Being a god was a heady tonic, and the Lindens could not let it go.

17 The Day the Grid Disappeared

It started out as a day like any other in Second Life. It was the next-to-last Sunday in October 2005, the day before a major new patch of the virtual world's software was to be installed. What made the day exceptional was the small spherical object one resident quietly added to the stock of user-created content that makes SL unusual among virtual worlds.

Adorned with an image of the G-Man from the Half-Life single-player action games, the object had soon rezzed a copy of itself and then there were two, floating side by side, low above the landscape of the Grid. A moment later, each of those had replicated again, and there were four. Soon after that, there were eight, and then there were sixteen. Like the cell division that marks the beginning of life, the exponential growth continued. The spheres multiplied, overflowing the boundaries of the server in which they'd started and spilling over into neighboring regions, then into the regions that bounded those.

Eventually, according to some reports, there were 5.4 billion of them.

Who knows how long it took or what the exact sequence of events was, whether the servers went down one by one or crashed spectacularly all at once. But by late afternoon on that Sunday they had all winked out. All of them. Second Life was no more.

In a world whose residents can create not only fantasy castles and other marvels but scripted objects that can interact with each other, with avatars, and with applications outside the virtual world as well, accidents will happen. From time to time, an ambitious builder or scripter may overreach his or her talents. Create a linked chain of objects that employ the SL physics engine and you can strain a server's resources to the breaking point. Servers will crash.

Whether an "accident" hit Second Life on October 23, though, is open to interpretation. Was it an "accident" that the self-replicating objects had been named GriefSpawn by their creator? Was it mere coincidence that this creative mind had been a member of the W-Hats, a group of residents renowned for their inflammatory builds and harrassment of others?

Signs point to no, that what happened on the day the Grid disappeared was not an accident at all, but the most effective denial-of-service attack Second Life had ever seen, and it came from within the world itself.

Residents, needless to say, were dismayed. Though there's no comparison in terms of loss of life and other damages, having Second Life flooded with GriefSpawn spheres was a bit like having your city hit by a hurricane: Businesses were forced to close, residents were forced to evacuate, and though the world was back online relatively quickly, it was days or weeks before the full extent of the damage was known.

The amount of damage will be difficult to calculate, though, because the GriefSpawn attack has had lasting effects that go beyond whatever immediate destruction and business loss was caused. The code-meisters over at Linden Lab were obviously not very happy on GriefSpawn day. But they must have been relieved that it came the day before a major patch, for they took the opportunity to sneak a change into Second Life's new version that was designed to prevent such attacks in the future.

To many residents, however, the cure was worse than the disease.

To create a self-replicating object on the scale of the GriefSpawn that crashed all of Second Life, the parent object has to give a copy of the replication script to the children it creates, like cells passing along their DNA. So to prevent such attacks in the future, Linden Lab coded new limitations into the function that passes inventory from one object to another, making it impossible to do so unless the objects you'd created were located on land you owned. The change was slipped in just under the wire for the new release. And by Monday, residents were outraged.

This was virtual homeland security at its finest. One resident had crashed the Grid; all seventy-five thousand of them now had their hands tied. Many of the most robust builds and business applications in Second Life had relied on the transfer ability to work anywhere in the virtual world. Now you could play around with such functions in your back yard, but that was about it. To protect against future attacks, the new release actually rolled back functionality. And not just any functionality, but one of the key features that had allowed Second Life to become, for a great many people, the only virtual world that matters.

The perpetrator was punished too, of course, reportedly given a permanent ban by Linden Lab. But there's almost no doubt he or she will be back. A borrowed credit card and a new IP address is all it takes. Perhaps the perp has learned a lesson, perhaps not. But the gods had spoken, the way the world worked had been changed.

Fortunately, that change was reversed soon after it was put into place. Popular outcry once again had its effect. But if the new law had stayed on the books much longer, the world of Second Life might have been in for far greater losses than any caused by the occasional griefer's global attack.

Second Life stands or falls on what it's possible to create there. With Linden Lab providing only a landscape (and sometimes not even that), the residents effectively constitute the largest content-creation team in existence, and one that pays for the privilege. In return they garner fun, fame, and, in more than a few cases, fortune.

But to make such a place truly vibrant, much more must be possible there than the creation of shiny dream palaces. In fact, more must be possible than the creation of only the fine, attractive, or even tediously dull things that many residents add to the Grid. Real life works the same way, after all. The physics of the world around us allows for damage and destruction as well as beauty and utility. We have learned to harness the forces of our world for things like nuclear power and computer technology, but that has also made possible things like briefcase bombs and spam. In a world in which the latter wasn't possible, the former world disappear as well.

What's special about cyberspace is that the men and women behind the code control the physics of their worlds. The avatars of Second Life are free to fly around at will. But a few keystrokes on the part of the coders could change that. Until late October, the physics of Second Life allowed object-to-object transfers. Because of a crime, those physics were briefly changed.

And that's where things get tricky. Real-world crimes don't, of course, lead to changes in the physical laws of the world in which we live. They lead to changes in the civil and criminal laws. That's why we have such laws, because "bad" things *are* possible. Criminalizing murder doesn't eliminate the threat, it simply raises the risks associated with committing the crime.

Murder, of course, is something most people would agree should be eliminated from the world, if only it were possible. But incarceration is also possible under the physics of our world. Most people wouldn't want to change this, as it's one of the threats we use to convince people not to do things like commit murder. It's a tool of social engineering that makes our society a comfortable place to live. But if Joe Psychopath next door were to lock away your neighbor down the street, it wouldn't be called incarceration, it would be called kidnapping. If you could change the physics of our world, would you want to get rid of jails just so you could get rid of kidnappers?

In a sense, that's how Linden Lab chose to deal with the GriefSpawn. The criminal laws of Second Life haven't changed; global attacks were strictly a no-no before October 23 and they remain against the "rules" today. But rather than put more cops on the street or find a better way to register and ban individual users, the company chose to eliminate a good in order to eliminate an evil.

It should be said that Linden Lab continues to look for improvements that would allow more good while eliminating still more evil. But that's not the point. Because no matter how foolproof the physics of your world are, there will always be a way to grief it. Ask any coder and he or she will tell you the same thing: There is no application without a bug, and no security system without a crack in it. The limited time and resources of a development team simply can't compete with the nearly unlimited curiosity and commitment of those who hope to find those bugs and cracks. And once found, of course, someone will eventually exploit them, whether your physics likes it or not.

Linden Lab did find a new way to deal with the problem several months after the GriefSpawn episode, when a similar attack was perpetrated by another member of the W-Hats. This time, though, someone was watching, and the company managed to contain the attack in much the same way as firefighters will work to stop a rapidly spreading fire by depriving it of fuel. When a new grief-sphere hit the Grid in late November, Linden Lab itself took a swath of sims offline, creating a virtual fire-break, so that the objects would be contained in one corner of the Grid.[1] The strategy worked like a charm. How effective such measures will be in the future remains to be seen (monitoring the Grid and policing for such attacks can be an overwhelming task), but the moment was promising. Finally, it looked as if the company itself was beginning to accept that its code would not suffice as the sole oversight for its world.

Philip Rosedale, the founder and CEO of Linden Lab, says he is not building a game, he is "building a country." If so, it is a country whose citizens have no formal voice, and which is run suspiciously as if it were, in fact, a game. Second Life's seven thousand-word Terms of Service document contains all the same caveats as that of any game company's. Users do retain the intellectual property rights to their creations, but Linden Lab or anyone else on the Grid can use those creations as they see fit. LL can kick you out or delete your stuff "for any reason or no reason." And the Terms of Service and Community Standards, the documents that effectively constitute the civil, criminal, and constitutional laws of the world, change so often and with so little notice that it's impossible to know exactly where you stand at any given moment. As a virtual world, Second Life is the coolest thing going. As a country, it is failing badly.

18 The Metaverse Is Born

By February 2006, Peter Ludlow had had enough. He had been watching the metaverse slowly emerge since he started the *Herald* in October 2003, but now other people could do the watching. Uri announced his retirement in the *Herald* on February 15, in his own inimitable style.

> Famed cyberjournalist and virtual media mogul Urizenus Sklar announced his retirement today, shortly after a hunting trip with Dick Cheney and executives from Haliburton and IGE. In a statement released by the *Herald* Offices, Urizenus (Uri to his multitudinous friends) announced that he would be turning the *Herald* over to his trusted editorial director, Walker Spaight, and would be leaving Second Life as well, returning only for occasional hunting vacations in Jessie.[1]

The next day one of Ludlow's students told him, somewhat prophetically, "You know, no one ever really retires from life online." It wasn't a retirement, but it did turn out to be a long sabbatical. Walker Spaight took over duties as publisher, growing the operations of Herald Enterprises, while staying true to the mission of snarky investigations into the conflicts and drama that ravaged the relations between Second Life residents, and between residents and Linden Lab. But Walker's offline work left him little time to contribute, and the *Herald* limped along for some months on life support, largely just providing an outlet for the occasional resident who wanted to write about the interesting build they'd found or complain about the latest injustice. Walker advertised for a managing editor, but no suitable candidates presented themselves.

Eventually, though, a writer with sufficient moxie emerged to fit the bill. Pixeleen Mistral was a virtual sailing enthusiast who made her first mark as a *Herald* sports correspondent. She soon branched out to the political desk, perfectly hitting the *Herald*'s "Always Fairly Unbalanced" tone, and though she resisted at first, Walker eventually recruited her to be the new managing editor.[2]

Uri had been following events in Second Life in a relatively detached way, dropping in on his property in Jessie every month or so. But about the time Pix took over the *Herald*, Uri began to follow what was happening in Second Life more closely. What he saw blew his mind. In his absence, the metaverse was finally taking shape! But it wasn't pretty. All of Uri's worst fears were being realized.

For starters, large corporations were pouring into Second Life as fast as they possibly could. In an interview subsequently posted in the *Herald*, Uri described it as watching bull hippos rut racing through a China shop to get to a hippo cow. Sony, Nissan, Toyota, Adidas, American Apparel, and IBM were all pouring into the space.

This in itself was not a problem; what concerned Uri was the realization that these corporations were being sheperded in by several newly formed development companies that were largely staffed by members of the Feted Inner Core. The Electric Sheep Company, Millions of Us, Infinite Vision Media, and Aimee Weber Studios were terraforming islands and building virtual stores and corporate headquarters for real-world corporations, and the principals of those development corporations were the members of the privileged class that Prokofy Neva had raged against in the forums.

But now the FIC were getting not just pats on the back and special favors when it came to disputes with other residents, they were receiving contracts worth up to hundreds of thousands of dollars, according to *Business Week* magazine.[3] In many cases, real world corporations were coming to Linden Lab seeking advice, and were being funneled directly to the friends of Linden Lab. As the volume of work grew, though, Linden Lab was hard-pressed to continue to hand out juicy contracts. Instead, they started a developers list, similar to the lists maintained by software companies like Microsoft. In Microsoft's case, though, getting on the dev list is merely a matter of fulfilling Microsoft's certification requirements. Linden Lab had no such formal process in place, and many residents and would-be developers continued to complain about favoritisim.

Uri decided his sabbatical had gone on long enough. He checked in with Walker and Pixeleen about returning as a contributing editor, and found they were delighted to have him. On his return, Uri found that the *Herald* was operating at a much higher level than during his tenure. Instead of five stories a week, it was not unusual for there to be five stories a *day* published—and it generally seemed that all of them were important.

Once back on the Grid, Uri puzzled over the new expensive builds that the SL development firms were building for the large corporations. The Nissan build seemed particularly problematic to Uri. Why, in a land of magical snail race chariots and dragons and flying saucers was Nissan delivering scale models of a Nissan Sentra? Was this the most creative thing they could come up with?

Uri was baffled by the way real-world companies approached marketing in what was fundamentally a user-generated social space. The cars were individually gorgeous, of course, with reflected light "baked" into the textures on the cars, and the giant vending machine that dispensed them exhibited an engineer's love for keeping computer processing to a minimum: it had no curves, no torii, nothing that would be computationally costly. But so what?

To Uri, it would have made more sense for Nissan to have built a virtual junkyard, and to have hired some gearheads to sit around and talk cars with visitors who came by. Instead there was a giant vending machine dispensing cars one after another. One could almost hear it saying, "Take your car, it is perfect. Move along please. Next."

It seemed to Uri that the issue went to the very essence of Linden Lab and its relation to Second Life. The company had a crack team of forward-thinking technical people who seemed unable to focus on the social aspect of Second Life, even though that aspect had already proven to be the heart of the world. The Lindens had identified the gifted builders, naturally picking people like themselves with a creative engineering bent. But that didn't capture what Second Life was really about. To Uri, it appeared the Lindens were just delivering eye candy.

Uri suspected that the new builds were failing to attract visitors, and this was confirmed when *New World Notes* reporter Hamlet Linden looked up the "dwell" figures—numbers that reflected the relative number of visitors to each location. If Hamlet's numbers were correct, people were avoiding the new corporate builds like the plague. Uri went to visit a cluster of eight islands that had been built for corporate customers by one of the FIC development corporations. It was mid-afternoon, and there was one visitor.

Not all the builds were designed to generate high traffic, of course. Many were built for one-off events that were designed to generate publicity and hype in the real world press—"hypervents" in *Herald* parlance. And while people didn't necessarily spend time on Nissan Island some people did take Nissan Sentras back to their own plots of land and claimed to thoroughly enjoy them (although it wasn't clear to Uri how, since there was no significant road system in Second Life). Walker was skeptical when the Electric Sheep Company announced it would bring Major League Baseball's Home Run Derby to Second Life. Why not just watch it on television? But the residents who attended had a great time, rezzing giant baseball paraphernalia and generally goofing off and carrying on while the event took place. Though corporate builds might not hew to the existing paradigm of the world, it seemed that residents would find ways to make them their own on their rare visits.

Of course this raised an altogether new problem for corporate marketers. They were learning what virtual world makers had learned many years before: In virtual worlds you have little control over how people use (or abuse) the content you place in the world. A classic example of this occurred when NBC planned a hypervent in which it would hold a virtual version of the lighting of the giant Christmas tree at New York's Rockefeller Center. The event was sharded, so that it took place on nearly twenty sims simultaneously, allowing one thousand people to attended the event. Linden Lab, though, unable to keep pace with its world's rapid growth, could not provide the virtual land. So the Electric Sheep Company, who produced the event, turned to Second Life's land baron Anshe Chung, who rented the company the land on which to erect the models of Rockefeller Center. The next day, however, Prokofy Neva noted that one of the hastily arranged rental sites was sitting smack next to a Gorean sim dedicated to role-playing the sexual slavery of women.

NBC could not have been happy with that (provided they knew who or what Goreans were), but even more vocal about their displeasure were the many residents of Anshe Chung's Dreamland Sims, who were furious to wake up one morning and find their lovely ocean views spoiled by a giant block of midtown Manhattan buildings. They protested in the forums, saying that Anshe was violating her own zoning regulations. She claimed her understanding of the builds only involved a skating rink and a restaurant (living in Wuhan China, she probably had no idea what came with the Rockefeller Center package). All in all it showed that in the metaverse your next door neighbors may be from radically different cultures (Chinese, or as the case may be, Gorean) and controlling events, misunderstandings, and how projects unfolded can be difficult if not impossible.

Some of the corporations did show some creativity with the uses of the content supplied by *other* corporations. Several employees of IBM found a use for their Toyota Scions, placing them in a neat row behind a ramp and using them as obstacles for their virtual motorcycle jumps.[4] At least IBM was "getting it"; they understood that life online was about being creative and doing things that you couldn't do in the physical world. The *Herald* staff was further heartened when a paparazzo scored a screenshot from the forbidden twelve-island complex owned by IBM; it showed a dock with some elite Second Life pleasure boats and a dispenser for the *Second Life Herald*![5] For the most part though, the corporate newcomers were either not really present—certainly not socially present—or were fumbling about trying to find a message.

The large corporations and development companies weren't the only ones not quite getting it. Public relations and marketing corporations were racing into Second Life too, hoping to find the harvest of eyeballs that had eluded them for most of Web 2.0. It seemed they were going to have a rough start in Second Life as well. A PR manager for Ogilvy had listed a number of "virtual firsts" including the first concert in Second Life (Suzanne Vega, he thought), the first hotel chain in Second Life (Starwood Aloft, he thought), the first sporting event in Second Life (the Home Run Derby) and on and on. But these were false firsts; there had been plenty of concerts in Second Life and more than a few hotels, and Uri had witnessed sporting events the day he arrived on the Grid in August 2003. Other bloggers had protested Ogilvy's claims, but the corporations weren't listening. When a new media marketing company announced that it was going to be the first corporation to launch in Second Life, Uri blew a gasket.

In one of the most incendiary posts he had ever written, Uri teed off on the PR and marketing flaks that were charging into the virtual space with no respect for local history.

> What are we to say about this? Is this an attempt to rewrite history? More likely, I would say it is a case of a bunch of desperate clueless fucktards trying to show how bleeding-edgy they are, and, given that SL is the bleeding-edgy flavor of the month, they are wrapping themselves in the Linden cape of bleeding-edginess. But they are being exposed as clueless frauds. If you are a corporation paying these people good money, get your money back now!, because they don't know the first thing about

this place and they are pissing people the fuck off. Whether they know anything about new media is another question, but I find it hard to imagine that they are anything more than old media dinosaurs wearing ill-fitting pixel clothing. The seams are showing. They don't even know how to move their slide bars.[6]

The post spread like wildfire among PR blogs and eventually made its way to Adrants (the most widely read advertising blog). The PR gadfly Amanda Chapel of the admirably snarky blog Strumpette asked Uri to write a column that she then tastefully entitled "Fucktards in Cyberspace."

I joined Second Life in August of 2003. At the time it was a sleepy little enclave of cyberspace with a few thousand residents, most of them fringe culture programmers, artists, and way-out-of-the-box entrepreneurs, each of them a brand new flavor of pioneer. These pioneers collectively decided they were not playing a game, but actually building a new continent, a place where people were free to express their creativity, develop new ideas, create wealth and socialize in ways that were otherwise constrained in meatspace due to geographical separation, lack of tools for content creation, and unlevel social and economic playing fields.

For two and a half years I watched Second Life residents work like dogs, often without remuneration to build the wonderful mind-blowing place that it is today. All forms of fantastic structures and vehicles emerged in the space, from psychedelic cities to dark medieval fortresses to delicate gravity-defying elven castles. Artificial life forms appeared, reproduced and evolved in gorgeous gardens, while the skies were dotted by magnificent and elegant otherworldly flying machines. Virtual sporting events ranged from elven archery tournaments to giant snail races.

In February of 2006, I took a sabbatical from Second Life to pursue other projects. When I returned eight months later I was flabbergasted by what I saw. Second Life, now with 1 million subscribers, was being invaded by an army of old world meatspace corporations, ranging from Reebok and American Apparel to GM and Nissan. The traditional newsmedia was hyperventilating in its awe of the old meatspace corporations and the "innovative" things they were doing in Second Life, and could not stop writing about it.

But what were these corporations in fact contributing? Rather than use Second Life to create new and exotic things, the corporations brought their old tired ideas with them. Fantastic flying vehicles gave way to scale models of Scions and Sentras. Psychedelic builds and castles and mushroom hotels gave way to scale models of the next Starwood Hotel. Flaming jet boots gave way to scale models of Adidas. Golden battle suits gave way to American Apparel yuppieware. Giant snail races gave way to pathetic in world broadcasts of the Major League Baseball's home run derby in a traditional-looking stadium.

And then came the public relations and media marketing firms, trying to show what groovy hepcats they were. They came late to a world they didn't understand and hyped what they thought they saw without research, reflection, or understanding.[7]

Uri's rant received a sympathetic hearing from a number of quarters, including, surprisingly, PR and marketing people who were desperately trying to come to grips with the new medium of 3-D social spaces. New Second Life resident, PR guy, and author of *The End of the 30 Second Spot,* Joseph Jaffe came in for heavy criticism when his new media consulting company Crayon launched in Second Life, but he invited Peter Ludlow to his podcast (Across the Sound). Soon after, Uri, Jaffe, Amanda Chapel, and several other PR people began meeting in-world to try to sort out ways of being helpful rather than destructive in a social space like Second Life. So there was hope.

Anshe Chung also took notice of the Uri's rant. Anshe had a deep appreciation of the history of the Second Life community. She had also grown into an incredibly powerful economic figure during Uri's absence. She had developed her own continent off of the Second Life mainland. Called Dreamland, it was so large it constituted about 10 percent of the entire virtual land mass of Second Life. Anshe broadcast a ballot to all the tenants in her domain, asking in effect if they wished to ban unrepentant PR flacks who made false claims of "firsts" in their marketing spiels. The ballot initiative passed; the PR flacks would be banned from Dreamland if they persisted in their unsupported hype.

It was a fascinating development (although troubling from a free speech perspective). Anshe was showing that it would be possible to establish regional authorities, or, for that matter, regional dictators within Second Life, and that democratic procedures might be instituted in those regions. Anshe's subsequent press release laid out the specifics of the law and how she would enforce it, including provisions for a jury trial if it came to that.[8]

Events like this suggested that the metaverse might still crystallize into a place where real world democratic and social institutions could be created and voted upon without constant interference from the platform owners, in this case Linden Lab. But Anshe was an unusual choice to be the Thomas Jefferson of this world; raised in Communist China (as a child she had been chosen to give speeches at important Communist events) she confided in Uri that she just didn't understand the Western press. Indeed, she was not above threatening inaccurate reporters with libel suits (as another Second Life newspaper learned).

In spite of this encouraging show of emerging regional governance structures, in most ways, it seemed that all the old problems were still in play when Uri returned from sabbatical. In late 2006, the mainland grid was still overrun with griefers; in-world tools like the Search utility were constantly breaking down; and there were hacks of the Second Life client software taking place everywhere you looked, many of them threatening the economic security of the residents of Second Life. The relationship between Linden Lab and the users of its world was frayed at best. And then, in early November, an event occurred that tied all of these concerns together in one neat package: The CopyBot affair.[9]

The *Herald* had covered its share of hacks and mods in its day, and it had also covered a fair number of griefers, not to mention scandals like the theft of textures in Second Life. It had certainly covered the uneasy relation between residents and Linden Lab, but it had never seen anything like this.

What happened was this: a group of residents called libsecondlife had been working on reverse engineering the Second Life client. Their results were to be open-source and made available on a wiki. Though the idea of monkeying around in the client code alarmed many residents, their efforts had the approval of Linden Lab chief techology officer Cory Ondrejka, who saw no harm in having a user-produced client in development, given that the server code that was the background of the world would remain in the company's hands. The project's original intention was to develop programming interfaces that might help users create more intuitive, custom-designed interfaces and external applications for Second Life. Unfortunately, one of their early work products was a bit of software code that generated an unprecedented level of *Sturm und Drang* on the Grid by playing directly to the fears residents had of their content being stolen.

Known as CopyBot, the code could produce a copy of any object that it targeted in Second Life, including avatars, cars, clothing, or anything else that existed on the Grid. While it could not copy scripts, it could do a fine job on shapes and textures. Videos of it in action soon turned up on YouTube, and it was an impressive sight. An avatar running CopyBot could seemingly touch anything, and with godlike powers generate a copy right before your eyes.

The libsecondlife programmers had been careful to make sure CopyBot didn't store any of the information it copied. When you logged off, the copies vanished. But it was a simple matter for one of them to alter the code so that CopyBot became a Frankensteinish vacuum, sucking up content from all over the Grid and storing it in an avatar's inventory for later use.

Needless to say, content creators went ballistic.

The CopyBot protests that broke out like flash mobs all across the grid were at least as impressive as CopyBot itself. Dozens of content creators shuttered their shops and put up invisible walls to prevent entry. Movement across the mainland became nearly impossible given all the barriers, and for a moment it looked like economic activity would all but grind to a halt.

Pixeleen and Prokofy churned out stories for the *Herald*, seemingly by the hour, that swung between resident protests, leaked chat logs, denials, and prevarications from libsecondlifers and Linden Lab. When the dust finally settled, it became clear that much more was going on than initially met the eye.

It soon became clear, for example, that some of the people working with the SL Development companies had close ties with libSL, and had participated in the project to some degree. This fueled speculation throughout the Grid and in the pages of the *Herald* that CopyBot was actually a commissioned piece of work, a charge that the *Herald* editorial staff was never able to confirm, but which several different sources maintained was the case.

Some people couldn't understand why shopkeepers were upset. Textures, after all, were information, and information wanted to be free. Stealing copyrighted information, of course, was against the law. And it was a legal defense that Linden Lab put forth: If you think someone is ripping off your product, file a take-down notice under the Digital Millennium Copyright Act, they advised. The law was on the books, they said, so use it.

But this struck many users as unfair. Many had entered Second Life and started businesses in the wake of intense and unrelenting PR from Linden Lab calling attention to how very many people were able to make money, even earn a living in the world. The in-world interface allowed you to label an object as "no copy," which suggested that the software would ensure that object would be protected. But now it was as if they were being told "sorry, that protection is no longer offered in our world."

In *Code and Other Laws of Cyberspace* Lawrence Lessig explained how the social values we prize are built into our world. It isn't by laws alone, or by social pressures alone, or by engineering alone, but a combination of the three. We don't pass laws against stealing skyscrapers nor do we teach our children that it would be wrong to do so. There is no point. It is just a feature of the physics of our world that you canot steal them. The value is safeguarded by the physics. Not all values are protected that way, but some are.[10]

The CopyBot affair was significant because it undermined users' beliefs that it was the physics of the world that protected their values. The Lindens had made it appear that way, but then they pulled the rug out from under the users. The Lindens seemed to be saying "Sorry, but this value is no longer protected by the physics of this world, it is no longer protected by the code. In fact, it is not protected by us at all." And, "Go to a real world court if you have issues with that."

Of course, it would probably be impossible for Linden Lab to protect users from copyright and trademark infringements altogether, making those beliefs a bit naive. In an excellent analysis of the problem Raph Koster explained that the end users must have the objects and images resolved on their computer screens at home or work and this means that the information necessary to recreate those objects must be transmitted to the end users' computer. This means that clever users can copy all the objects they want and reproduce them at will within the world.[11]

Koster is certainly correct that there is no failsafe solution to the problem of copying, but many residents hoped that it could be made more difficult. Neither engineering solutions nor real-world legal institutions are foolproof, but perhaps in concert they could make the situation better. Was there any harm in using code *and* laws *and* social mores to solve the problem? Unfortunately, it seemed that Linden Lab wanted no part of the responsibility.

The CopyBot affair was a key moment in the evolution of Second Life. Clearly, the world was growing faster than Linden Lab's ability to secure its stability and maintain the values the company claimed were integral to SL society. It was almost as if the world was being pulled in two radically different directions. The era of utopian self-expression insulated from the exigencies of the wider Web was clearly over. But how much sway the real world would have remained to be seen. The real world and the virtual world were colliding like never before, and it was anyone's guess whether the energy released in that collision would be too destructive for the metaverse to handle.

The truth is that the metaverse will likely become much more fragmented as more people enter it. In any case, there is simply no way that Linden Lab will be able to support the Grid by itself if its growth is to be truly global. Even Philip Rosedale has conceded this point.

Where the servers that run the metaverse of the future will eventually reside is with the residents of virtual worlds. What Linden Lab, among others, envisions is a model of the metaverse in which its various components are distributed among many locations, a world whose residents are responsible for the hardware that runs their virtual environment. Once that begins to happen, the virtual world could begin to change in radical ways, and that day may be upon us sooner than even the Lindens realize.

As of this writing many of the Second Life content developers see the handwriting on the wall; the future of the metaverse does not lie with Second Life's clunky software and inept community management, it lies in a broad spectrum of proprietary and open-source versions of online 3-D social spaces linked together by a standard internet protocol. Many developers who work in such environments are working behind the scenes with online virtual world software developers to help make such a pluralistic metaverse a reality.

Second Life will probably not be the platform that will sustain the metaverse. It was, however, the prototype that proved the concept—it kicked open the doors. It showed people that if done correctly, 3-D virtual spaces could be effective tools for business, education, collaboration, socializing, and entertainment, and it showed development companies that a lot of money could be made in building the metaverse, so much money that the development companies can no longer afford to wait for Second Life to fix its problems (a task even the Lindens described as swapping jet engines while the plane is in flight). Alternative open-source platforms like Open Croquet that once languished for lack of interest are now viewed as viable alternative solutions to building the infrastructure of the metaverse, and, as of this writing, several proprietary "stealth" alternatives are also under development behind the scenes. And, finally, very soon Linden Lab will make public all or part of the source code that runs the world of Second Life. As these developments unfold, many more things will become possible.

Imagine a metaverse of even only ten thousand servers, many more powerful than those in existence today, each one of which could support one hundred avatars or more as well as a nice country estate, a mall, and a museum or an office complex on its sixteen acres of virtual land. And imagine that many of those servers are under the control of individuals, people who are actively involved in the coding and development of their corner of the world. You might teleport from one sim to the next and find that here the user in charge has reversed gravity and now you are walking on the ceiling. Or you might be out shopping and find yourself suddenly in a tax-free sim. You might have plans to open a retail outlet of your own and want to rent a plot of land on someone's server—so tax rates will be important to you, and if you're selling skirts and dresses, which way gravity goes will be important as well. You may have any number of sims to choose from in which to establish your online board room; all manner of other commercial services will be available as well. Your children might play together in a sim where "mature" content was strictly regulated by both the code and the administrator; they might attend classes in a similar place. Your online dating service might not just match you up with a likely partner who lived near you in the real world, but let you go on virtual dates with that person in the metaverse as well; in some sims you might even be able to have cybersex with them, depending on what the person behind the server had done with its code. Perhaps the unleashing of this technology will even spawn corners of the metaverse where platform managers nurture the community aspect of their spaces, where they give users the tools to provide their own governance structures and dispute-resolution systems, and where the policies of the platform managers are clear and fairly applied.

A scenario in which *millions* of users maintain their own corners of the virtual world, and in which many millions more visit such places, is not so far-fetched. In fact, it has been seen before in the development and adoption of the World Wide Web. The key to the Web's growth was the fact that in the spring of 1993 the technology behind it was made freely available to all users without any payment necessary.[12] Two and a half years later, Netscape sparked the Web revolution with its landmark IPO, and ten years after that there are more than 11.5 billion publicly indexable Web pages.[13] Virtual worlds will have to undergo a similar transformation to become a free, open-source model, but once they do, there's no telling how widespread and powerful they could become.

It was the morning of November 28, 2006. Anshe Chung was going to hold an in-world press conference that day announcing that she had become the first person to acquire a million U.S. dollars worth of assets inside a virtual world. (Another first!) The *Herald* had followed her from the very beginning, from her days as a "tea house girl" in the erotic clubs of Second Life. The paper had tracked her slow and unrelenting accumulation of wealth in Second Life by buying, subdividing, and developing virtual real estate. The *Herald* had followed the extortion attempts on her by the W-Hats, and the Lindens' indifference to her and what she had accomplished (she told Uri that they had refused to announce her accomplishment or even to appear with her at the press conference—she wasn't one of the chosen ones; she wasn't FIC). But with or without the blessings of the Lindens she was now a millionaire, and there was no taking that away.

Anshe's story was a perfect metaphor for what had happened to virtual worlds in the three years since the *Herald* had gone into business. She had gone from the erotic club scene to becoming a powerful economic force in the still wild and woolly world of the fledgling metaverse.

Though her track record wasn't perfect, Anshe was part of the new metaverse. She understood that the metaverse would be built on a foundation of community; that one could stand up to the gods of the platform and insist that they do the right thing; that voting mechanisms and governance structures could be introduced as crucial components of the new society emerging in cyberspace.

In the phenomen that was Anshe, Uri saw great hope, but a positive outcome was by no means assured. He thought of an event that had occurred a year earlier at a workshop sponsored by Edward Castronova.[14] During a cocktail reception after the workshop, Ludlow felt someone tug on his arm. It was Raph Koster, then chief creative officer of Sony Online Entertainment, the man largely responsible for creating the landmark MMO Ultima Online.

"Hey," Koster said. "There's a student here that was in the battle with the Sleeper." Ludlow's knees buckled at the news. In the early days of the *Herald*, it was the story of the brave guilds of Rallos Zek that had inspired him, and had served as a metaphor for much of his understanding of the relation between the owners of virtual worlds and their citizens. Koster pointed out the former combatant, who was studying games at Indiana University, and Ludlow introduced himself. He felt it was like meeting someone who had walked on the moon.

Ludlow soon discovered there had been a misunderstanding. "I hear you were in one of the guilds that fought the Sleeper on Rallos Zek," he said.

"No, I wasn't on Zek," the student responded.

"But Raph said you were in the battle against the sleeper."

"I wasn't in it, but I saw it."

"I don't understand."

"I was a game master. I was in the room when we respawned the sleeper."

It suddenly dawned on Ludlow that this was not one of the brave warriors that had finally defeated the unkillable monster known as the Kerafyrm; this was one of the faceless men behind the curtain, the hand of Sony Online Entertainment, the company that ran EverQuest. Here was a wizard himself.

He wasn't what Uri expected. The kid had been only eighteen at the time of the battle, and far from being a corporate suit he looked like he had never worn a suit in his life. This was no longer like meeting Neil Armstrong; it was more like meeting Satan and finding that he looked like Ashton Kutcher. But expectations aside, Ludlow realized he now had the chance to answer the question that had nagged at him for nearly two years. It was the same question he'd wanted to ask Electronic Arts when they'd killed Urizenus. He was finally going to find out why. Why on earth did they do it? Had the company really failed to understand the heroic nature of the moment? Had the Sony execs who'd pulled the trigger really been blind to everything that was best about their game?

His heart racing, Ludlow could barely get his question out. "But why? Didn't you realize what you were doing? Why did you do it? How could you do it? Why did you stop them from killing the Sleeper?"

The kid took a drink and answered matter-of-factly.

"Because, man. Sony told me it wasn't supposed to happen."

There was the problem. If virtual worlds continued to be ruled by monolithic, unimaginative corporations that could see no further than the laws of their software, and if we followed along blindly, there was little hope. Even if the metaverse became widely distributed there would be no great victory if people did not think carefully about the rules of the worlds they were creating—if they did not reflect on the values they were encoding into their corners of the metaverse.

But some people could imagine another way. The guilds of Rallos Zek could. So could the writers for the *Herald*. It was true that the *Herald* had no real power, but it could be a witness to what was happening, and it could offer people an alternative picture of how things *could* be. It would be up to others to decide what kind of worlds they wanted, but at least the *Herald* could question the current trajectory of virtual worlds. What the guilds of Rallos Zek had showed and what the survival and success of the *Herald* had showed was that imagining another way could lead to things *being* another way. Here too was hope.

With that thought in mind, Peter Ludlow sat down at his computer at home, and checked the Second Life website to see if any other *Herald* employees were online. Pix and Prokofy were there. So were Walker and Budka. Gina Fatale and Fiend Ludwig were online as well. Ludlow smiled, poured himself a cup of coffee, and logged on.

Appendix A: A Declaration of the Rights of Avatars

Raph Koster

When a time comes that new modes and venues exist for communities, and said modes are different enough from the existing ones that [the] question arises as to the applicability of past custom and law, and when said venues have become a forum for interaction and society for the general public regardless of the intent of the creators of said venue, and at a time when said communities and spaces are rising in popularity and are now widely exploited for commercial gain, it behooves those involved in said communities and venues to affirm and declare the inalienable rights of the members of said communities. Therefore herein have been set forth those rights which are inalienable rights of the inhabitants of virtual spaces of all sorts, in their form henceforth referred to as avatars, in order that this declaration may continually remind those who hold power over virtual spaces and the avatars contained therein of their duties and responsibilities; in order that the forms of administration of a virtual space may be at any time compared to that of other virtual spaces; and in order that the grievances of players may hereafter be judged against the explicit rights set forth, to better govern the virtual space and improve the general welfare and happiness of all.

Therefore this document holds the following truths to be self-evident: That avatars are the manifestation of actual people in an online medium, and that their utterances, actions, thoughts, and emotions should be considered to be as valid as the utterances, actions, thoughts, and emotions of people in any other forum, venue, location, or space. That the well-established rights of man approved by the National Assembly of France on August 26th of 1789 do therefore apply to avatars in full measure saving only the aspects of said rights that do not pertain in a virtual space or which must be abrogated in order to ensure the continued existence of the space in question. That by the act of affirming membership in the community within the virtual space, the avatars form a social contract with the community, forming a populace which may and must self-affirm and self-impose rights and concomitant restrictions upon their behavior. That the nature of virtual spaces is such that there must, by physical law, always be a higher power or administrator who maintains the space and has complete power over all participants, but who is undeniably part of the community formed within the space and who must therefore take action in accord with that which benefits the space as well as the participants, and who therefore also has the rights of avatars and may have other rights as well. That the ease of moving between virtual spaces and the potential transience of the community do not limit or reduce the level of emotional and social involvement that avatars may have with the community, and that therefore the ease of moving between virtual spaces and the potential transience of the community do not in any way limit, curtail, or remove these rights from avatars on the alleged grounds that avatars can always simply leave.

Articles:

1. Avatars are created free and equal in rights. Special powers or privileges shall be founded solely on the common good, and not based on whim, favoritism, nepotism, or the caprice of those who hold power. Those who act as ordinary avatars within the space shall all have only the rights of normal avatars.

2. The aim of virtual communities is the common good of its citizenry, from which arise the rights of avatars. Foremost among these rights is the right to be treated as people and not as disembodied, meaningless, soulless puppets. Inherent in this right are therefore the natural and inalienable rights of man. These rights are liberty, property, security, and resistance to oppression.

3. The principle of all sovereignty in a virtual space resides in the inalterable fact that somewhere there resides an individual who controls the hardware on which the virtual space is running, and the software with which it is created, and the database which makes up its existence. However, the body populace has the right to know and demand the enforcement of the standards by which this individual uses this power over the community, as authority must proceed from the community; a community that does not know the standards by which the administrators use their power

is a community which permits its administrators to have no standards, and is therefore a community abetting in tyranny.

4. Liberty consists of the freedom to do anything which injures no one else including the weal of the community as a whole and as an entity instantiated on hardware and by software; the exercise of the natural rights of avatars are therefore limited solely by the rights of other avatars sharing the same space and participating in the same community. These limits can only be determined by a clear code of conduct.

5. The code of conduct can only prohibit those actions and utterances that are hurtful to society, inclusive of the harm that may be done to the fabric of the virtual space via hurt done to the hardware, software, or data; and likewise inclusive of the harm that may be done to the individual who maintains said hardware, software, or data, in that harm done to this individual may result in direct harm done to the community.

6. The code of conduct is the expression of the general will of the community and the will of the individual who maintains the hardware and software that makes up the virtual space. Every member of the community has the right to contribute either directly or via representatives in the shaping of the code of conduct as the culture of the virtual space evolves, particularly as it evolves in directions that the administrator did not predict; the ultimate right of the administrator to shape and define the code of conduct shall not be abrogated, but it is clear that the administrator therefore has the duty and responsibility to work with the community to arrive at a code of conduct that is shaped by the input of the community. As a member of the community himself, the administrator would be damaging the community itself if he failed in this responsibility, for abrogation of this right of avatars could result in the loss of population and therefore damage to the common weal.

7. No avatar shall be accused, muzzled, toaded, jailed, banned, or otherwise punished except in the cases and according to the forms prescribed by the code of conduct. Any one soliciting, transmitting, executing, or causing to be executed, any arbitrary order, shall be punished, even if said individual is one who has been granted special powers or privileges within the virtual space. But any avatar summoned or arrested in virtue of the code of conduct shall submit without delay, as resistance constitutes an offense.

8. The code of conduct shall provide for such punishments only as are strictly and obviously necessary, and no one shall suffer punishment except it be legally inflicted according to the provisions of a code of conduct promulgated before the commission of the offense; save in the case where the offense endangered the continued existence of the virtual space by attacking the hardware or software that provide the physical existence of the space.

9. As all avatars are held innocent until they shall have been declared guilty, if detainment, temporary banning, jailing, gluing, freezing, or toading shall be deemed indispensable, all harshness not essential to the securing of the prisoner's person shall be severely repressed by the code of conduct.

10. No one shall be disquieted on account of his opinions, provided their manifestation does not disturb the public order established by the code of conduct.

11. The free communication of ideas and opinions is one of the most precious of the rights of man. Every avatar may, accordingly, speak, write, chat, post, and print with freedom, but shall be responsible for such abuses of this freedom as shall be defined by the code of conduct, most particularly the abuse of affecting the performance of the space or the performance of a given avatar's representation of the space.

12. The security of the rights of avatars requires the existence of avatars with special powers and privileges, who are empowered to enforce the provisions of the code of conduct. These powers and privileges are therefore granted for the good of all and not for the personal advantage of those to whom they shall be entrusted. These powers and privileges are also therefore not an entitlement, and can and should be removed in any instance where they are no longer used for the good of all, even if the offense is merely inactivity.

13. A common contribution may, at the discretion of the individual who maintains the hardware, the software, and the data that make up the virtual space, be required in order to maintain the existence of avatars who enforce the code of conduct and to maintain the hardware and the software and the continued existence of the virtual space. Avatars have the right to know the nature and amount of the contribution in advance, and said required contribution should be equitably distributed among all the

citizens without regard to their social position; special rights and privileges shall never pertain to the avatar who contributes more except insofar as the special powers and privileges require greater resources from the hardware, software, or data store, and would not be possible save for the resources obtainable with the contribution; and as long as any and all avatars are able to make this contribution and therefore gain the powers and privileges if they so choose; nor shall any articles of this declaration be contingent upon a contribution being made.

14. The community has the right to require of every administrator or individual with special powers and privileges granted for the purpose of administration, an account of his administration.

15. A virtual community in which the observance of the code of conduct is not assured and universal, nor the separation of powers defined, has no constitution at all.

16. Since property is an inviolable and sacred right, and the virtual equivalent is integrity and persistence of data, no one shall be deprived thereof except where public necessity, legally determined per the code of conduct, shall clearly demand it, and then only on condition that the avatar shall have been previously and equitably indemnified, saving only cases wherein the continued existence of the space is jeopardized by the existence or integrity of said data.

17. The administrators of the virtual space shall not abridge the freedom of assembly, save to preserve the performance and continued viability of the virtual space.

18. Avatars have the right to be secure in their persons, communications, designated private spaces, and effects, against unreasonable snooping, eavesdropping, searching and seizures, no activity pertaining thereto shall be undertaken by administrators save with probable cause supported by affirmation, particularly describing the goal of said investigations.

19. The enumeration in this document of rights shall not be construed to deny or disparage others retained by avatars.

—January 26, 2000

Appendix B: *Herald* Obituary: In Memory of Candace Bolter, aka Kale

Peter Ludlow

On March 28, 2005, *Herald* co-founder and legal editor Candace Bolter passed away after a long struggle with a string of illnesses ranging from cancer to heart disease to lupus. She was twenty-seven years old.

Often too sick to leave her bed, Candace was a powerful advocate for the *Herald* in our run-ins with Maxis and EA and naysayers in the blogging community. She visited *Terra Nova* regularly and took on the likes of Jeff Cole, Brian "Psychochild" Green, and "Phineas" Schwanz, who were concerned that an anti-video game campaign would be spawned by the controversy surrounding the *Herald*. Candace had a very firm grip on the legal issues surrounding the case and consulted with several lawyers on the matter. (She herself planned on going into law school after completing her Ph.D., and was accepted to U.C. Berkeley's Law School but was too ill to attend.)

In the months following EA's moves against the *Herald*, Candace pursued a number of interesting legal issues in TSO and then Second Life, and she conducted a classic interview with Cory Linden on the flouting of intellectual property rights by SL users.[1]

I also assigned her some projects that were, in her view, pretty silly, and she used the pseudonym I. P. Lithium when publishing those efforts. One such case was when she had to speak to Relina, who claimed to have been loved and then scorned by Mr-President in TSO.[2]

Mostly though, Candace was always deeply concerned about others and their well-being (both in-game and in RL). As sick as she was, she was incredibly sensitive to the dispositions of those around her and always worked hard to cheer up someone she felt was depressed. She always had time to dispense the kind of spiritual and metaphysical advice that befit a philosopher and virtual shaman.

But now, I sit here wondering: was I so self-absorbed that I let her help me with my stupid problems when she was suffering in ways I can't even imagine? Probably. But fortunately for me, Candace was forgiving, and by her dictates my penance for any arbitrary crime was listening to Paul Westerberg and drinking single-malt scotch.

And so, as I slip in a Westerberg CD and uncork my bottle of Ardbeg, I just want to say: Candace, the scotch is good but I still hate Paul Westerberg. That, and we miss you so much . . .

Notes

Acknowledgments

1. http://www.alwaysblack.com/blackbox/bownigger.html.

2. http://gillen.blogspot.com/2004/03/new-games-journalism-this-may-turn.html.

1 The Death of Urizenus

1. Originally found at http://www.alphavillherald.com, the *Herald* can now be read at http://www.secondlifeherald.com/.

2. See chapter 9.

3. Johannes, "China plans to invest $1.8 Billion in Online Gaming," http://chinanetinvestor.blogspot.com/2005_08_01_archive.html (August 2, 2005).

4. Edward Castronova, "Virtual Worlds: A First-Hand Account of Market and Society on the Cyberian Frontier (CESifo Working Paper No. 618, December 2001, http://papers.ssrn.com/abstract=294828).

5. Mark Wallace, "The Game Is Virtual. The Profit Is Real," *The New York Times*, Sunday Business (May 29, 2005).

6. See chapter 7.

7. Cao Li, "Death Sentence for Online Gamer," *China Daily*, http://www2.chinadaily.com.cn/english/doc/2005-06/08/content_449600.htm (June 8, 2005).

8. http://jobs.ea.com/about.html.

9. David Becker, "Online Gaming: A Revolution Ahead," *ZDNet News*, http://news.zdnet.com/2100-9595_22-922731.html (May 24, 2002).

10. Amy Harmon, "A Real-Life Debate on Free Expression in a Cyberspace City," *The New York Times* (January 15, 2004).

11. In fact, the Sleeper probably had more like one hundred million hit points, according to Al Brandes, who has studied the episode in more depth than anyone probably should. See http://www.albrandes.com/skden/articles/sleeper.asp.

12. Andrew Phelps, Assistant Professor, Department of Information Technology, Rochester Institute of Technology, Rochester, NY, and founding faculty member of the Game Programming Concentration, http://www.corante.com/gotgame/archives20031101.html#61354 (November 1, 2003).

13. Urizenus, "New Year's Wishes From Urizenus: May We Slay the Kerafyrm in Our World," *Alphaville Herald*, http://www.dragonscoveherald.com/blog/index.php?p=65 (December 31, 2003).

2 Inside the Virtual World

1. Blizzard Entertainment, press release, http://www.blizzard.com/press/031705-worldwide.shtml (March 17, 2005).

2. Blizzard Entertainment press release, http://www.blizzard.com/press/051219.shtml (December 19, 2005).

3. Robert Holt, *All Things Considered*, http://www.npr.org/templates/story/story.php?storyId=4537744 (March 16, 2005).

4. Rick Adams, "A History of 'Adventure,'" http://www.rickadams.org/adventure/a_history.html, and Don Woods, interview with Mark Wallace, August 2005.

5. Don Woods, interview with Mark Wallace, August 2005.

6. Tracy Kidder, *The Soul of a New Machine* (New York: Avon, 1982), 260.

7. David Cuciz, "The History of MUDs," *GameSpy*, http://archive.gamespy.com/articles/january01/muds1/index3.shtm (January 2001).

8. MUD1 can still be played on the Web at http://www.british-legends.com/.

9. *GameSpy.com*, http://archive.gamespy.com/articles/january01/muds1/index4.shtm (January 2001).

10. "Massively Multiplayer Online Games: The Past, The Present, and The Future," *GameSpy.com*, http://archive.gamespy.com/amdmmog/week2/ (series September 23 to November 14, 2003).

11. From Andrew Kirmse's personal Web site, http://www.ieatcode.com/meridian/.

12. Explored throughout this book, but especially in chapter 16.

13. In 2001, several former Meridian developers formed Near Death Studios, Inc., which resurrected the game and maintains it to this day.

14. http://archive.gamespy.com/amdmmog/week2/index.shtml.

15. http://www.aschulze.net/ultima/stories9/beta.htm and http://archive.gamespy.com/amdmmog/week2/index.shtml.

16. Andy Phelps, interview with Mark Wallace, June 2005.

17. Neal Stephenson, *Snow Crash* (Bantam Books, 1992).

3 Slinging Bolts at the Robot Factory

1. William Blake, *The Book of Urizen* (1794).

2. Marcy Burstiner, "Electronic Arts to Buy Maxis for $125 Million," *Wired News*, http://wired-vig.wired.com/news/business/0,1367,4273,00.html (June 5, 1997).

3. Urizenus, Interview with Don Hopkins, *Alphaville Herald*, http://www.dragonscoveherald.com/blog/index.php?p=110 (February 12, 2004).

4. Lev Grossman, "Sim Nation," *Time* magazine (November 25, 2002).

5. http://terranova.blogs.com/terra_nova/2005/06/_ive_been_asked.html.

6. Deep Max, "More Promises Promises Promises Promises," *Alphaville Herald*, http://www.dragonscoveherald.com/blog/index.php?p=150 (March 30, 2004).

7. Peter Ludlow, ed., *High Noon on the Electronic Frontier: Conceptual Issues in Cyberspace* (Cambridge, MA: MIT Press, 1996) and *Crypto Anarchy, Cyberstates, and Pirate Utopias* (Cambridge, MA: MIT Press, 2001).

8. Walter Isaacson, *Benjamin Franklin: An American Life* (New York: Simon and Schuster, 2003).

9. A former student of Ludlow's when he had taught at SUNY Stony Brook, Squirrel had caught Ludlow's attention with an evaluation of his course that appeared in *The Stony Brook Press*, which Given edited, in December 2000. It was unattributed, but was clearly the work of Squirrel: "Ludlow is the greatest teacher ever to grace this campus. It's that simple. If you have any brain cells left in that bong—I mean head—you'll be riveted. . . . He gives extra points for being especially clever and doesn't take shit from moronic students. Get into something he's teaching by hook or by crook." With his encyclopedic knowledge of online games, Ludlow figured Squirrel would bring valuable knowledge and experience to the project, as well as a helping of energy and attitude. Besides, after an evaluation like the one in the *The Press*, how could Ludlow not sign him up?

10. Urizenus, "A Letter from the Publisher: Our Mission at *The Alphaville Herald*," *Alphaville Herald*, http://www.dragonscoveherald.com/blog/index.php?p=3 (October 24, 2003).

11. Urizenus, "TSO: High School Redux?" *Alphaville Herald*, http://www.dragonscoveherald.com/blog/index.php?p=15 (November 8, 2003).

4 A Day in the Life of a Techno-Pagan Newsroom

1. The Gorean lifestyle is based on John Norman's science-fiction series of Gor novels, in which enslaved women are sexually subjugated, routinely "disciplined," and humiliated by men (and, in some cases, by "free women").

2. Hamlet Linden, aka James Wagner Au, "Man and Man on Woman on Woman," *New World Notes,* http://secondlife.blogs.com/nwn/2005/01/man_and_man_on_.html (January 2005).

3. Walker Spaight, "Turning the Pages at the SL Public Library," *Second Life Herald,* http://www.dragonscoveherald.com/blog/index.php?p=629 (January 16, 2005).

4. Sherry Turkle, *Life on the Screen: Identity in the Age of the Internet* (New York: Simon and Schuster, 1995) and *The Second Self: Computers and the Human Spirit* (New York: Simon and Schuster, 1984).

5. Sheryl Hanson, "'Voleur' Means 'Thief,' Part I," *Alphaville Herald,* http://www.dragonscoveherald.com/blog/index.php?p=25 (November 19, 2003).

6. Urizenus, "Voleur Part 2: Interview with Voleur/Evangeline," *Alphaville Herald,* http://www.dragonscoveherald.com/blog/index.php?p=29 (November 24, 2003).

7. Urizenus, "Evangeline: Interview With a Child Cyber-Prostitute in TSO," *Alphaville Herald,* http://www.dragonscoveherald.com/blog/index.php?p=45 (December 8, 2003).

5 Dollars and Cyberspace

1. For an explanation of servers and "sharding" in virtual worlds, see chapter 2.

2. Many money traders in TSO relied on a complex system of automated "bots" to produce vast quantites of simoleans for them. RB introduced Uri to a shadowy underground of money traders who took elaborate measures to hide their activities from EA representatives, and Uri, in turn, introduced them to the *Herald*'s readers. See chapter 12 for further explanation.

3. Urizenus, "Interview with SARP's AJ: Hey, you've got us all wrong!" *Alphaville Herald,* http://www.dragonscoveherald.com/blog/index.php?p=91 (January 23, 2004).

4. http://cgi.ebay.com/ws/eBayISAPI.dll?ViewItem&category=33887&item=8199384295&rd=1.

5. The Phantom, "Founder Account for Sale on eBay," *Alphaville Herald,* http://www.dragonscoveherald.com/blog/index.php?p=67 (January 2, 2004).

6. http://cgi.ebay.com/ws/eBayISAPI.dll?ViewItem&item=8204270353&category=41013&ssPageName=WDVW&rd=1.

7. Urizenus, "Pet Pull Frenzy! An interview with Becca from Pet Addicts," *Alphaville Herald*, http://www.dragonscoveherald.com/blog/index.php?p=211 (May 3, 2004).

8. Friends of the money-trader RB had automated this process. See chapter 12.

9. Wage Slaves, 1UP.com, http://www.1up.com/do/feature?cId=3141815 (July 5, 2005).

10. David Barboza, "Boring Game? Here a player," *New York Times*, http://www.iht.com/articles/2005/12/08/business/gaming.php (December 8, 2005).

11. "Wage Slaves," *1UP.com*, http://www.1up.com/do/feature?cId=3141815 (July 5, 2005).

12. Embassy of *The People's* republic of China in the United States of America, http://www.china=embassy.org/eng/gyzg/t268200.htm.

13. United Nations Statistics Division, National Accounts Main Aggregates Database, table: Per Capita GDP in US Dollars, http://unstats.un.org/unsd/snaama/dnllist.asp.

14. Edward Castronova, "Virtual Worlds: A First-Hand Account of Market and Society on the Cyberian Frontier," CESifo Working Paper No. 618, available at http://papers.ssrn.com/abstract=294828 (December 2001).

15. Montserrat Tovar, "Interview with Mr-President," http://www.dragonscoveherald.com/blog/index.php?p=174 (April 8, 2004).

16. Or in some cases, you turn over the goods and get no money in return. Compounding the problem is the fact that some auction and payment Websites provide no protection for the sale of virtual goods. Author Julian Dibbell, who undertook a year-long experiment in trying to earn his living in Ultima Online (chronicled in his latest book, *Play Money* [Perseus 2006]), tried to navigate this problem in an amusing conversation with a PayPal customer service representative, in which Dibbell pressed for an explanation of the difference between selling tickets for a football game (which are covered by PayPal's nonpayment protection policy) and selling a password to a game account (which is not covered). His encounter is chronicled on his Weblog at http://www.juliandibbell.com/playmoney/2003_10_01_playmoney_archive.html#106645520484229563.

17. Electronic Arts press release, http://retailsupport.ea.com/corporate/pressreleases/uo_ebay.html.

18. Jay Lyman, "Gamer Wins Lawsuit in Chinese Court Over Stolen Virtual Winnings," *TechNewsWorld*, http://www.technewsworld.com/story/32441.html (December 19, 2003).

19. Budka Groshomme, "Opening the Cupboard Door," *Second Life Herald*, http://www.dragonscoveherald.com/blog/index.php?p=710 (March 11, 2005). Psychologist Abraham Maslow conceived of psychology as a hierarchy of human needs, from the

physiological to the need for security, for love, for esteem, and for self-actualization. See http://en.wikipedia.org/wiki/Maslow.

20. Mark Wallace, "The Game Is Virtual. The Profit Is Real," *The New York Times*, Sunday Business (May 29, 2005).

21. Mark Wallace, "The Game Is Virtual. The Profit Is Real," *The New York Times*, Sunday Business (May 29, 2005).

22. Walker Spaight, "The *Herald* Profile: Anshe Chung," *Second Life Herald*, http://www.dragonscoveherald.com/blog/index.php?p=645 (January 25, 2005).

23. Philip Rosedale, interview with Mark Wallace, May 2005.

24. Mark Wallace, "The Game Is Virtual. The Profit Is Real," *The New York Times*, Sunday Business (May 29, 2005).

25. Urizenus Sklar, "Interview with Opfor founder Jack Orlowski (aka bicycle maker William Bukowski)," *Second Life Herald*, http://www.dragonscoveherald.com/blog/index.php?p=353 (August 6, 2004).

26. Chip Poutine, "Little House on the Sandbox," http://virtualsuburbia.blogspot.com/2006/07/little-house-on-sandbox.html (July 18, 2006).

27. "Second Life Teaches Life Lessons," *WrongPlanet.net*, http://www.wrongplanet.net/modules.php?name=News&file=print&sid=203 (April 6, 2005).

28. Philip Rosedale, interview with Mark Wallace, May 2005.

29. James Grimmelmann, "The State of Play: On the Second Life Tax Revolt," http://research.yale.edu/lawmeme/modules.php?name=News&file=article&sid=1222 (September 21, 2003).

30. Bruce Sterling Woodcock, "MMOGCHART.COM," http://www.mmoprgchart.com.

31. "Korea Leads in New Technology: FEER," http://korea.net/news/news/newsview.asp?serial_no=20020712001 (July 13, 2002).

6 The Case of the Broken Jaw

1. See chapter 9 for a discussion of the Gorean subculture.

2. Alpha Riot Grrrlz, "Profanity Filter or Thought Filter?" *Alphaville Herald*, http://www.dragonscoveherald.com/blog/index.php?p=75 (January 9, 2004).

3. http://www.philosophicalgourmet.com/overall.htm.

4. Larry Sklar, *Space, Time and Spacetime* (Berkeley: University of California Press).

5. Candace Bolter, "EA's Indifference on Record Here & Now," *Alphaville Herald*, http://www.dragonscoveherald.com/blog/index.php?p=36 (December 2, 2003).

6. Urizenus, "Maxis Targetting Whistle-Blowers?" *Alphaville Herald*, http://www.dragonscoveherald.com/blog/index.php?p=43 (December 6, 2003).

7. Urizenus, "MAXIS is Deleting In-Game References to *Alphaville Herald*, *Alphaville Herald*, http://www.dragonscoveherald.com/blog/index.php?p=44 (December 8, 2003).

7 Crossing the Line: Scamming, Griefing, and Real-World Crime

1. Urizenus, "Interview with Celestie, the Abusive Granny," *Alphaville Herald*, http://www.dragonscoveherald.com/blog/index.php?p=38 (December 2, 2003).

2. Urizenus, "Interview with Celestie, the Abusive Granny."

3. Urizenus Sklar, "'Extortion!': Anshe Chung Accuses SL Gangs of Using Criminal Tactics to Force Below Market Land Sales," *Second Life Herald*, http://www.dragonscoveherald.com/blog/index.php?p=626 (January 14, 2005).

4. John Suler, "The Bad Boys of Cyberspace," in *The Psychology of Cyberspace*, http://www.rider.edu/~suler/psycyber/badboys.html (1997).

5. See comments thread, http://www.alphavilleherald.com/archives/000208.html.

6. Urizenus, "Alert!: Lead Archetict Clone Strikes Again and Again and Again," *Alphaville Herald*, http://www.dragonscoveherald.com/blog/index.php?p=216 (May 5, 2004).

7. Urizenus Sklar, "Another Day in Jessie," *Second Life Herald*, http://www.dragonscoveherald.com/blog/index.php?p=350 (August 4, 2005).

8. Tony Walsh, "Virtual Nipples Make Ripples," *Clickable Culture*, http://secretlair.com/index.php?/clickableculture/entry/virtual_nipples_make_ripples/ (February 2, 2005).

9. Alexander Sliwinski, "Blizzard of GLBT Gaming Policy Questions," *In Newsweekly*, http://www.innewsweekly.com/innews/?class_code=Ga&article_code=1172 (January 25, 2006).

10. http://www.washingtonpost.com/wp-dyn/content/article/2006/03/10/AR2006031001934.html.

11. "Blizzard CEO Responds to GLBT Issue," *Edge Online*, http://www.edge-online.co.uk/archives/2006/03/blizzard_ceo_re.php, March 10, 2006.

12. Walker Spaight, "Blizzard: Don't Ask, Don't Tell. But Go Ahead and Call People 'Fag' All You Like," *Second Life Herald*, http://www.secondlifeherald.com/slh/2006/01/blizzard_dont_a.html, January 27, 2006.

13. http://www.thottbot.com/?n=616211.

14. "Players that loot an item out of turn or against the group's wishes do not fit in the criteria of a scammer, and will not be investigated by the [game-master] Staff," http://www.blizzard.com/support/wowgm/?id=agm01726p.

15. Neal Stewart, "Controversial German Designer Returns from Her 8th Suspension," *Second Life Herald*, http://www.dragonscoveherald.com/blog/index.php?p=686 (February 24, 2005).

16. Urizenus Sklar, "BallerMoMo King: 'they know they can't fuck with me,'" *Second Life Herald*, http://www.dragonscoveherald.com/blog/index.php?p=589 (December 28, 2004).

17. Matthias Zander and Urizenus Sklar, "He's Baaaaaack! BallerMoMo Returns, Attempts to Instigate Interclub Warfare," *Second Life Herald*, http://www.dragonscoveherald.com/blog/index.php?p=636 (January 19, 2005).

18. http://www.secretlair.com/index.php?/clickableculture/entry/second_life_hacker_reportedly_admits_guilt/.

8 Down the Rabbit Hole

1. Urizenus Sklar, "Interview with SSG's Snow White," *Alphaville Herald*, http://www.dragonscoveherald.com/blog/index.php?p=32 (November 26, 2003).

2. Urizenus, "Interview with Former SSG General, Master Bam," *Alphaville Herald*, http://www.dragonscoveherald.com/blog/index.php?p=34 (December 1, 2003).

3. Urizenus, "History of the Sims Shadow Government, Part 1: The Prehistory of SSG," *Alphaville Herald*, http://www.dragonscoveherald.com/blog/index.php?p=54 (December 14, 2003).

4. Urizenus, "'Voleur' Means 'Thief,' Part 1," *Alphaville Herald*, http://www.dragonscoveherald.com/blog/index.php?p=25 (November 19, 2003); and "Voleur Part 2: Interview with Voleur/Evangeline," http://www.dragonscoveherald.com/blog/index.php?p=29 (November 24, 2003).

5. "'Voleur' means 'Thief,' Part 1" and "Voleur Part 2: Interview with Voleur/Evangeline."

6. Jim Schaefer, "Sex and the Simulated City," *Detroit Free Press* (January 27, 2004).

7. "Sex and the Simulated City."

8. http://syminalist.tripod.com/simsoutofline/.

9. Clay Shirky, speaking on social software at ETech, a conference on emerging technologies, April 2003.

10. Urizenus, "Sims Shadow Government," *Terra Nova*, http://terranova.blogs.com/terra_nova/2003/11/sims_shadow_gov.html (November 27, 2003).

11. Urizenus, "Interview with SSG's Snow White," *Alphaville Herald,* http://www.dragonscoveherald.com/blog/index.php?p=32 (November 23, 2003).

9 "Cyber Me, Baby!": Sex, Love, and Software in the Virtual World

1. Julian Dibbell, "A Rape in Cyberspace; or How an Evil Clown, a Haitian Trickster Spirit, Two Wizards and a Cast of Dozens Turned a Database into a Society," *Village Voice* (December 21, 1993), reprinted in Peter Ludlow, ed., *High Noon on the Electronic Frontier: Conceptual Issues in Cyberspace* (Cambridge, MA: MIT Press, 1996).

2. Pat the Rat, "Pat the Rat: Beyond the Valley of the Webcams," *Alphaville Herald,* http://www.dragonscoveherald.com/blog/index.php?p=133 (March 10, 2004).

3. Urizenus Sklar, "Teledildonics Comes to SL!!?," *Second Life Herald,* http://www.dragonscoveherald.com/blog/index.php?p=902 (July 31, 2005).

4. Urizenus, "Interview with Anonymous, on Alphaville's Bondage, Discipline and Sadomasochism Community," *Alphaville Herald,* http://www.dragonscoveherald.com/blog/index.php?p=60 (December 20, 2003).

5. Urizenus, "Interview with Gorean Mistress Maria LaVeaux and Her Slave, Toy," *Alphaville Herald,* http://www.dragonscoveherald.com/blog/index.php?p=69 (January 2, 2004).

6. Neal Stewart and Pirate Cotton, "Review: Sexy Skyboxes—Second Life's Mile High Clubs," *Second Life Herald,* http://www.dragonscoveherald.com/blog/index.php?p=725 (March 19, 2005).

7. Urizenus Sklar, "Looking Up Taco Rubio at the Upskirt Museum," *Second Life Herald,* http://www.dragonscoveherald.com/blog/index.php?p=574 (December 17, 2004).

8. http://shadowfyre.com/portkar/html/index.php.

9. David Thomas, "Architecture and Vice: Fantasy in the Magic Kingdom of Second Life," *The Escapist,* issue #4, http://www.escapistmagazine.com/issue/4/8 (August 2005).

10. Walker Spaight, "Off the Grid with Walker Spaight: The Making of a Post Six Grrrl," *Second Life Herald,* http://www.dragonscoveherald.com/blog/index.php?p=743 (March 25, 2005).

11. Ren Reynolds, "Welcome to oh oh oooh6," http://terranova.blogs.com/terra_nova/2006/01/welcome_to_oooh.html (January 1, 2006).

12. http://sociolotron.amerabyte.com/.

13. Montserrat Tovar, "Diary of a Newbie #4: Meeting Evangeline," *Alphaville Herald,* http://www.dragonscoveherald.com/blog/index.php?p=139 (March 17, 2004).

14. Tovar, "Diary of a Newbie #4: Meeting Evangeline."

15. Squirrel, "Do You Have What it Takes to be a Slave/Escort," *Second Life Herald*, http://www.dragonscoveherald.com/blog/index.php?p=559 (December 10, 2004).

16. Pat the Rat, "E-L-I-T-E spells DRAMA! As Dancers Defect to The Deck, Big John Vows: "I will burn u down!," *Second Life Herald*, http://www.alphavilleherald.com/archives/000501.html (October 16, 2004).

17. Urizenus Sklar, "RIP Club Elite," *Second Life Herald*, http://www.dragonscoveherald.com/blog/index.php?p=787 (April 20, 2005).

18. ESA press release, http://www.theesa.com/archives/2005/07/video_game_indu_1.php.

19. Urizenus Sklar, "GTA San Andreas Banned Down Under. Is SL Next?," *Second Life Herald*, http://www.dragonscoveherald.com/blog/index.php?p=909 (August 3, 2005).

10 Murdered!

1. For the *Herald*'s December 2003 archives, see http://www.dragonscoveherald.com/blog/index.php?m=200312.

2. Urizenus, "Maxis Targetting Whistle-Blowers?," *Alphaville Herald*, http://www.dragonscoveherald.com/blog/index.php?p=43 (December 6, 2003).

3. As related in chapter 6.

4. Urizenus, "Maxis Harassment of *Alphaville Herald* Continues: Urizenus Suspended," *Alphaville Herald*, http://www.dragonscoveherald.com/blog/index.php?p=47 (December 10, 2003).

5. Urizenus, "EA/Maxis Permanently Terminates Urizenus Account," *Alphaville Herald*, http://www.dragonscoveherald.com/blog/index.php?p=48 (December 10, 2003).

6. http://secondlife.blogs.com/nwn.

7. Farhad Manjoo, "Raking muck in 'The Sims Online,'" http://www.salon.com/tech/feature/2003/12/12/sims_online_newspaper/index_np.html (December 12, 2003).

8. http://games.slashdot.org/games/03/12/13/221218.shtml?tid=153.

9. http://www.penny-arcade.com/view.php?date=2003-12-15.

10. James Grimmelmann, "Sims Online Censors Online Journalist," *LawMeme*, http://research.yale.edu/lawmeme/modules.php?name=News&file=article&sid=1291 (December 14, 2003).

11. Urizenus, "Obituary: Censorship Dies, Victim of The Blog," *Alphaville Herald*, http://www.dragonscoveherald.com/blog/index.php?p=58 (December 18, 2003).

12. Amy Harmon, "A Real-Life Debate on Free Expression in a Cyberspace City." *New York Times* (January 15, 2004), A1.

13. Mark Ward, "The Dark Side of Digital Utopia," *BBC News* (December 22, 2003).

14. In reflecting on Brown's comment, Ludlow later wondered whether the exec hadn't accidentally backed into a deep truth: Perhaps Brown really was a railroad tycoon in the moments when he snapped up B&O and Short Line, simply by virtue of being one in the context of the game. In his best contemporary philosopher's style, Ludlow took Brown's quote as the basis for an academic paper on "the myth of fiction" ("From Sherlock and Buffy to Klingon and Norrathian Platinum Pieces: Pretense, Contextualism, and the Myth of Fiction," available at http://www-personal.umich.edu/~ludlow/Fiction.rtf, or forthcoming in Ernest Sosa and Enrique Villanueva, eds., *Philosophical Issues 16: Philosophy of Language* [Nous annual supplement], Blackwell Publishers). In the paper, he argued that just as real people, places, and things often find their way into works of fiction, so do fictional institutions sometimes find their way into "reality." The Klingon language, for instance (see http://en.wikipedia.org/wiki/Klingon_language), had its origins on a short-lived 1960s television series, but is now spoken by a number of people around the world (including someone at Google, apparently: see http://www.google.com/intl/xx-klingon/). Similarly, the *Herald* had originated as a game-world publication, but had somehow become a real Web-based newspaper.

15. See chapter 12.

16. Dave Kindred, "MLB Is No Match for Minnesota," *Sporting News*, http://64.233.167.104/search?q=cache:WOgdcnf95tYJ:i.tsn.com/voices/dave_kindred/20011119.html (November 19, 2001).

17. Greg Lastowka, "*Alphaville Herald* Hits the Big Time," *Terra Nova*, http://terranova.blogs.com/terra_nova/2003/12/alphaville_hera.html (December 14, 2003).

18. *Marsh v. Alabama*, see Peter S. Jenkins, "The Virtual World as a Company Town—Freedom of Speech in Massively Multiple Online Role Playing Games," *Journal of Internet Law* 8:1, see http://www.ssrn.com/abstract=565181 (July 2004).

19. F. Gregory Lastowka and Dan Hunter, "The Laws of Virtual Worlds," http://papers.ssrn.com/sol3/papers.cfm?abstract_id=402860.

20. Jenkins, "The Virtual World as a Company Town."

21. Jack M. Balkin, "Virtual Liberty: Freedom to Design and Freedom to Play in Virtual Worlds," *Virginia Law Review* 90, no. 8, http://www.yale.edu/lawweb/jbalkin/articles/virtual_liberty1.pdf (December 2004).

22. Eric Goldman, "Speech Showdowns at the Virtual Corral," 21 *SANTA CLARA COMPUTER & HIGH TECH. L.J.* 845 (2005).

23. Neal Stewart, "Editorial: Simulating Free Speech In Virtual Lives," *Second Life Herald*, http://www.dragonscoveherald.com/blog/index.php?p=693 (March 4, 2005).

24. See appendix A.

11 Behind the Pixel Curtain

1. Bethany MacLean, "Sex, Lies, and Videogames," *Fortune.com*, http://www.fortune.com/fortune/technology/articles/0,15114,1090767-1,00.html (August 22, 2005).

2. Rob Fahey, "More on the SEC Investigation," *GamesIndustry.biz*, http://gamesindustry.biz/content_page.php?section_name=pub&aid=1968 (July 22, 2003).

3. http://www.mercurynews.com/mld/mercurynews/business/11012030.htm.

4. Urizenus Sklar, EA Execs Dumping Stock. Insider Trading or . . . What?, *Second Life Herald*, http://www.dragonscoveherald.com/blog/index.php?p=694 (March 3, 2005).

5. Urizenus Sklar, "The Other Shoe Drops: Insider Selling at EA Is Followed by 13% Stock Drop—Stockholders Sue," *Second Life Herald*, http://www.dragonscoveherald.com/blog/index.php?p=748 (March 30, 2004).

6. David Becker, "EA Hit with Shareholder Lawsuits," *CNET News.com*, http://news.com.com/EA+hit+with+shareholder+lawsuits/2100-1047_3-5645435.html (March 29, 2005).

7. Milberg Weiss Bershad & Schulman LLP, court filing in re ELECTRONIC ARTS, INC. SECURITIES LITIGATION, http://securities.stanford.edu/USDC_CAND/1034/ERTS05_01/2005812_r08c_0501219.pdf (August 12, 2005).

8. Schubert & Reed LLP, EA Image Production Employee Overtime Litigation, http://www.schubert-reed.com/EAOvertime.htm.

9. Schubert & Reed LLP, Electronic Arts Programmers Overtime Litigation, http://www.schubert-reed.com/EAProgrammers.htm.

10. "Video Game Maker Settles Suit for $15.6M," *Associated Press*, http://www.forbes.com/feeds/ap/2005/10/05/ap2263401.html (October 5, 2005).

11. EA Spouse, http://www.livejournal.com/users/ea_spouse/ (November 2004).

12. Ed Frauenheim, "Electronic Arts Promises Workplace Change," *CNET News.com*, http://news.zdnet.com/2100-3513_22-5476714.html (December 3, 2004).

13. Urizenus Sklar, "EA to Employ 500 in China. Jeff Brown: It isn't outsourcing," *Second Life Herald*, http://www.dragonscoveherald.com/blog/index.php?p=528.

14. *KATHERINE REAB, GAIL LEE GRAHAM, STEVEN J. FINGER, JR. and IAN RONALDS, individually and on behalf of others similarly situated, Plaintiffs, v. ELECTRONIC ARTS, INC. and ORIGIN SYSTEMS, INC., Defendants*, Civil Case No. 00-B-

1839 (OES) UNITED STATES DISTRICT COURT FOR THE DISTRICT OF COLORADO 214 F.R.D. 623; 2002 U.S. Dist. LEXIS 26374; 8 Wage & Hour Cas. 2d (BNA) 1196 September 23, 2002, Decided, September 24, 2002, Filed.

15. Deep Max, "Will's Faustian Bargain with EA: How Maxis was Saved at the Cost of its Soul, by Deep Max," *Second Life Herald*, http://www.alphavilleherald.com/archives/000312.html (June 27, 2004).

12 Taking It to the Virtual Streets

1. Edward Castronova, "The State of Play: Warriors Revolt," *Terra Nova*, http://terranova.blogs.com/terra_nova/2003/11/the_state_of_pl.html (November 18, 2003).

2. http://secondlife.com/notes/2003_08_11_archive.php#20030812.

3. http://secondlife.com/notes/2003_09_08_archive.php#20030912a.

4. Urizenus, "SnowWhite and -Storm Resign SSG: Is It the End?," *Alphaville Herald*, http://www.dragonscoveherald.com/blog/index.php?p=77 (January 12, 2004).

5. Urizenus, "On the Map: Interview with Godfather Antonio Armone," *Alphaville Herald*, http://www.dragonscoveherald.com/blog/index.php?p=100 (February 7, 2004).

6. Kale, "Interview with Fans: Director of the Alphaville Government CIA," *Alphaville Herald*, http://www.dragonscoveherald.com/blog/index.php?p=39 (December 4, 2003).

7. Daniel Terdiman, "Mr-President Bids for Re-Election," *Wired.com*, http://wired-vig.wired.com/news/games/0,2101,62635-1,00.html (March 12, 2004).

8. Neal Conan, "Politics in Alphaville, an Online Community," *NPR's Talk of the Nation*, http://www.npr.org/templates/story/story.php?storyId=1828683 (April 7, 2004).

9. Mark Glassman, "Braving Bullying Hecklers, Simulants Run for President," *The New York Times*, http://query.nytimes.com/gst/abstract.html?res=F60612-FA3E5D0C728CDDAD0894DC404482 (April 1, 2004).

10. Urizenus, "The Other Fixed Election: Seth Galloway Speaks," *Alphaville Herald*, http://www.dragonscoveherald.com/blog/index.php?p=188 (April 21, 2004).

11. The Teflon Don, "Election Shocker! Mr-President Enlisted Mafia to Oversee Election," *Alphaville Herald*, http://www.dragonscoveherald.com/blog/index.php?p=158 (April 5, 2004).

12. Urizenus, "Mr-President Wins! But Voting Irregularities Cast Shadow Over Election," *Alphaville Herald*, http://www.dragonscoveherald.com/blog/index.php?p=171 (April 20, 2004).

13. Urizenus, "Elections *Were* Rigged. Mr-President Exposed as Puppet of JC Soprano," *Alphaville Herald,* http://www.dragonscoveherald.com/blog/index.php?p=182 (April 18, 2004).

14. Urizenus, "Jason Sim on Oprah: AVG Elections Were Rigged!," *Alphaville Herald,* http://www.dragonscoveherald.com/blog/index.php?p=326 (July 23, 2004).

15. Urizenus Sklar, "David Pierce Files Virtual Class-Action Suit Against AVG's Chad Thomas," *Second Life Herald,* http://www.dragonscoveherald.com/blog/index.php?p=333 (July 28, 2004).

16. Urizenus Sklar, "Chad Thomas Found Innocent," *Second Life Herald,* http://www.dragonscoveherald.com/blog/index.php?p=364 (August 20, 2004).

17. http://www.corante.com/gotgame/archives20031101.html#61354.

13 Into the Code: Exploits, Mods, and Hacks

1. Ben Zackheim, "World of Warcraft Exploit Could Mean Trouble for Public Gatherings," *Joystiq.com,* http://www.joystiq.com/entry/1234000023030840/ (February 8, 2005).

2. Rob Malda, "World of Warcraft Duping Bug Found," *Slashdot.org,* http://games.slashdot.org/games/05/07/19/1644250.shtml?tid=209&tid=10 (July 19, 2005).

3. *My Trip to Liberty City* can be viewed at http://nomediakings.org/mytrip.htm.

4. Urizenus, "Interview with Nyk: Legendary Mazebot Programmer," *Alphaville Herald,* http://www.dragonscoveherald.com/blog/index.php?p=118 (February 25, 2004).

5. Markee Dragon, "Confessions of a UO Gold Farmer," *MarkeeDragon.com,* http://www.markeedragon.com/u/ubbthreads/showflat.php?Board=uonews&Number=29818 (January 25, 2005).

6. Rich Thurman, interview with Mark Wallace, September 2005.

7. "Confessions of a UO Gold Farmer."

8. Though Thurman is out of the gold-farming business, he is now partners in a venture that will make some of his botting techniques available to any player. The Macroh Masheen (http://www.macrohmasheen.com) is a powerful scripting add-on that Thurman helped design and which allows players to add their own functionality to any online game.

9. Ian, "Maze is Back! But Maxis Fumbles the Fix," *Alphaville Herald,* http://www.dragonscoveherald.com/blog/index.php?p=173 (April 13, 2004).

10. Described in chapter 7.

11. Edward Castronova, "Free Rogue Server Achieves Significant Population," *Terra Nova*, http://terranova.blogs.com/terra_nova/2004/01/free_rogue_serv.html (January 12, 2004).

14 The Resurrection of Urizenus Sklar

1. Larry Sklar, *Space, Time and Spacetime* (Berkeley: University of California Press, 1977).

2. Urizenus "Scammers Moving to Second Life?" *Alphaville Herald*, http://www.dragonscoveherald.com/blog/index.php?p=251 (May 25, 2004).

3. Urizenus, "Alpha Refugees Start with Clean Slate in Second Life," *Alphaville Herald*, http://www.dragonscoveherald.com/blog/index.php?p=262 (May 30, 2004).

4. See chapter 12.

5. Pat the Rat, "Papparazi Catch Simlebrities in SL," *Alphaville Herald*, http://www.dragonscoveherald.com/blog/index.php?p=254 (May 26, 2004).

6. Urizenus, "SL CEO Holds Another Town Meeting," *Alphaville Herald*, http://www.dragonscoveherald.com/blog/index.php?p=255 (May 27, 2004).

7. Urizenus Sklar, "New Name. Extended Mission," *Second Life Herald*, http://www.dragonscoveherald.com/blog/index.php?p=279 (June 14, 2004).

8. Urizenus Sklar, "Interview with Second Life CEO, Philip Rosedale," *Second Life Herald*, http://www.dragonscoveherald.com/blog/index.php?p=290 (June 21, 2004).

9. Urizenus, Sklar, "Introducing SL's First Mafia: The Valentino Family," *Second Life Herald*, http://www.dragonscoveherald.com/blog/index.php?p=296 (June 15, 2004).

10. Budka Groshomme, "Which Came First: The Creativity or the Creator?," *Second Life Herald*, http://www.dragonscoveherald.com/blog/index.php?p=759 (April 4, 2005).

11. Residents can check their fishing tournament standings at http://fish.neorealms.com/.

12. Mark Wallace, "A Virtual Holiday in the Virtual Sun," *The New York Times*, Escapes section (October 28, 2005).

13. Linden Lab press release, http://lindenlab.com/press_story_12.php.

14. Philip Rosedale, interview with Mark Wallace, May 2005.

15. See chapter 5.

16. See chapter 7.

17. See chapter 7.

18. Urizenus Sklar, "Ruby Wilde vs. Land Baron One Song," *Second Life Herald,* http://www.dragonscoveherald.com/blog/index.php?p=370 (August 21, 2004).

19. Chronicled by Hamlet Linden (aka games and technology journalist Wagner James Au), who works for Linden Lab reporting on the world of Second Life in his blog, *New World Notes*. For Hamlet's ten-part history of the Jessie war, see http://secondlife.com/notes/2003_07_07_archive.php#20030707.

20. Urizenus Sklar, "Tensions Rise on the Jessie/Stanford Border," *Second Life Herald,* http://www.dragonscoveherald.com/blog/index.php?p=367 (August 20, 2004).

21. Urizenus Sklar, "WAR!," *Second Life Herald,* http://www.dragonscoveherald.com/blog/index.php?p=372 (August 23, 2004).

22. Urizenus Sklar, "Essay: A History of the Second Jessie War," *Second Life Herald,* http://www.dragonscoveherald.com/blog/index.php?p=438 (September 17, 2004).

15 The Power of the Virtual Press

1. http://secondlife.com/corporate/tos.php.

2. Urizenus Sklar, "Avatar of the Year: One Song/Mr. Fairplay," *Second Life Herald,* http://www.dragonscoveherald.com/blog/index.php?p=593 (December 30, 2004).

3. Urizenus Sklar, "*Herald* Announces New Editorial Board," *Second Life Herald,* http://www.dragonscoveherald.com/blog/index.php?p=603 (January 6, 2005).

4. Walker Spaight, "Turning the Pages at the SL Public Library," *Second Life Herald,* http://www.dragonscoveherald.com/blog/index.php?p=629 (January 16, 2005).

5. Walker Spaight, "The *Herald* Profile: Anshe Chung," *Second Life Herald,* http://www.dragonscoveherald.com/blog/index.php?p=645 (January 15, 2005).

6. Walker Spaight, "Showdown in Street City," *Second Life Herald,* http://www.dragonscoveherald.com/blog/index.php?p=702 (March 6, 2005).

7. Walker Spaight, "The Making of a Post Six Grrrl," *Second Life Herald,* http://www.dragonscoveherald.com/blog/index.php?p=743 (March 25, 2005), and see chapter 9.

8. Walker Spaight, "Putting the Pr0n in Second Life," *Second Life Herald,* http://www.dragonscoveherald.com/blog/index.php?p=776 (April 15, 2005).

9. Neal Stewart, "'people think I'm teh sexy': A Conversation With SL's Charles Manson Stalker," *Second Life Herald,* http://www.dragonscoveherald.com/blog/index.php?p=660 (February 5, 2005).

10. Neal Stewart, "Extinct Native American Tribe Finds Second Wind," *Second Life Herald,* http://www.dragonscoveherald.com/blog/index.php?p=663 (February 6, 2005).

11. Neal Stewart, "Controversial German Designer Returns from Her 8th Suspension," *Second Life Herald*, http://www.dragonscoveherald.com/blog/index.php?p=686 (February 24, 2005).

12. Neal Stewart, "Sweatshop Discovered in Second Life Mieto Sim," *Second Life Herald*, http://www.dragonscoveherald.com/blog/index.php?p=704 (March 7, 2005).

13. Neal Stewart, "Review: Sexy Skyboxes—Second Life's Mile-High Clubs," *Second Life Herald*, http://www.dragonscoveherald.com/blog/index.php?p=725 (March 19, 2005).

14. Neal Stewart, "'R.I.P Ryan Dayton'—Teenage 'Air' Profits," *Second Life Herald*, http://www.dragonscoveherald.com/blog/index.php?p=791 (April 24, 2005).

15. Walker Spaight, "The Messenger's Message: There's A New Newspaper in Second Life," *Second Life Herald*, http://www.dragonscoveherald.com/blog/index.php?p=922 (August 9, 2005).

16. Advertisement: "TSLAS Nuclear Warhead," *Second Life Herald*, http://www.dragonscoveherald.com/blog/index.php?p=718 (March 17, 2005).

17. Urizenus Sklar, "Gosh W-hat a Surprise: W-Hats in the Middle of SL Hack Mess," *Second Life Herald*, http://www.dragonscoveherald.com/blog/index.php?p=884 (July 20, 2005).

18. Urizenus Sklar, "Bow Padre: Uri Remembers Pope JP2," *Second Life Herald*, http://www.dragonscoveherald.com/blog/index.php?p=764 (April 8, 2005).

19. Urizenus Sklar, "The Second Coming of Dyerbrook," *Second Life Herald*, http://www.dragonscoveherald.com/blog/index.php?p=525 (December 1, 2004).

20. Second Life forums, http://forums.secondlife.com/showthread.php?t=31559 (January 1, 2005).

21. Second Life forums, http://forums.secondlife.com/showthread.php?t=43275 (April 18, 2005).

22. Urizenus Sklar, "'All on the Same Page': IRC Chat Logs Support Linden/FIC Conspiracy vs. Prok," *Second Life Herald*, http://www.dragonscoveherald.com/blog/index.php?p=857 (June 29, 2005).

23. Clay Shirky, http://www.shirky.com/writings/group_enemy.html.

24. Urizenus Sklar and Walker Spaight, "2005 Avatar of the Year: Prokofy Neva," *Second Life Herald*, http://www.secondlifeherald.com/slh/2006/01/avatar_of_the_y.html (January 2, 2006).

25. Lawrence Lessig, *Code and Other Laws of Cyberspace*, (New York: Basic Books, 1999).

16 Ruling the Metaverse

1. http://www.eve-online.com.

2. Tom Francis, "Murder Incorporated," *PC Gamer*, UK edition (September 2005).

3. Francis, Murder Incorporated.

4. http://www.eve-online.com/faq/faq_06.asp.

5. http://secondlife.com/community/blotter.php.

6. See chapter 12.

7. Urizenus Sklar, "SL Land Heist! XLS Operatives Wipe Out Space Monkey Corporation," *Second Life Herald*, http://www.dragonscoveherald.com/blog/index.php?p=917 (August 6, 2005).

8. Sklar, "SL Land Heist!"

9. Prokofy Neva, "Lindens Seize Land in Internal GIGAS Dipute," *Second Life Herald*, http://www.dragonscoveherald.com/blog/index.php?p=914 (August 5, 2005).

10. Urizenus Sklar, "Interview with Second Life CEO, Philip Rosedale," *Second Life Herald*, http://www.dragonscoveherald.com/blog/index.php?p=290 (June 21, 2004).

11. Urizenus Sklar, "Betrayed! Lindens Phuck Gaming Open Market!," *Second Life Herald*, http://www.dragonscoveherald.com/blog/index.php?p=936 (August 27, 2005).

12. Second Life forums, http://forums.secondlife.com/showthread.php?t=65426.

17 The Day the Grid Disappeared

1. Walker Spaight, "Newsflash: Linden Firelane Foils Latest W-Hat Attack," *Second Life Herald*, http://www.dragonscoveherald.com/blog/index.php?p=1025 (November 23, 2005).

18 The Metaverse Is Born

1. Urizenus Sklar, "Urizenus Announces Retirement," *Second Life Herald*, http://www.secondlifeherald.com/slh/2006/02/urizenus_announ.html (February 15, 2006).

2. Walker Spaight, "*Herald* Announces New Editorial Board," http://www.secondlifeherald.com/slh/2006/10/herald_announce.html (October 12, 2006).

3. Robert Hof, "A Virtual World's Real Dollars," *Business Week* (March 28, 2006).

4. Urizenus Sklar, "IBM Finds Application for Second Life Scions," http://www.secondlifeherald.com/slh/2006/11/ibm_finds_appli.html (November 30, 2006).

5. Pixeleen Mistral, "Paparazzi Infiltrate IBM's Private Islands!," http://www.secondlifeherald.com/slh/2006/11/paparazzi_infil.html (November 19, 2006).

6. Urizenus Sklar, "A Gallery of Lies!," http://www.secondlifeherald.com/slh/2006/10/a_gallery_of_li.html (October 25, 2006).

7. Urizenus Sklar, "Fucktards in Cyberspace," http://strumpette.com/archives/218-Fucktards-in-Cyberspace.html (October 29, 2006).

8. Urizenus Sklar, "Anshe to Honor Residents' Vote: Dishonest PR Flocks to Be Banned from Dreamland Continent," http://www.secondlifeherald.com/slh/2006/11/anshe_to_honor_.html (November 11, 2006).

9. Pixeleen Mistral, "Mass Unrest in Manitoba!," http://www.secondlifeherald.com/slh/2006/11/mass_unrest_in_.html (November 14, 2006).

10. Lawrence Lessig, *Code and Other Laws of Cyberspace* (New York: Basic Books, 1999).

11. Raph Kester, "Copybot," http://raphkester.com/2006/11/15/copybot/ (November 15, 2006).

12. http://intranet.cern.ch/Chronological/Announcements/CERNAnnouncements/2003/04-30TenYearsWWW/Welcome.html.

13. http://en.wikipedia.org/wiki/World_Wide_Web.

14. See the Website of the Center for the Study of Synthetic Worlds, http://cssw1.org/.

Appendix A A Declaration of the Rights of Avatars

http://www.legendmud.org/raph/gaming/playerrights.html.

Appendix B *Herald* Obituary: In Memory of Candace Bolter, aka Kale

Second Life Herald, http://www.dragonscoveherald.com/blog/index.php?p=750 (March 31, 2005).

1. Kale, "Interview: Cory Linden on IP Issues in Second Life," *Second Life Herald,* http://www.dragonscoveherald.com/blog/index.php?p=360 (August 12, 2004).

2. I. P. Lithium, "Scorned Relina: I Was Mr-President's Secret Sim Love," *Alphaville Herald,* http://www.dragonscoveherald.com/blog/index.php?p=189 (April 24, 2004).